DEWEY'S NINE LIVES

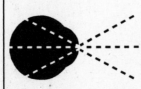

This Large Print Book carries the
Seal of Approval of N.A.V.H.

DEWEY'S NINE LIVES

THE LEGACY OF
THE SMALL-TOWN LIBRARY CAT
WHO INSPIRED MILLIONS

VICKI MYRON
WITH BRET WITTER

THORNDIKE PRESS
A part of Gale, Cengage Learning

Detroit • New York • San Francisco • New Haven, Conn • Waterville, Maine • London

Copyright © 2010 by Vicki Myron LLC.

Photo Credits: Pages (6), (73), (392), (480):courtesy of the author; Page (33): Shutterstock; Pages (74), (112): Barbara Pajiness; Pages (113), (162): William A. Bezanson; Pages (163), (201): Mary Nan and Larry W. Evans; Page (202): Vicki Klueverj; Pages (264), (312): Lynda Caira; Page (313): Kristie L. Dvent; Page (355): Carol R. Riggs.

Thorndike Press, a part of Gale, Cengage Learning.

ALL RIGHTS RESERVED

While the author has made every effort to provide accurate telephone numbers and Internet addresses at the time of publication, neither the publisher nor the author assumes any responsibility for errors, or for changes that occur after publication. Further, the publisher does not have any control over and does not assume any responsibility for author or third-party websites or their content.

Thorndike Press® Large Print Nonfiction.

The text of this Large Print edition is unabridged.

Other aspects of the book may vary from the original edition.

Set in 16 pt. Plantin.

LIBRARY OF CONGRESS CATALOGING-IN-PUBLICATION DATA

Myron, Vicki.
    Dewey's nine lives : the legacy of the small-town library cat
who inspired millions / by Vicki Myron with Bret Witter. —
Large print ed.
        p. cm. — (Thorndike Press large print nonfiction)
    Originally published: New York : Dutton, 2010.
    ISBN-13: 978-1-4104-2875-2
    ISBN-10: 1-4104-2875-3
    1. Cats — Anecdotes. 2. Human-animal relationships —
Anecdotes. 3. Dewey (Cat) — Anecdotes. 4. Large type books.
I. Witter, Bret. II. Title. III. Title: Dewey's 9 lives.
SF445.5.M974 2010b
636.8—dc22
                                                      2010035060

Published in 2010 in arrangement with Dutton, a member of Penguin Group (USA) Inc.

Printed in the United States of America
1 2 3 4 5 6 7 14 13 12 11 10

To Glenn,
for his amazing love and support

CONTENTS

PROLOGUE
DEWEY

"Thank you, Vicki, and thank you, Dewey. . . . I don't believe in angels, but Dewey comes close."

— Christine B., Tampa, FL

I disagree with the person who wrote that letter, because I do believe there are angels walking among us, helping us grow. I believe in "teachable moments," when we can learn something valuable about life if our eyes and hearts are open to the world around us. These angels of opportunity, as I like to think of them, come in all forms. They appear thanks to the important people in our lives, but also through chance meetings and strangers. I believe Dewey Readmore Books, the famous library cat of Spencer, Iowa, was one of those angels. He taught so many lessons, and touched so many lives, that I can't dismiss it as chance. And I don't believe in coincidence.

But I know what that young woman is saying. She is saying that Dewey, through his actions and his example, transformed her life. She can't find the words to describe that power, but she knows it is special.

Well, I have a phrase for it: Dewey's Magic. It is the phrase I used each time I saw his ability to change the way people thought about themselves. No one saw that Magic more than I, because of all the people in the world, I knew Dewey best and was touched by him most. I'm just an ordinary Iowa girl, the long-serving director of a small-town library less than a dozen miles from the farm where I was born and raised, but for nineteen years I was privileged to share my journey with Dewey. And Dewey . . . he was special. He impacted lives. He inspired a town. He became famous around the world, headlined magazines and newspapers, and was the subject of the #1 *New York Times* bestselling memoir *Dewey,* which as "Dewey's Mommy" I was privileged to write. Dewey's Magic, that's what it was. He was just a cat, but he had a way of inspiring our better selves. He made everyone fall in love with him. He touched the world. No one who met him ever forgot Dewey Readmore Books.

His story began quietly, on a brutally cold weekend in January 1988. The temperature was minus fifteen degrees, the kind of cold that burns your lungs and peels the skin from your face (or at least it feels that way). That kind of cold, often accompanied by ferocious winds, is the worst thing about living in the great northern plains. You learn to tolerate it, but you never adapt. There are times in northern Iowa when it just isn't wise to go outside.

But despite the deep freeze, someone had been out in downtown Spencer, because at some point that Sunday, a tiny homeless kitten was shoved into the book return slot on the back wall of the Spencer Public Library. I hope it was an act of mercy, that someone saw a tiny eight-week-old, one-pound kitten shivering in the snow and wanted to protect it. If that was the case, they were misguided. The library book return was nothing more than a metal tube that led, after a four-foot drop, into a sealed metal box. In effect, it was a refrigerator. There were no blankets, pads, or soft linings. There was only cold metal. And books. For at least ten hours and maybe as long as twenty-four, little Dewey sat in bitterly cold utter darkness, with nothing to comfort him but books.

I entered the story early Monday morning when I opened the book return box and found the tiny kitten inside. When he looked up longingly into my eyes, my heart stopped. He was so cute . . . and so in need. I cradled him in my hands until he stopped shivering, then gave him a warm bath in the library sink and dried him with the blow-dryer we used for children's craft projects. That's when Dewey took over, tottering on frostbitten feet to each person on the library staff and nuzzling them sweetly with his nose.

I decided, right then, that the library should adopt him. It wasn't just that I fell in love with Dewey the moment he looked at me with his glorious golden eyes. I knew, for those eyes and his determination to thank every staff member for his rescue, that he would fit perfectly into my plan to warm up the cold institutional nature of the Spencer

Public Library. He had such a loving and outgoing personality, such a heartwarming presence, that he made everyone feel good.

And at that moment, that's *exactly* what Spencer, Iowa, needed. The town was reeling from a farm crisis, with 70 percent of the downtown storefronts empty and farms in the county going bankrupt by the dozen. We needed a feel-good story. We needed something positive to talk about, and a lesson in persistence, hope, and love. If someone could shove a tiny kitten into a dark and freezing metal box, and that kitten could emerge with his trust and compassion intact, then we could endure our misfortunes, too.

But Dewey wasn't a mascot. He was a flesh-and-blood companion, an animal always open and loving the moment anyone stepped into the library. He warmed hearts one lap at a time, and maybe even more important, he had a knack for knowing who really needed him.

I remember the retired patrons who visited every morning. Many of them started staying longer and talking with the staff more after Dewey arrived.

I remember Crystal, a middle school student with severe physical disabilities who did nothing but stare at the floor until Dewey found her and started jumping onto her wheelchair as she was rolled through the door. Then Crystal started to look at the world around her. She started to make noises every week when she entered the library, and when Dewey came running and leapt on her chair, a smile burst out of her heart.

I remember our new assistant children's librarian, who had recently moved to Spencer to care for her sick mother. She and Dewey sat together every afternoon. I caught her one day with a tear in her eye and realized how much she had been suffering, and that only Dewey had been there for her.

I remember the shy woman who had trouble making friends. I remember the young man frustrated by his inability to find work. I remember the homeless man who never spoke to anyone but always found Dewey, placed him on his shoulder (the right shoulder of course; Dewey would sit only on your right shoulder), and walked with him for fifteen minutes. The man whispered; Dewey listened. I am convinced of that. And by listening, by being present, he helped them all.

But mostly, I remember the children. Dewey had a special relationship with the children of Spencer. He loved babies. He would creep to their carriers and snuggle beside them, a look of complete contentment on his face, even when they pulled his ears. He let toddlers pet him and prod him and squeal with delight. He befriended a boy with allergies who was heartbroken because he couldn't have a pet of his own. He spent afternoons with the middle school students who stayed in the library while their parents worked, chasing their pencils and hiding in their jacket sleeves. He would brush by every child at our weekly Story Hour before choosing one lap to curl up on — a different lap, I should mention, every week. Yes, Dewey had catlike habits. He slept a lot. He was picky about being petted on the belly. He ate rubber bands. He attacked typewriter keys (back then, we still had typewriters around) and computer keyboards. He lounged on the copier, because it blew warm air. He climbed on the overhead lights. You couldn't open a box anywhere in the library without Dewey suddenly appearing and jumping inside. But what he really did was something just as catlike but more profound: He opened the hearts of the people of Spencer, one at a time, to the beauty and love in our wonderful little town in the middle of the great Iowa plains, and to one another.

That was the real Dewey Magic, his ability to spread his joyous, friendly, and relaxed attitude toward life to everyone he met.

15

The fact that he became famous? That was pure charisma. I intended, of course, for him to become well known in Spencer. I worked hard to help him change the image of the library, to make it a gathering place as opposed to just a warehouse for books. I was amazed that anyone outside northwest Iowa would care. But slowly at first, and then in a torrent, they came, drawn by the story of the special cat who inspired a town. The journalists came first — from Des Moines, England, Boston, and Japan. Then the visitors started to arrive. An older couple from New York on a cross-country drive who, after visiting Dewey, sent money on his birthday and Christmas every year of his life. A family from Rhode Island, who were in Minneapolis (five hours away from Spencer) for a wedding. A sick little girl from Texas who, I was sure, had asked her parents for this one gift. It was amazing to watch the accidental blossoming of fame. People met Dewey; they spent time with him; and they loved him. They went home and told other people about him, and then those people came to visit him, and they left impressed, and the next thing we knew, we were receiving a telephone call from a newspaper in Los Angeles or a news reporter in Australia.

So when Dewey died peacefully at the age

of nineteen, having served the community of Spencer and its public library every day with enthusiasm and grace, I wasn't really surprised that his obituary, first published in Sioux City, ran in more than 275 newspapers. Or that the library received letters by the thousands from around the world. Or that hundreds of fans signed his condolence book and attended an impromptu memorial. For two months, we were besieged by reporters and admirers and requests to talk about Dewey. And then, slowly, the clamor died down. The cameras turned off, and Spencer went back to being the quiet little town it had always been. Those of us who had loved Dewey were, finally, left to our personal grief. Dewey the celebrity was gone; the memories of Dewey our friend remained, held privately in our hearts. When I finally buried Dewey's ashes outside the window of the children's section of the library he had loved so much, it was at dawn on a freezing December morning with only the assistant library director at my side. And that's the way he would have wanted it.

I knew he had left a legacy, because Dewey had changed me. He had changed members of the library staff. He had changed Crystal the disabled girl, and the homeless man, and the children who came each week for Story

17

Hour, many of whom brought their own children to see him in his later years. I knew how important he was because people kept telling me their Dewey stories, confiding in me in a way. In the end, he touched more than the town of Spencer. But it was those of us who had known him and loved him and heard his story that he changed. His legacy would live on in us.

I thought that was it. I really did.

And then something amazing happened. I wrote a book about Dewey, and people around the world responded. The book was meant as a tribute to my friend, a thank-you for his service to Spencer and his impact on my life. I knew he had fans. I thought they might want to read the full story. I was not prepared for the passionate response. So many of the people who attended my book events didn't just like Dewey, and didn't just enjoy the book. They *loved* them both. They felt touched by the story. And they felt changed. I remember one woman in Sioux City who broke down in tears as she told me that her mother, a Spencer piano teacher and church organist, had taken her every Saturday for cinnamon rolls and a trip to the library to see Dewey. Then her mother developed Alzheimer's and slowly forgot her husband, her children, even her own identity.

Her daughter drove two hours from Sioux City to visit her every week, and she always brought her own cat with her. The cat was black and white, nothing like copper-colored Dewey at all, but every week her mother smiled and said, "Oh, it's Dewey. Thank you for bringing Dewey." The daughter could barely get those last words out, she was crying so hard.

"I went out in the parking lot after I met you," she told me some time later, "and sat in my car and cried for fifteen minutes. The tears wouldn't stop. My mother had been dead for twelve years, but it was the first time I had really cried for her. Thinking about Dewey, remembering how much my mother loved him, was the end of the grieving process."

The strangest thing? I didn't know this woman, Margo Chesebro, or her mother, Grace Barlow-Chesebro (although from her daughter's description of a smart, strong, independent woman who believed in the magic of animals, I'm sure I would have liked her). And yet, they had known and loved Dewey. He had been a regular and important part of their lives, important enough that Grace would somehow retain his memory in her damaged mind, even as she lost forever the names of her children and became

19

convinced her husband was her long-dead brother. There was no way, I realized then, that I could ever *truly* know the extent of the lives Dewey had touched.

And then there were the people who had never known Dewey, the strangers who were so touched by his story, they felt compelled to write to me. It started almost immediately after the book's publication. "I've never written to an author before but I was so moved by Dewey's story. . . ." Or, "Dewey was an angel, thank you for sharing him with the world."

As the months went on, and the book topped the national bestseller lists, the letters became more frequent, until I was receiving dozens every day. After a year, I had received more than three thousand letters, e-mails, and packages, almost all from people who had never heard of Dewey before reading the book. I received a pillow cross-stitched with the image of Dewey from the book's cover. I received several paintings of him. A former resident of Spencer, who had moved away but had never forgotten, commissioned a sculpture of Dewey for the library. (I knew Dewey's Magic was at work when I saw where the artist's studio was located: Dewey, Arizona.) I can't even count how many drawings, ornaments, and carvings of cats I have received from fans. I have a bookcase in my house just to display them — and it's overflowing.

One person sent me twenty dollars to buy roses for Dewey. Another sent five dollars to place catnip on his grave. A woman at a call center in Idaho told me that every time someone calls from Iowa, she asks about Dewey, hoping to find someone who knew him. Another man sent a picture of the jar in which he collects spare change. It featured a picture of Dewey. The man was donating his change, from that time forward, to animal rescue.

I read every card, letter, and e-mail. I wanted to respond, but there was no way to keep up with the volume, especially since I was often on the road, meeting Dewey's fans. (But please rest assured, letter writers, that I bought those roses and that catnip for Dewey's grave.) The sentiments expressed in the letters, and the way Dewey continued to change people's lives, touched me more, I suspect, than these fans ever imagined.

A young man who had suffered a devastating divorce and career setback that left him bitter and angry wrote to say that Dewey's life "opened my heart."

A woman with severe MS told me how, after reading *Dewey,* she got down on the floor to kiss the head of the dog that lived in her group home. Afterward, she was unable to get back up without assistance, but she was happy she had done it, because the dog died a week later.

A man in England wrote to say that he had lost his wife several years before. He realized only after he read *Dewey* that the two cats she left behind — two animals he had resented after her death — had actually carried him through. Without those cats to care for, he wrote, he would have been in a "black depression" he might never have endured.

The letter from a young woman in Florida was typical. Just before reading *Dewey,* the young woman wrote, she had ended an abusive two-year relationship with a borderline alcoholic that had destroyed her self-respect and forced her into debt and foreclosure. "I felt foolish," she said, "and most of all, I felt like a failure. Then I read your book.

"Now I'm happy to say," she continued later, "that I'm starting back to school on Monday. I am focusing on putting the pieces of my life back together. It didn't happen because of your book, but your book gave me strength, it made me resolute. Most of all, it reminded me that I was not done.

"So thank you, Vicki, and thank you, Dewey. . . . I don't believe in angels, but

Dewey comes close. Even in death, he has touched lives such as my own through you. You were truly blessed to have such a special person in your life, but I don't have to tell you that. I just know I have been blessed to have Dewey in my life, even if I never met him in person."

Did I react when I read that letter? Of course. To touch someone so deeply, and to help them see the promise in their life, is a gift I will forever cherish. It makes me proud. And that gift was given to me by Dewey.

Since the publication of the book, I have heard not only from strangers. Old friends and family members who had been lost from my life have reached out to me, too. I've met people, such as my cowriter, editors, and agent, who have become true friends. (The illustrator of Dewey's children's books was even named Steven James: the same as my beloved brother who died of cancer at twenty-three — Dewey's Magic again!) I even heard from my ex-husband again. He was a sweet, intelligent man, but he was also a severe alcoholic who did more damage to my life — and his own — than anyone I have ever met. Although we shared a daughter, I hadn't heard from him in eleven years, until he wrote me a letter after reading the book. He had been sober for a decade. He had married his first childhood sweetheart, and they were living happily in Arizona. He sent me pictures. He looked good. He was always a good-looking man. He looked happy, and so did his wife. He sent me a T-shirt that read "Be careful, or I'll put you in my novel," another one of his jokes. There were no hard feelings about the book; it had all been true. "I'm sorry," he told me simply. And he ended the letter: "I'm proud of you." I was very proud of him, too.

I have also heard from fellow librarians, from fellow farm kids and native Iowans, from other single mothers and people whose loved ones committed suicide (it was a brother, in my case) and fellow breast cancer survivors. I have heard from women who shared my terrible experience of an unnecessary hysterectomy in the 1970s, including a woman in Fort Dodge, Iowa, whose surgery was performed by the same doctor as mine, at around the same time. "The surgery almost killed me," she told me at a book signing. "I was in a coma for a week. My health, like yours, has never been the same." We hugged each other. She cried. Sometimes, I've realized, it's nice to know you're not alone.

Community, we call that. *Community.* I

believe, very strongly, in the power of community, whether it is a physical town, a shared religion, or a love of cats. I believe *Dewey* is a book about regular people that shows what's good and possible in ordinary lives, and that this is one of the reasons it has touched so many hearts. People appreciate Spencer, Iowa. They like our cornfields and architecture, and they also like what we represent: simplicity, old-fashioned hard work, but also creativity, commitment, and love. (The doctor who helped with my double mastectomy, Dr. Kohlgraf, told me he was able to finally woo a top surgeon from California to join his practice after twenty years of trying. She had read the book and loved it. She wanted to live in a place like Spencer.) The honesty and the values expressed in the book — "Find your place. Be happy with what you have. Treat everyone well. Live a good life. It isn't about material things; it's about love. And you can never anticipate love." — transcend boundaries. I'm talking international boundaries, too. Dewey's story has been a bestseller in England, Brazil, Portugal, China, and Korea. I've been invited for appearances in Turkey. A man from Milan, Italy, came to Spencer just to see the town where Dewey lived. People all over the world have told me they are coming to visit the famous Spencer, Iowa, and more important, they are keeping the book and passing it down to future generations as a family heirloom. Do you think it's because they care so much about my story? No. Of course not. They want to share the power of love that is woven into the pages.

They want to experience, in other words, the Magic of a special animal named Dewey Readmore Books, a cat that somehow, from inside the walls of a small Iowa library, managed to touch the world. As I said at the beginning, all of this is for and because of Dewey. There would have been no book without him. As the young woman from Florida wrote, each reader of the book experienced Dewey's Magic in their own lives, even though they never met him in person.

So Dewey lives! Even though he has gone, he lives as a memory, a reminder, an example of what's right in the world. Most importantly, I realized as I read letters day after day, he lives in all the other animals that share his tenderness, playfulness, attentiveness, and devotion. My favorite fact from the letters was that 30 percent came from male fans, including two cat-loving sheriffs, and they all started "I'm sure you never receive any letters from men. . . ." Don't worry, real men love cats, too! But the most important thing I read over and over again was this: Dewey touched my heart, because *he reminded me of my own pet.*

Slowly, it dawned on me that Dewey had tapped into the deep love people around the world feel for their animals. And that *Dewey,* the book, had given these people something just as important: a way to share that love. In a way, I think, the book made it acceptable to tell a stranger, even if that stranger was only me: "I love my cats. They are important. They are my friends. They've changed my life. When they die, I miss them terribly." As a young man wrote, after telling me of how broken he felt after a difficult divorce and how his two cats had been the only bright spot in an otherwise dismal time:

At first I thought to myself, my God, how can I love two animals so much? There must be something wrong with me. My life must be so empty. I was embarrassed to admit to myself how important these cats were in my life. Then I read your book and realized there was nothing wrong with loving an animal to the depths that I do. In a way, your book made it okay for me to love my cats the way I do and it made it okay for me to explore our love further, to deepen our relationship and intertwine our lives even more.

Thank you.

For so long, the word people conjured when they heard about a deep relationship between a cat and a person was: *sad*. But I was passionate about my cat. And I wasn't the only one. Not even close. I think Dewey, through his generosity of spirit and endearing personality — through the Magic of his life in a small-town library — became a symbol of that vital connection so many human beings feel with the animals in their lives.

In *Dewey's Nine Lives,* you will read nine stories of extraordinary cats and the people who loved them. Three of the chapters are set in or around Spencer, Iowa, and feature Dewey stories that didn't make it into the first book — because I didn't know of them at the time. The other six stories are about people who wrote to me after reading *Dewey*. They are the purest of contributors: fans who wrote only to express their admiration and love for Dewey and their own animals, expecting nothing in return.

Are these the best stories that could have come out of those three thousand letters? I don't know. In most cases, after all, I was reacting to a sentence or two.

"We housed homeless and abused cats on a foster home basis. . . ."

"He survived a coyote attack, a smack by a bear, walking thirty miles to return to me after a vindictive woman took him to another place just to hurt me."

"I have never been loved by anyone, not even my daughter or my parents, the way I have been loved by my Cookie."

When my cowriter and I followed up on the letters with phone calls, we heard stories about people and cats that were completely unexpected. Some were better. Some worse. All were genuine, heartfelt stories about real people and their animals. After *Dewey,* people advised me to write about the cat found in a sofa donated to the Goodwill, or the burned cat they saw on the local news, or the one-eyed, lop-eared cat that lived his whole life in a Chicago beer bar. But I thought: Why? What's the connection with Dewey? Those are cute stories, but where is the love? If I'm going to tell other stories, I want them to be based on the same foundation as *Dewey*: the special bond between a cat and a person. I wanted to write stories about people whose lives had been changed by their love for their cat.

The people in this book don't think of themselves as heroes. They didn't do anything, as I like to say, that would get them on the *Today* show or the morning news. They are ordinary people, leading ordinary lives, with ordinary animals. I can't tell you if theirs are the best stories in those letters, but I can assure you of this: I like every person in this book. They are the kind of people I grew up with in Spencer, and they are the kind of people I want as my friends. Together with their cats, they embody everything I believe Dewey stood for: kindness, perseverance, morality, hard work, and the strength to always, no matter what the circumstances, stay true to your values and yourself. If the resonance of Dewey's story was based in part on its values, then I wanted these people to reflect those values, too. And I think they do. I am proud to have gotten to know every one of them.

I can't tell you that you will like every action taken by the people in this book. You will not, because I don't agree with some of them myself. As hard as I try, for instance, I cannot condone the fact that Mary Nan Evans didn't have her cats spayed sooner. I just can't. Others let their cats roam outside, even though it is well known that this shortens their life expectancy. Some cats might seem too pampered, or smothered, or anthropomorphized. I know there will

30

be objections. After all, I received hate mail after my first book because I let Dewey eat Arby's Roast Beef sandwiches in his last year of life. I loved that cat with all my heart; I gave everything I could to him; he lived nineteen wonderful years — nineteen! — and yet people still harassed me and called me a murderer because, at the end of his life, in an act of mercy that tore the heart right out of my chest, I put him to sleep.

If you feel the temptation to criticize, please stop and think of this: Every person in this book loved their animals, fiercely and deeply. Every one of them acted in the best interest, as they understood it, of the animals they loved. If they made decisions you disagree with, that is not an indictment of their character. They are simply different from you. Or they lived in a different time, with a different understanding of how animals and people thrive together. Or, very often, both. No story has been changed for this book. Nothing has been glossed over. This is not *The Cat Whisperer* or a guide to kitten care. This is a collection of stories about the way real cats and real people live.

This book is not *Dewey: The Sequel,* nor is it meant to be. There is only one *Dewey* (the book), just as there is only one Dewey (my amazing cat). But there are thousands

31

of stories. There are millions of cats that could, if given the chance, change a life. They are out there, living with the people featured in this book and millions of others like them. They are also out there in much worse circumstances: in rescue shelters, in feral cat colonies, or fighting for survival alone on the frozen streets, waiting for their chance.

Of all the lessons I've learned over the past twenty years, perhaps the most important is this: Angels come in all forms. Love can arrive from anywhere. One special animal can change your life. He can change a town. In a small way, he can change the world.

And so can you.

ONE
DEWEY AND TOBI

"She was a quiet cat. She was gentle and . . . she never wanted to get in any trouble with anybody, she just wanted to live and let live, you know what I mean?"

For much of the world, my beloved Spencer, Iowa, with a population of about ten thousand, is a small town. The streets, mostly numbered on a square grid that extends twenty-nine blocks north-south (with a river in the middle) and twenty-five blocks east-west, are easy to navigate. The stores, primarily extending along Grand Avenue, our main street, are sufficient without being overwhelming. The one-story library, near the corner of Grand Avenue and Third Street, in the heart of downtown, is intimate and welcoming.

But size is relative, especially in a place like Iowa, a state with one-sixth the population of Florida but almost twice as many incorporated towns. Many of us here are from even smaller towns than Spencer, like Moneta, the place I consider my hometown even though I grew up on a farm two miles away. Moneta was six blocks. It had five commercial buildings, if you include the bar and the dance hall. At its height, its population was just over two hundred people. That's fewer people than come through the door of the Spencer Public Library every single day.

So around here, in Iowa farm country, Spencer is large. It's the kind of town people drive to, not through. It's the kind of town where you recognize most of your fellow citizens but don't necessarily know their names. A town where everyone hears about the closing of a business and has an opinion, but not everyone is directly affected. When a farm goes under in Clay County, where Spencer is located, we might not remember the farmer, but we remember someone like him, and we care and understand. Whether we're from an old line of blue-collar farmers, or one of the recent Hispanic immigrants who fill many of the rungs of the vast industrial agricultural economy, we share more than a straight-lined, carefully marked plot of earth called Spencer, Iowa. We share an attitude, a work ethic, a worldview, and a future.

But we don't all know each other. As the director of the Spencer Public Library, that was always clear to me. I could walk through the library at any moment, on any day, and recognize the regular visitors. I knew many of their names. I had grown up with a lot of them, and often I knew their families, too. I remember, more than a decade ago, a library regular sliding toward oblivion over a series of months. I had known him since high school, and I knew his past. He had been heavily involved in drugs, kicked the habit, but was clearly in trouble again. So I called his brother, an old friend, who drove in from out of state to arrange for care. That is the blessing of a town like Spencer: Connections run deep. Help and friendship are often only a phone call away.

But the library drew visitors from nine counties — when I retired we had eighteen thousand card-carrying members, almost twice the population of Spencer — so there was no way I could know everyone. One of the many regular visitors I recognized but never knew was a woman named Yvonne Barry. She was fifteen years younger than I, so I hadn't gone to school with her. She wasn't from Clay County originally, so I didn't know her family. The staff would watch the homeless man who came every morning to visit Dewey, because we wanted to make sure he was doing all right, but Yvonne was always well dressed and groomed, so there never seemed to be a reason to worry. And she was intensely quiet. She never initiated conversation. If you said, "Good morning, Yvonne," the most you received was a whispered, "Hello." She liked magazines, and she always checked out books. Beyond that, I knew only one thing about her: She loved Dewey. I could see that in the smile on her face every time he approached her.

Everyone thought she had a unique relationship with Dewey. I don't know how many times someone whispered to me, in strictest confidence, "Don't tell anybody, because they'll be jealous, but Dewey and I have something special." I'd smile and nod and wait for someone else to say the exact same thing. Dewey was so generous with his affection, you see, that everyone felt the connection. For them, Dewey was one of a kind. But for Dewey, they were one of three hundred . . . five hundred . . . a thousand regular friends. I thought he couldn't possibly cherish them all.

So I assumed Yvonne was another occasional companion. She spent time with Dewey, but they didn't run to each other. I don't remember Dewey waiting for her. But somehow, in the course of Yvonne's visit, they always seemed to end up together, wandering the library on a secret, silent quest, happy as clams.

It wasn't until Dewey's passing that Yvonne started talking. A little. For nineteen years, I had kept up a steady stream of Dewey chats with many of the library regulars. After his death, he seemed like all we could discuss. It wasn't until the end of the initial rush, though, when the cold slog of February settled over us and the realization that Dewey was gone had dug deep into our bones, that Yvonne approached me, quietly and nervously, and talked about Dewey. She told me how much she had looked forward to seeing him. How much he had understood her. How gentle and brave he was. She told me, more than once, about the day Dewey slept on her lap for an hour, and how special that made her feel.

"That's nice," I told her. "Thank you."

I appreciated her thoughtfulness, especially since I knew how hard it was for her to initiate conversation. But I was busy, and I never asked her anything more. Why should I? Dewey sat on everyone's lap. Of course it was special.

After a few short conversations, Yvonne stopped talking. She faded back into the background, and her special moment with Dewey became just another brushstroke on the giant portrait of his life. It wasn't until two years later, after I heard how thrilled she was that her name appeared in *Dewey*, that I sat down with her. By then, I had collected so many sweet but simple stories from regular library users about Dewey — stories that amounted to little more than "I can't explain it, he just made me happy" — that I doubted there was much to this one.

But Yvonne's story was different. There was something about her moment with Dewey that reminded me why I have always loved libraries. And small towns. And cats. Yvonne was so closed off, I must admit, that I didn't learn much about her. I thought I had, at the time, but when I read this story,

I realized that she remained, and always will remain, something of a mystery.

What I learned instead is how different lives can be, even when they are lived alongside each other. And how easy it is to get lost, even in a straightforward little town like Spencer, Iowa. I learned how hard it is to know someone, and how little that matters if your heart is open to their needs. We don't have to understand; we just have to care.

That is something, once again, I learned from Dewey. That was his Magic. In the end, I guess, this is another story about him.

Yvonne grew up in Sutherland, Iowa, a town of about eight hundred people, thirty miles southwest of Spencer. Her father was what you might call a tinkerer. He worked a small rented farm near County Road M12, served in a series of low-level county government positions, and owned an old water truck that he filled from a well on their property and drove around to local feedlots. I've known a lot of men like him: quiet and a bit shambling, often unnoticed but always there, a good guy searching for the leg up that never arrives. Eventually, after he was voted out of office, the family drifted out of the farm lease and into a house in town. Her father took up factory work. Yvonne, five years old and the youngest of five children, took to caring for the cats that roamed their new property.

I remember those rural childhood days myself: the long, slow seasons, the hours spent playing with my brothers in the yard while my parents worked to make the farm produce. I still remember, as if it was yesterday, the afternoon my dad brought home Snowball, the first animal I ever loved. It was a hot early summer day, and I stood in the yard watching him coming closer and closer out of the knee-high corn. Dad was sweating so badly under his hat, it almost looked like tears, and as I followed his slipstream into the house, I could see he had something in his hands, even though I didn't know what it was.

"It must have been born in the field," he told my mother, "because there were a bunch of them hidden down there. The mother and other babies were killed by the plow. This one," he said, holding up the kitten, which was covered in blood, "had its back legs cut off."

Most farmers would have left the badly injured animal to die, letting nature have its way, but when my dad saw the kitten was still alive, he picked it up and rushed home.

My mother, as much an animal lover as my father, took over from there, nursed it for a month with milk from a bottle. She gave it warm blankets at night, and let it stay in her sweltering kitchen by day. I watched over her shoulder as she cared for it, amazed by the kitten's recovery. By midsummer, Snowball's stumps had healed. A lot of people think cats are lazy, but the effort Snowball made! The determination! In no time, it seemed, she developed the ability to balance on her front two legs, with her back end held straight up. Then she learned to hop, with her rear end swinging in the air like a highfalutin lady, and her tail pointed toward the sky. I loved it. That summer, Snowball and I played together every day. I ran around the farmyard, laughing and shouting, and she hopped after me, her back end waving. In the fall, at the end of each school day, I jumped off the bus, threw down my book bag, and raced into the farmyard, yelling for her. She didn't live long, and when she died I was inconsolable for a while, but I will never forget the way Snowball danced around that yard, in slow motion, like she was doing the jitterbug hop. Her determination, and the lesson from my parents to respect and cherish every living thing, were the lasting legacies of my summer with Snowball.

How different was five-year-old Yvonne's experience? I don't know. I don't know if she played with her older siblings, or if she was left alone in the yard. I don't know if she chose the company of cats out of loneliness or out of a natural love. I do know her parents, like a lot of farm people, didn't think much of cats and didn't help her care for the ones that kept appearing in their yard. "The cats were always dying or disappearing," Yvonne told me. "It broke my heart. But my parents would never buy them food, no matter how often I asked. They said they couldn't afford it."

My clearest childhood memory is of my father, with that injured cat in his hands, talking with my mother. Yvonne's clearest memory is of a photograph. She was six. Her mother wanted a picture of her kids with their favorite cats. Yvonne couldn't find her favorite, a black-and-white kitten known as Black-and-White. Her mother told her to quit looking already and stand with her brother and sister, who were both holding up wiggling cats to the camera.

"Come on, now, smile," her mom commanded.

"I can't find my kitten."

"It doesn't matter. Just smile."

Afterward, Yvonne stared off into the

neighboring fields, biting her lip. There are flat empty spaces in Iowa, even in the towns, where you can watch the world stretch away from you. You can see forever out there if you keep looking, but eventually Yvonne turned away, walked over to her mother, and asked if she would take a picture of her with one of the other cats.

"No," her mom said. "I'm out of film."

"I wanted to cry," Yvonne told me, "but I didn't. I knew they would make fun of me."

Ten years later, when Yvonne was sixteen, her father got a job at the Witco factory, and the family moved to Spencer. I remember venturing into Spencer when I was a teen-ager living in the nearby town of Hartley. It was terrifying. The girls at Spencer High School seemed so worldy, so willing to dress fashionably and talk to boys and linger on street corners, as if they were one step away from being Pink Ladies in *Grease*. I remem-ber thinking they were physically bigger than us country kids, that they could crush us if they wanted. That was Spencer to me, yet I had every advantage. My grandmother lived in town, so I knew the streets and shops; I went to Hartley High School, one of the larger schools in the surrounding area; I was an outgoing, popular girl who almost never felt out of place or overwhelmed. So I can imagine what it must have been like for Yvonne, a shy girl who had never spent time in Spencer, never succeeded in school, and never been comfortable with social situations, even in Sutherland. I understood what she meant when she told me her year and a half at Spencer High School was torture.

Her parents gave her one thing to ease the loneliness: a cat. Just before the move to Spencer, Yvonne's aunt May's cat gave birth to a litter of half-Siamese kittens. As soon as Yvonne saw them, she fell in love. Somehow, she convinced her parents to let her adopt one of the half-Siamese kittens. When they arrived for the adoption, the rambunctious brood was sprinting around the yard, rumbling and tumbling and throwing dirt in one another's faces. Yvonne was overwhelmed. She stared at them and wondered, *How am I ever going to pick my cat?*

Then one kitten, who must have been hiding, crept over and looked up at her with big shy eyes, as if whispering, in the quietest and sweetest voice imaginable: "Hi."

"Okay, I'll take you," Yvonne whispered back.

She named the kitten Tobi. She was browner and rounder than a typical Siamese but had the luxurious softness and gorgeous blue eyes so typical of the breed. And soft wasn't just a description of her fur. Tobi was a soft cat. Soft spoken. Soft in manner. She wasn't courageous, either. She ran when anyone entered a room; she ran when she heard a door open anywhere in the house; she sprinted to the safety of Yvonne's bed when she heard footsteps on the stairs. She went outside only once, running right past Yvonne as she stood in the doorway. Yvonne stepped out onto the concrete stoop and saw Tobi disappearing around the corner of her parent's Spencer house. She ran the other way around the house and met her in the backyard. Tobi came tearing toward her and leapt straight into her arms, a look of terror on her soft little face.

"Oh, don't do that again, kitty," Yvonne begged. "Please don't do that again." It was impossible to tell who was more scared.

"Tobi was a cuddler." That was the way Yvonne described her. "She always wanted to be on top of me. She slept in my bed every night."

"I bet that made you feel good," I replied.

"Yeah, it did," she said. Then she sat looking at me, waiting for my next question.

After high school, Yvonne joined her father at the Witco plant. The factory produced handheld hydraulic tools, known as grease guns, that squirt grease into small spaces inside car engines and other machines. After her struggles at Spencer High School, the line was a relief. The work was fast-paced and physically demanding, but Yvonne was young and strong. She could fasten bolts as quickly as anyone on the line, and it didn't require talking to her colleagues.

"It wasn't the best job in the world," she told me, as if uncomfortable with her obvious pride in a task well done. "But it was work." And there is nothing better, as I well know, than meaningful work.

Yvonne didn't have much of a social life outside the factory, but whenever she finished a shift, she could count on one thing: Tobi would be waiting. The kitten liked high places, away from kicking feet and swinging arms, and she often watched for Yvonne from the top of the bookcase. Other times, Tobi was staring from the top of the stairs when Yvonne opened the front door. If the house was empty, Tobi followed her around: to the kitchen, to the den. But when someone came home, they both headed to Yvonne's room and closed the door. Tobi, Yvonne soon realized, spent most of the day in her bed, under her covers, waiting for the only person she felt comfortable with to return. And while the idea never consciously crossed her mind, that was exactly what

Yvonne wanted: a friend who would always be there for her.

In her twenties, Yvonne moved out of her parents' house and into a fourplex apartment house with her older sister. Tobi loved the quiet. Yvonne loved being on her own. She thrived on the assembly line, affixing small bolts to grease guns. For years, Spencer's grid of numbered streets had intimidated her, and everyone she passed seemed like a stranger. But slowly she developed an appreciation of the patterns, and she began to recognize the faces around her. She shopped in the stores along Grand Avenue or at the new mall on the south side of town. She bought clothes at the Fashion Bug and Tobi's favorite food, Tender Vittles, at a little locally owned pet store. One Halloween, she bought a scary mask. She put it on and tromped heavily up the stairs. She came through the door to the bedroom with a low moan — "ahhhhhhh" — and Tobi's beautiful blue Siamese eyes popped right out of her head. She started to rear back, her fur fluffing out in fear, and Yvonne felt so bad that she tore the mask right off.

"Ah, Tobi," she said. "It's only me."

Tobi stared for a few more seconds, then turned and looked away, as if to say, *I knew that.*

The next day, Yvonne decided to scare Tobi again. She put on the mask and stomped through the bedroom door. Tobi took one look and turned away in disgust, as if to say, *Please. I know it's you.*

Yvonne laughed — "You're a smart one, aren't you, Tobi?" — and gave her a hug. Life was simple, but life was good. Yvonne Barry had found her comfort zone; she had found a companion; and she was happy. Her life was lived in repeated details, small moments in time. At Christmas, Yvonne built a little tunnel out of presents, and Tobi sat in that tunnel for days. "I thought she was unique. Oh, Tobi loves the Christmas tree. But then I found out a lot of other cats did that, too."

In the evening, in her bedroom, she spun Tobi in a swivel chair, the little cat lunging at her hand every time she passed by. Even decades later, Yvonne smiled at the memory. Tobi loved that swivel chair. And if Tobi loved it, then Yvonne loved it.

When the local economy turned sour in the mid-1980s, and Yvonne lost several of her weekly shifts, she moved back in with her parents. I don't know how Yvonne really felt about this, because she wouldn't say, but I don't think it was much of a change. "My rent was too high" was all she told me. "I asked my parents if I could come back, and they said okay.

"Sometimes, my dad wiggled his finger under his newspaper," she continued. "Tobi would jump for it, and dad would laugh. We called it the old newspaper game. But mostly, you know, with my parents, Tobi just sat on the back of the chair, staring out the window while dad read the paper."

I don't know what to make of a story like that. Was there more laughter and fun in that house than I imagined? Did Tobi break through a quiet man's shell? Or was the old newspaper game a brief moment of levity in an otherwise quiet and dusty world? I want to hear the laughter, but I can't help but imagine the hours and days and weeks — even months, if I understood Yvonne's inflections correctly — between rounds of the old newspaper game. I can't help but imagine an older man sitting silently in his chair, a newspaper shielding him from view; a little cat looking away to stare out the window; and a young woman watching them, half hidden in the doorway. Yvonne's siblings had moved out, and I can't believe much more than emptiness filled the long hours in the quiet house. Her mother read romance novels in her bedroom. Her father watched baseball on television. Yvonne and

Tobi slunk upstairs, as quiet as mice, to play spin-the-cat-on-the-chair.

But then, only a couple blocks away, there was Dewey.

A library is more than a storeroom for books. In fact, most of the smart librarians I know believe one of its primary functions doesn't involve books at all. That function is openness and availability. In a world where many people feel displaced by society, a library is a free place to go. How many times have you heard an impoverished child, now successfully grown up, say a library saved his life? Yes, the knowledge stored in the books, and now on the computers, expanded his universe beyond the narrow slice of world he inhabited. But the library also provided something else: space. If there was fighting at home, the child could escape into silence. If he felt neglected, he could find human interaction. It's not even necessary, in a library, to talk to anyone. That's a wonderful thing about the way people are wired. Often, it's enough to simply be in the presence of one another, even if we never say a word.

When I became the director of the Spencer Public Library, my first priority was to make the library more open, accessible, and friendly. New books and materials were part of my plan, but I also wanted to change the attitude. I wanted people to feel comfortable in our space, like they were part of a community instead of visitors to a municipal building. I had the walls painted brighter colors and the imposing black furniture replaced with more comfortable tables and chairs. I started a fund to buy artwork for the walls and sculpture for the tops of the shelves. I instructed the staff to smile at every visitor and say hello. When Dewey appeared in the book return box less than six months later, I saw immediately he would fit perfectly with the plan. I knew he was a calm kitten; I knew he would never cause problems. But I thought he would just be background, like another piece of artwork to make the library feel like a home.

But Dewey had no intention of being background. From the second his paws healed (he suffered frostbite in the book return box) and he could walk the library without discomfort, Dewey insisted on being front and center. The paradox for a librarian is that, for a library to work, you can't be *too* friendly. You want people to feel welcome, but you don't want them to feel hassled. A library is not a social environment. You can enter anytime, but you only have to be as involved as you want. It's your choice. If you want conversation, you can chat all day. If you want anonymity, the library promises that, too. Many people, especially those who are marginalized or nervous in social situations, love the library's mix of privacy and public space — the chance to be surrounded by people without the pressure of interacting with them.

This can create a conundrum for librarians in the case of, for instance, Bill Mullenberg. For decades, Bill was the principal of Spencer High School, a job that was not only respected and important but required him to talk with hundreds of people every week. I know retirement was difficult for him, because it is always hard to leave behind your life's work. But Bill's transition was made much harder by the death of his beloved wife.

After she died, he started coming to the library every morning to read the newspaper — and I knew it wasn't to save the subscription cost. Bill was lonely at home by himself, and he wanted a place to go. What was the staff to do? We said hi, but it would have been against the ethos of a library to force the conversation past small talk. Besides, we were busy. Spencer didn't pay us to be friends or therapists; everyone on staff had to work forty hours every week, at least, just to keep the place running.

That's when Dewey waltzed in. As a cat, he didn't have the social limitations of a librarian. And as our social director and official greeter, he didn't have other work to keep him busy in the back offices. Dewey thought nothing of walking up to strangers and jumping on their laps. If they pushed him away, he'd come back two or three times, until he got the message he wasn't wanted. Then he'd walk away, no harm done. A pushy cat, after all, is not nearly as annoying as an overly "helpful" librarian, because there's no feeling that they are judging you or pressuring you or asking you about things you'd rather not share.

The effect when a visitor embraced Dewey's presence, however, was profound. Within a month of Bill accepting Dewey as a lap mate, Bill's demeanor changed. For one thing, he was smiling. I think the first time I'd seen him smile since his wife died was the second or third time Dewey jumped into his lap, pushed aside the newspaper, and demanded affection. Now he was smiling all the time, just as he had in his old job. He was interacting more with the staff, and he was staying longer each morning to hang out and chat. Watching Bill, I realized for the first time that Dewey was more than fuzzy artwork walking around the floor.

After Dewey arrived, visits to the library increased dramatically. I'm not sure he brought people through the door for their first visit, but I think he convinced them to come back. Yvonne, for instance, didn't visit the library until Dewey was four or five months old. She had read the article about him in the *Spencer Daily Reporter* shortly after his rescue, but it wasn't until summer that she decided to stop in. By then, Dewey was half grown. With his bushy tail, brilliant copper fur, and magnificent ruff, he already looked like the pampered, patrolling King of the Library. Which he was. Cool, confident Dewey was completely at ease in his surroundings. The first time Yvonne saw him, he was strutting around as if he owned the place.

What a beautiful cat, she thought.

I don't know how they met. I assume Dewey approached Yvonne, because that's what he always did, but she may well have been drawn to him. He was easy to talk to, for lack of a better phrase, since there's no social pressure in petting a cat. It wasn't until they were well into their relationship that I noticed, in passing, that Dewey was usually at her side. He rubbed her leg, sniffed her hand when she petted him, listened to her whispered greetings. When she wadded a piece of paper into a ball and threw it to him, he pounced on it, rolled on his back, and kicked it into the air with his back legs. So she threw more.

She bought him trinkets at the mall, the same toys she bought for Tobi. She liked to hold the toys out at different heights and make Dewey leap for them. One day, she held a toy at head height, about five feet off the floor. "Come on, Dewey," she told him. "You can do it."

Dewey stared up at the toy, then looked down. *He can't do it,* Yvonne thought. Then Dewey turned and sprang — like a rocket, as Yvonne remembered it, *just like a rocket* — and grabbed the toy out of her hand. She stared at him in amazement, then started to laugh. "You fooled me, Dewey," she said. "You fooled me."

In November, she came to Dewey's first birthday party. She's not in the video, but I'm not surprised. Yvonne is one of those people who stands beside you for an hour until you look over and say, "Oh, I didn't see you there." She is the quiet but industrious worker who never seems to come out of his office; the neighbor you rarely see; the woman on the bus who never looks up from her book. It's wrong to think of this as sad, or unfulfilling, because who are we to judge anyone's internal life? How are we to know what a person's days are like? Emily Dickinson's neighbors thought of her as a sad spinster living quietly in her parents' house, when in fact she was one of the greatest poets in the history of the English language and a frequent correspondent with the most accomplished writers of her day. Shyness isn't a problem, after all; it's a personality type.

Dewey, of course, was exactly the opposite. Watching him in that birthday video is to see a true ham at work. Children were crowded around him, jostling for position, but Dewey never seemed startled. No matter how much they grabbed and shrieked, he enjoyed the attention. He lapped it up almost as fervently as he licked his mouse-shaped, cream cheese–covered cat food birthday cake. Dewey didn't have a problem biting into that cake right in front of his adoring crowd. And I bet, after the video was turned off, he did something just as magical: He walked up to Yvonne — or at least made eye contact with her — and made her feel special for coming.

I know for a fact that happened a year later, at a library party in 1989. About two hundred people came to celebrate the reopening of the library — it had been closed briefly for remodeling — and I was busy giving tours of the improvements. Yvonne was there, on the edge of the crowd, probably feeling like she was back in high school, because anonymity in a library is a blessing but anonymity at a party is awkward and unsettling. Her discomfort ended, however, when she saw Dewey weaving through the crowd. No one was paying attention to him, and that fact clearly irked him to no end. Then he spotted Yvonne and waltzed over. She picked him up. She held him to her heart. Dewey put his head on her shoulder and started purring.

"Someone took a picture of us," Yvonne told me several times in our conversations. "I don't know who it was, but they took a picture of us. It was only my back. It was Dewey's face. But there was a picture of us together."

I don't want to make too much of Dewey's relationship with Yvonne. I don't want to imply that her life was centered around the library. I know she led a circumscribed existence, and I know she was no Emily Dickinson, but I also know that Yvonne Barry has kept a large piece of her soul hidden from view. I know she corresponded regularly with friends. I know, like most of us, she had a love-hate relationship with her job.

She was proud of her work but increasingly frustrated at being passed over for higher-paying positions. I know she loved her family, and beneath their silences was a complex and multifaceted web of relationships. What those facets were . . . they're hers to keep, as she has chosen, for herself alone.

What she shared with me was Tobi. I think Dewey, perhaps because he was so different from her, was Yvonne's social outlet. Tobi was Yvonne's best friend. She loved to be *with* Dewey, but she loved Tobi. And Tobi loved her in return. More than anything in the world, Tobi cared about Yvonne Barry, and she was excited whenever Yvonne walked through the door. Tobi and Yvonne weren't opposites, you see, they were soul mates. When Yvonne told me, "She was a quiet cat. She was gentle. She never wanted to get in any trouble with anybody; she just wanted to live and let live, you know what I mean?" my first thought was, *She could be talking about herself.*

They were also dedicated to each other. "I never took any trips overnight," Yvonne told me, "because I couldn't bring myself to leave Tobi." They traveled together once, to visit her sister Dorothy in Minneapolis. For the first fifteen miles, Tobi screamed and slammed her face against the bars of her cage. It wasn't until Milford, Iowa, that she realized she wasn't going to the veterinarian's office and settled down. For a few miles, she meowed at Yvonne, as if hoping for an explanation. But how can a cat understand a concept like Minnesota? Eventually, she slunk to the back of her carrier and lay down . . . for five hours. In Minneapolis, Tobi went straight to the guest bedroom. She used her litter, ate her Tender Vittles, and hid under the bedcovers until Yvonne came in each night. Then Tobi climbed up and nestled against Yvonne's neck, overjoyed to have her best friend back. "I love you, Tobi," Yvonne whispered, snuggling up to her cat. Except for the drive, it was like any other weekend of their lives.

It's tempting to say that's the reason Yvonne loved Tobi so much: The cat was the only constant in her life. But, in reality, I think Yvonne's life was mostly constants. The same job on the assembly line, doing the same task. The same errands. The same meals. The same silent evenings at home with her parents. Even her life with Dewey had a comforting familiarity because she knew he would always be there. They may not have had a lot of excitement, but Tobi and Yvonne had their routine. They had each other. And that was enough.

But there's one thing about cats we must all face: Most of the time, we outlive them. Thirteen years of love was a small slice of life for Yvonne, but it was a lifetime for Tobi. By 1990, the cat was visibly slowing down, and her arthritis made it difficult to climb up and down the stairs. Her fur thinned, and more and more often, Yvonne came home to find Tobi curled so tightly in their bed that she didn't want to wake up.

Around the same time, Yvonne discovered the Bible. She says the catalyst was the buildup to the first Gulf War. The threat of violence made her anxious and unsure about the future, and she felt unhappiness bearing down like a weight. I have no reason to doubt that, but there might have been other pains more difficult for a quiet person to discuss. Like her frustration with the Witco plant, where management refused to promote her to a better position even though she knew she could handle the work. And the soreness in her knees, caused by standing for eight hours a day at the assembly line. And her mother's deteriorating health. And couldn't part of it have been, with as much as Tobi meant to her, the inevitable and obvious decline of her beloved cat?

As war approached, and Tobi's health faltered, Yvonne's religious reading increased.

She had initially been drawn to biblical prophecies of war and destruction, but it was the hope and comfort of the Lord that ultimately inspired her. Six months after picking up the Bible for the first time, as the troop carriers rolled across the Iraqi border and explosions blackened the Baghdad sky, Yvonne Barry knelt beside her bed and asked Jesus to enter her heart.

"I felt like I had stuck my finger in a light socket," she said of that moment. "I felt so different, and after that, I had the most peaceful night's sleep of my life. And I knew something had changed."

Yvonne began reading her Bible for at least an hour every day. She started attending First Baptist Church twice on Sundays and every Thursday for prayer group. There was often a group activity of some sort at the church, and Yvonne found herself drawn to their communion. On quiet nights at home, she sought comfort in the Book. Sometimes Tobi was there, curled at her side, but the cat spent most of her time sleeping in a hooded basket, which Yvonne filled with sheep's wool to keep her warm. Yvonne heard Fancy Feast helped cats live longer, so she started buying Fancy Feast instead of Tender Vittles, even though she couldn't really afford it. She adored Tobi; she cared for her as she always had. But after dinner, instead of spinning Tobi in her swivel chair, Yvonne went back to her Bible, leaving Tobi more and more on her own.

And then, a year after Yvonne became a Christian, Tobi started stumbling. One summer evening, she fell in the bedroom and urinated on herself. She looked up at Yvonne, scared to death, begging her to explain. Yvonne took her to Dr. Esterly, who gave her the bad news. Tobi's liver had failed. The vet could keep her alive for a few days, but she would be in a great deal of pain.

Yvonne looked at the floor. "I don't want that," she whispered.

She held Tobi in her arms. She stroked her as Dr. Esterly prepared the needle. The cat laid her head against Yvonne's elbow and closed her eyes, as if she felt safe and comfortable with her friend. When she felt the prick, Tobi let out a terrible yowl, but she didn't bolt. She simply looked up into Yvonne's face, terrified, wondering, then slumped over and slipped away. Yvonne, with the help of her father, buried her in a far corner of their backyard.

She had so many happy memories. The Christmas tree. The spinning chair. The nights together in bed. But that last yowl, a sound unlike any Tobi had ever made . . . it was something Yvonne could not forget. It tore her, and a great rush of guilt came flooding out. Tobi dedicated her life to Yvonne, but in her last years, when Tobi was old and sick and needed her most, Yvonne felt she had turned away. She hadn't spun her in the swivel chair; she hadn't built Christmas present tunnels; she hadn't noticed how sick Tobi was getting.

That night, she went to prayer meeting. Her eyes were puffy and red, and the tears were still on her cheeks. Her fellow worshippers kept asking, "Are you okay, Yvonne? What's the matter?"

"My cat died today," she told them.

"Oh, I'm so sorry," they said, patting her on the arm. Then, with nothing more to say, they walked away. They meant well, Yvonne knew. They were good people. But they didn't understand. To them, it was just a cat. Like the rest of us, they didn't even know Tobi's name.

The next day, when she visited the Spencer Public Library, Yvonne didn't feel any better. In fact, she felt worse. More guilty. More alone. She had no desire, she realized, to even browse the library books. Instead, she went straight to a chair, sat down, and thought about Tobi.

A minute later, Dewey came around the

corner and walked slowly toward her. Every time he had seen her, for at least the last few years, Dewey had meowed and run to the women's bathroom door. Yvonne would open the door, and Dewey would jump on the sink and meow until she turned on the water. After staring at the column of water for half a minute, he'd bat it with his paw, jump back in shock, then creep forward and repeat the process again. And again. And again. It was their special game, a ritual that had developed over a hundred mornings spent together. And Dewey did it every single time.

But not this time. This time, Dewey stopped, cocked his head, and stared at her. Then he sprang into her lap, nuzzled her softly with his head, and curled up in her arms. She stroked him gently, occasionally wiping away a tear, until his breathing became gentle and relaxed. Within minutes, he was asleep.

She kept petting him, slowly and gently. After a while, the weight of her sadness seemed to lighten, and then lift, until, finally, it felt as if it were floating away. It wasn't just that Dewey realized how much she hurt. It wasn't just that he knew her, or that he was a friend. As she watched Dewey sleeping, she felt her guilt disappear. She had done her best for Tobi, she realized. She had loved her little cat. She wasn't required to spend every minute proving that. There was nothing wrong with having a life of her own. It was time, for both of their sakes, to let Tobi go.

My friend Bret Witter, who helps me with these books, has a pet peeve (pun intended). He hates when people ask him, "So why was Dewey so special?"

"Vicki spent two hundred eighty-eight pages trying to explain that," he says. "If I could summarize it for you in a sentence, she would have written a greeting card instead."

He thought that was clever. Then he realized the question always made him think of something that happened in his own life, something that didn't involve cats or libraries or even Iowa but that might provide a short answer nonetheless. So he'd crack about the greeting card, then tell a story about growing up with a severely mentally and physically handicapped kid in his hometown of Huntsville, Alabama. The boy went to his school and his church, so by the time the incident happened in seventh grade, Bret had spent time with him six days a week, nine months a year, for seven years. In that whole time, the boy, who was too handicapped to speak, had never gotten emotional, never expressed happiness or frustration, never brought attention to himself in any way.

Then one day, in the middle of Sunday school, he started screaming. He pushed over a chair, picked up a container of pencils, and, with an exaggerated motion, began throwing them wildly around the room. The other kids sat at the table, staring. The Sunday school teacher, after some initial hesitation, began yelling at him to settle down, to be careful, to stop disrupting the class. The boy kept screaming. The teacher was about to throw him out of the room when, all of a sudden, a kid named Tim stood up, walked over, put his arm around the boy "like he was a human being," as Bret always tells it, and said, "It's all right, Kyle. Everything is okay."

And Kyle calmed down. He stopped flailing, dropped the pencils, and started crying. And Bret thought, *I wish I had done that. I wish I had understood what Kyle needed.*

That's Dewey. He always seemed to understand, and he always knew what to do. I'm not suggesting Dewey was the same as the boy who reached out — Dewey was a cat, after all — but he had an empathy that was rare. He sensed the moment, and he responded. That's what makes people, and animals, special. Seeing. Caring. Loving. Doing.

It's not easy. Most of the time, we are so busy and distracted that we don't even realize we missed the opportunity. I can look back now and see that the first ritual Yvonne developed with Dewey, before the bathroom-water-swatting, was catnip. Every day, she clipped fresh catnip out of her yard and placed it on the library carpet. Dewey always rushed over to sniff it. After a few deep snorts, he plowed his head into it, chewing wildly, his mouth flapping and his tongue lapping at the air. He rubbed his back on the floor so the little green leaves stuck in his fur. He rolled onto his stomach and pushed his chin against the carpet, slithering like the Grinch stealing Christmas presents. Yvonne always knelt beside him, laughing and whispering, "You really love that catnip, Dewey. You really love that catnip, don't you?" as he flailed his legs in a series of wild kicks until, finally, he collapsed exhausted onto the floor, his legs spread out in every direction and his belly pointed toward the sky.

Then one day, with Dewey in full catnip conniption (the library staff called it the Dewey Mambo), Yvonne looked up and saw me staring at her. I didn't say anything, but a few days later, I stopped her and said, "Yvonne, please don't bring Dewey so much catnip. I know he enjoys it, but it's not good for him."

She didn't say anything. She just looked down and walked away. I only meant for her to cut her gift back to, for instance, once a week, but she never brought another leaf of catnip to the library.

At the time, I thought I was doing the right thing, because that catnip was wearing Dewey out. He would go absolutely bonkers for twenty minutes, then Yvonne would leave and Dewey would pass out for hours. That cat was catatonic. It didn't seem fair. Yvonne was enjoying Dewey's company, but his other friends weren't getting a chance.

In hindsight, I should have been more delicate in handling the catnip incident. I should have understood that this wasn't just a habit for Yvonne, it was an important part of her day. Instead of examining the root of the behavior, I looked at the outward actions and told her to stop. Instead of putting my arm around her, I pushed her away.

But Dewey — he never did that. A thousand times, in a thousand different ways, Dewey was there when people needed him. He did it for dozens of people, I'm sure, who have never opened up to me. He did it for

Bill Mullenburg, and he did it for Yvonne, exactly as Tim had done it with Kyle in Bret's Sunday school class. When no one else understood, Dewey made the gesture. He didn't understand the root causes, of course, but he sensed something was wrong. And out of animal instinct, he acted. In his own way, Dewey put his arm around Yvonne and said, *It's all right. You are one of us. You will be fine.*

I'm not saying Dewey changed Yvonne's life. I think he eased her sorrow, but he by no means ended it. A month after Tobi's passing, Yvonne lost her temper on the assembly line and was not only fired but escorted out of the building. She had been frustrated by management for a long time, but I can't help but believe the last straw was the pain of Tobi's death.

It didn't stop there. A few years later, her mother died of colon cancer. Two years after that, Yvonne was diagnosed with uterine cancer. She drove six hours to Iowa City, for six months, to receive treatment. By the time she beat the cancer, her legs had given way. She had stood in the same position on the assembly line eight hours a day, five days a week, for years, and the effort had worn down her knees.

But she still had her faith. She still had

her routines. And she still had Dewey. He lived fifteen years after Tobi's death, and for all those years, Yvonne Barry came to the library several times each week to see him. If you had asked me at the time, I would not have said their relationship was particularly special. Many people came into the library every week, and almost all of them stopped to visit with Dewey. How was I to know the difference between those who thought Dewey was cute, and those who needed and valued his friendship and love?

After Dewey's memorial service, Yvonne told me about the day Dewey sat on her lap and comforted her. It still meant something to her, more than a decade later. And I was touched. Until that moment, I didn't know Yvonne had ever had a cat of her own. I didn't know what Tobi meant to her, but I knew Dewey had comforted her, as he had always comforted me, simply by being present in her life. Little moments can mean everything. They can change a life. Dewey taught me that. Yvonne's story (once I took the time to listen) confirmed it. That moment on her lap epitomized Dewey's understanding and friendship, his effect on the people of Spencer, Iowa, in a way I had never considered before.

I didn't notice when Yvonne stopped coming to the library after Dewey's death. I knew her visits had become less frequent, but she disappeared just as she appeared: like a shadow, without a sound. By the time I went to visit her two years after Dewey's death, she was living in a rehabilitation facility with a brace on her right leg. She was only in her fifties, but the doctors weren't sure she would walk again. Even if she recovered, she had no place to go. Her father was in the nursing home next door, and the family house had been sold. Yvonne told the new owners, "Don't dig down in that corner of the yard because that's where my Tobi is buried."

"Tobi's still down there," she told me. "At least her body anyway."

There was a Bible on her nightstand and a scripture taped to her wall. Her father was in Yvonne's room in a wheelchair, a frail old man who had lost his ability to hear and see. She introduced us, but beyond that, Yvonne hardly seemed to notice he was there. Instead, she showed me a small figurine of a Siamese cat, which she kept on a tray beside her bed. Her aunt Marge had given it to her, in honor of Tobi. No, she didn't have any photographs of Tobi to share. Her sister had put all of Yvonne's belongings into storage, and she didn't have the key. If I needed a photograph, she said, there was always the one of her and Dewey, taken at the library party twenty years before. Someone, somewhere, probably had a copy.

When I asked her about Dewey, she smiled. She told me about the women's bathroom, and his birthday party, and finally about the afternoon he spent on her lap. Then she looked down and shook her head sadly.

"I went to the library several times to see his grave," she said. "I've been inside. I looked around. It just doesn't seem the same. No Dewey. I mean, I saw the statue of him and I thought, *That's nice, it looks just like Dewey,* but it wasn't like Dewey was really there.

"I don't go to that place anymore. It was that cat, you know. Dewey, he'd always be there. Even if he was hiding somewhere, I'd just say to myself, 'Well, I'll see him next time.' But then I went and no Dewey. I looked at the place where he used to sit and it was empty and I thought, *Well, nothing to do here.* It just feels like a building with books in it now."

I wanted to ask her more, to figure something out, to learn something profound about cats and libraries and the crosscurrents of loneliness and love underneath the surface of even the most peaceful towns and the most peaceful lives. I wanted to know her because, in the end, it felt as if she was barely present in her own story.

But Yvonne just smiled. Was she thinking of that moment with Dewey on her lap? Or was she thinking of something else, something deeper that she would never share, and that only she would ever understand?

"He was my Dewey Boy." That's all she said. "Big Dew."

Two
Mr. Sir Bob Kittens (aka Ninja, aka Mr. Pumpkin Pants)

"I simply wanted to thank you for putting into such eloquent words what many of us who have loved a cat, or any animal, feel every day. They are our family, and we love them just as deeply and miss them just as desperately when they are gone."

I've known a lot of cats in my life, so I know

that all cats are different, even the special ones. Some cats are special because they are sweet. Some cats are special because they are survivors. Some cats are special because they were exactly what someone needed at exactly the time they needed it: a soul mate, a companion, a distraction, a friend. And some cats are just plain crazy.

That would be Mr. Sir Bob Kittens, formerly known as Ninja, who lives in an ordinary suburban house in Michigan with his family, James and Barbara Lajiness and their teenage daughter, Amanda. Mr. Kittens is not the cuddly cat. He's the quirky cat, the cat with attitude, the one who does his own thing, usually in a way you can't quite comprehend. Maybe that's why he was the last kitten adopted from his litter at the Humane Society of Huron Valley in Ann Arbor, Michigan. Or maybe it was the note on his cage: NINJA, it read. Then: DOESN'T GET ALONG WITH OTHER CATS OR DOGS. Apparently, he fought them instead.

When Barbara Lajiness met Ninja, it was not love at first sight. Yes, he was gorgeous, with big amber eyes, bright orange fur, and the longest whiskers she had ever seen on a kitten. Yes, he seemed intelligent and well behaved. But he wasn't active. He wasn't climbing and clamoring for attention like

the other kittens in the shelter. He wasn't
. . . well, he wasn't doing anything. He was
just lying alone in his big empty cage, hardly
bothering to look at the strangers wandering
by.

"He's great with people," the volunteer
said when she saw Barbara looking at Ninja.
"It's just other animals he has a problem
with."

Barbara's husband and daughter wanted
him. They had sensed something special in
his mischievous eyes and seemingly calm
disposition. When Barbara held him, she
felt it, too. A potential energy, perhaps, that
seemed barely contained. So she put him
down and told her daughter sorry, she wasn't
ready. The family had lost their beloved cat
only a month before. Barbara didn't tell her
daughter this, but she was terrified of becoming emotionally invested in another living thing that would only end up dying on
her.

But Ninja was so sleek and beautiful. And
her daughter and husband were so adamant.
And every time she went back to the shelter,
which she never should have done but just
couldn't help it, it became more and more
clear to Barbara that poor Ninja was never
going to get adopted. Not in that isolation
cell that made him seem like the worst in-

mate in the prison, and not with that sign on his cage. "He wasn't a Mr. Cuddle, purr-like-a-freight-train cat," Barbara recalled, "but he deserved a home. Every animal deserves a home. It was sad that no one had a place in their lives for him." Barbara cared about saving animals, and here was a cat that obviously needed saving. He needed a good, loving, pet-free (obviously) home, and that is exactly what she could provide. She couldn't turn away. Her whole life, largely thanks to her mother, Barbara Lajiness had never turned away from a creature in need.

"Why do you call him Ninja?" Barbara asked the volunteer as she was filling out the final paperwork and paying for his adoption.

"Don't worry," the volunteer replied with a smile. "You'll see."

Barbara's parents divorced in 1976. She was eight years old, and even at that young age, she knew it was coming. Her parents hadn't been getting along for years, and life at home had been uncomfortable and tense as two people who had gone separate ways struggled to make it work. Her mother was focused on the family. Her father wanted to have fun: to go drinking, to stay out late without the kids, to travel. When he came home, he was angry and frustrated with his life. Barbara had two teenage brothers, and they didn't appreciate either his absence or his anger. For a while, everyone yelled. Then nobody talked. Barbara's outlet, even at that young age, was the family cat, Samantha. *That's good,* the little girl thought when her brothers told her their father had moved out for good. *Now it might be calm in the house.* What a sad, sad thought for an eight-year-old child.

But she soon found out that life without her father was far worse than she had expected, at least financially. Almost instantly, the family plummeted from a comfortable, middle-class existence to the poverty line. Her father had a steady job working for Michigan Bell, the local telephone company. Before they were married, her mother had worked for Michigan Bell, too, as a telephone operator. She gave up her job to raise her children. Eighteen years later, she discovered that even in good times, jobs for middle-aged women with skimpy résumés were scarce. In 1976, in the hardscrabble communities around Flint, Michigan, they were nonexistent. There was barely enough work for the men who had once been employed by General Motors but were losing their jobs as the company took their factories overseas. The only job Evelyn Lambert could find to support her children was at a nursing home, cooking breakfast for the residents. Her shift started at 3:00 A.M. She was paid minimum wage.

It wasn't considered acceptable work for a mother. In 1976, in the small town of Fenton, Michigan, the commuter town outside Flint where the Lamberts lived, no work was considered acceptable for a mother. In Fenton, women didn't get divorced; they didn't work outside the home; they didn't leave their children alone for long stretches of time. Nobody wanted even to acknowledge what had happened to Evelyn Lambert. It was too real somehow, and who knows, it might be contagious. Some of the neighbors openly pitied her, something Barbara's mother could never stand. Others shunned her. Barbara found herself mocked at elementary school, where everyone seemed to know everything about her mom. Her friends were no longer allowed to come over and play, since there was no one to watch them. In only a few months, Barbara realized, her social status had fallen apart as quickly as the family finances. It didn't help that her father had moved to Grand Blanc, a nearby suburb of Flint, and was spending his time and money on a woman more interested in living the way he wanted to live.

Finally, a neighbor reached out to them. Her name was Ms. Merce, and she lived a few houses down and across the street. Ms. Merce, along with a few other local women, had started an organization called Adopt-a-Pet. The local humane society, in those days, was essentially an animal disposal unit. They kept the animals only a day or two before putting them to sleep. They were killing animals by the hundreds, and Ms. Merce and her friends didn't think that was any way for a civilized society to act. Adopt-a-Pet took in animals and kept them as long as it took to find a home. These days, no-kill animal shelters are common throughout the world. But more than thirty years ago, in Flint, Michigan, this was an incomprehensible concept. Cats and dogs were just animals, and animals didn't have much value. They were disposable playthings that died or ran away and were replaced. Adopt-a-Pet was bucking the attitude of an entire community.

When Ms. Merce asked Evelyn if she would be an animal foster parent, Barbara's mother was eager to volunteer. Why? Barbara hesitated for a long time before saying simply, "I guess Mom was just hardwired to help animals." That's probably somewhat true. Evelyn Lambert had always shown an embarrassing (at the time) level of concern for all living things. She didn't believe in herbicide, so her lawn was full of weeds. She didn't believe in waste, so she used old food containers as planters. She preferred herbal remedies to doctors' visits and despised insecticides. She believed in the sanctity of life. Every life, even insects. She was wired for compassion.

But she was also clearly lonely. And aimless in her unfulfilling job. And stung by the rejection of her husband and community. And eager to make a statement by adopting a cause that her husband would never have endorsed and her small-minded neighbors would never understand. What started as a favor for Adopt-a-Pet became, seemingly overnight, a cause. Almost as quickly, the nebulous idea of "animal foster care" became ten cats of various ages, colors, and conditions living together in one small suburban house.

It was not an easy time. Money was tight. Barbara's mother watered down the milk to stretch it for a few extra days and made a schedule every Sunday that showed exactly what could be eaten by the children while she was away at work. The biggest treat was a can of soda, which Barbara and her brother Scott had to split, and the biggest argument was always over who had drunk more than their share. Sometimes, there was barely food on the table by Friday night, even as Barbara's father was off in the next town with another woman, eating at expensive restaurants and taking out-of-state vacations.

Barbara took on the responsibility of running the household. She felt compelled to do it, as much out of fear as love. A few weekends after her parents' divorce, her neighbors offered to take her on a camping trip. Before the camper reached the end of the block, Barbara started screaming to be taken home. She was deathly afraid that if she left, her mother would be gone when she returned. She turned that terror, that fear of abandonment, into activity. She fed and watered the cats, emptied their litter, and cleaned their messes. She cooked meals in the microwave and washed the dishes when she and Scott were through. Every night before going to bed, she made sure everything was clean and in its proper place, so that her mother wouldn't have to worry when she arrived home in the middle of the night. If it snowed, nine-year-old Barbara put on her jacket and shoveled the driveway so that her mother could pull right into the garage. She was working to hold their world together, in her own way, as much as her mom.

There weren't many gifts, even at Christmas. The first year without Dad, the family waited until Christmas Eve to buy a Christmas tree because that's when the trees were cheapest. On the way home, Barbara and her fifteen-year-old brother, Scott (the oldest brother, Mark, was eighteen and not spending much time with the family), started fighting in the backseat. As they turned into the snowy driveway, their mother starting waving at them to stop.

"Quiet down," she yelled.

They didn't.

"Right now. I mean it. Right now."

The kids sat, shocked, and stared with their mother at the dark house in the silent suburban neighborhood. For a moment, there was nothing but the snow and the wind. Then they heard the tiny meow.

The next second, Evelyn Lambert was out of the car and clambering around in the snow. Her reputation as the "crazy cat lady" had already buzzed around Fenton, and if someone had an animal they didn't want, they often left it in the Lambert front yard. Over the next few years, the family would turn into the driveway dozens of times to find a sad-eyed animal staring at their car.

If it was a dog, they took it into the Adopt-a-Pet office. If it was a cat, they usually kept it because, well, that's what the Lamberts did. They helped cats in need.

This time, it was Scott who finally found the cat. The throwers had been aiming for the cat lady's house, no doubt, but they must have gotten the wrong address, because the wet and shivering kitten was buried in the snowbank across the street. Barbara remembers vividly the sight of her brother, a crazy smile on his face and a headband around his ears, walking up the driveway with the light from the garage reflecting off the snow and a tiny, shivering, coal-black kitten huddled inside his jacket.

She remembers pulling the kitten out of her brother's jacket, snuggling him to her cheek, and saying, "He smells like Hamburger Helper."

Then she smiled. She hadn't been expecting any presents that Christmas, but suddenly, as if by magic rather than cruelty and indifference, one had appeared.

She named the kitten Smoky. Although the Lambert house was full of cats, some adopted quickly and some around for months, Smoky was different. When Barbara held him that night, Smoky had hugged her and rubbed against her cheek. That's when she knew he was hers. Forever. Barbara's mother called him Black Spaghetti because he was like a limp noodle in her presence. Smoky loved his girl so much that he would let her do anything to him. She dressed him in doll clothes; she pushed him around in a stroller; she carried him on his back in her arms like a newborn baby. When she played dress-up, she wore him over her shoulders like a shawl. He was totally relaxed in her hands. The other cats slept on the first floor of the house or, in the warmer months, in the unfinished basement. Smoky curled up with Barbara every night.

She loved the other cats, too. They had been her companions in the lonely afternoons when her friends ignored her, and her mother was at work. But Smoky was her friend and confidante. She didn't want to burden her mother, who was already burdened enough, so she told Smoky her problems. Many times, they sat together in her room with the door closed. "I'm really sad today," she confided in him. Or "I'm scared and lonely. I don't know what's going to happen." If her mother yelled at her for spilling water on the floor while washing dishes, Smoky understood it wasn't her fault, she was only a child, and she was trying her best. When she came back from another soul-crushing visit to her father, whom she increasingly hated, Smoky snuggled against her side and purr, purr, purred. He let her pet him on the head and play with his paws. There was nothing more comforting than pushing on Smoky's footpads and watching his claws come out and retract, come out and retract. He just stared at her, blinking slowly in that sleepy way cats do, purring deep and strong. He never complained.

He was there when, at ten years old, Barbara's father broke the news. He had a new girlfriend by then, and they were leading a glamorous life in an upper-class suburb of Detroit: vacations, stylish clothes, wine tastings. One weekend, he took Barbara and Scott to a movie, something their mother couldn't afford. As they were settling into their seats, he turned to Barbara and said, "I got married."

"No, you didn't," she said.

"Yes, Barbara, I did. Last month."

Barbara sat in the dark movie theatre, crying. She didn't know what she expected, or why she was upset. Her father was married to someone else. It was done. It had already happened. She didn't even know why it bothered her. She had known forever that he wasn't coming back.

She didn't talk to Smoky about it. That

night, she just held him and cried. He snuggled against her and purred.

It was hard on her mother, too. It was hard to watch her husband living a fancy life; hard to watch him occasionally (very occasionally, according to Barbara) give her children things she couldn't afford; hard to watch him find happiness with someone else. The economy in the late 1970s was bad across the nation; in Flint, Michigan, it was abominable. Jobs were disappearing, abandoned houses were burning, and the unemployment rate was spiking above 20 percent. Whole neighborhoods collapsed as General Motors closed assembly lines, and the workers were often on strike. One day, when the family took a rare trip to the Courtland Mall, someone stole the spare tire off their car. That's how desperate the situation was in Flint. Against this backdrop of despair, Barbara's mother struggled through community college, while working full-time and raising three children, to earn an associate's degree in nutrition. She wanted to be in charge of a kitchen instead of just a cook, but her dreams of getting ahead were thwarted by frequent layoffs, increased competition for even the worst jobs, and the closing of one nursing home after another.

Barbara's mother had little sympathy for

the autoworkers. She didn't like the management of General Motors, which was rapidly moving jobs to Mexico, but she didn't particularly like the line workers, either. In nursing home kitchens, she was getting paid $3.35 an hour for backbreaking work on early morning and weekend shifts. The GM employees were making five times as much, with health insurance and benefits. The town was rife with rumors of workers who clocked in before going deer hunting, then came back to clock out for their full day's pay. At the bus and truck plants, people said, inspectors sometimes found vodka bottles inside half-built vehicles. Every time the autoworkers went on strike, half the town was vociferously for them. The other half — a spattering of heartless executives but mostly those unemployed or working bottom-of-the-pyramid jobs — felt like Evelyn Lambert, whose constant refrain was, "What do they have to complain about?"

"I would take that job in a minute," she said of the autoworkers, with increasing bitterness. "I'd take that pay. I'd take half that pay in a second."

But you couldn't get a position in the Shop, as the auto plants were known, unless you knew someone in the Shop, and Evelyn Lambert wasn't that lucky. So she continued to work long days for $3.35 an hour in the industrial kitchens of Flint. The hours were so long, and Evelyn was so often working multiple jobs, that there were whole weeks when Barbara didn't see her mother. She'd be at work when Barbara came home from school, and she wouldn't get home from her last shift until school started the next day. On her days off, she would take long walks. At the time, Barbara thought her mother was trying to escape, very briefly, from her responsibilities and frustrations. Looking back, she realized that her mother always came home from her walks carrying an arm-load of wood and dragging a bag full of soda cans. The wood was to heat the house in the winter. The cans were worth ten cents each at the recycling center. Between the soda can money, a religious devotion to clipping coupons, and some complicated calculations on exactly when to write checks so they would clear at the bank, Barbara's mother kept the household afloat. She often went hungry, but everyone else got fed.

That included the cats, which usually numbered about twelve. It's expensive to keep so many cats, especially when you're scraping for pennies, but Barbara's mother would never cut back on their needs, and she would let them leave only for legitimate adoptions.

It would be naïve not to think that Evelyn Lambert needed those cats to give her life direction and meaning. Even twelve-year-old Barbara understood that. But she also understood that her mother cared about the cats. She understood and loved each one of them, and that love comforted her. One of Barbara's favorite memories was seeing her mother relaxing in her favorite chair in one of her rare moments of peace, with big, lovable Harry sprawled on her lap. Harry talked constantly, and he had a great big rolling purr that never seemed to stop. Everybody called him Mr. Happy because that purr was like joy exploding out of him all the time.

Harry was Barbara's mother's favorite, a big sweet bear of a cat who always wanted a lap whenever Evelyn Lambert had one to offer. With that sweet personality, everyone assumed he'd be adopted right away. And he was. But two weeks later, the new owners brought him back. There was always an excuse when this happened: It scratched my sofa, it scratched my kid, its litter box stinks, or even, it's just not like I thought it was going to be. What was the excuse for Harry? Barbara only remembers that big Harry came back.

At that time, a year or two into being a foster parent, Evelyn Lambert let the cats roam freely inside and outside the house. Then one of the cats, Rosie, ate rat poison that had been left outside by the neighbor. Barbara's mother rushed her to the animal hospital, but it was too late. They had no choice but to put Rosie to sleep. A few weeks later, Harry wandered into the main road and was hit by a van. That was the moment that changed Evelyn Lambert's mind. Never again did she let any of her cats out of the house. After Harry's accident, she was a passionate advocate of keeping cats indoors. Now all the rescue agencies advocate this, of course, but in 1978 she was ahead of her time.

Fortunately, Harry survived the accident. A neighbor saw him lying on the side of the road and called the cat lady. Evelyn ran out with a blanket, eased Harry onto it as best she could, and rushed him to the veterinary clinic. Poor Harry had first been abandoned and then hit by a van, but the only effect on this kind soul was that, with a shattered hip, he walked sideways for the rest of his life. When he sat on Evelyn's lap, her head often bobbing as she teetered on the edge of exhausted sleep, Harry's leg always stuck out awkwardly to the side. But his injury never stopped those deep, booming purrs.

Barbara's brother Scott also had a favorite

cat. Her name was Gracie, and she was a thin gray kitten less than half the size of Happy Harry. She had been abandoned by her owner because she was incontinent and had trouble making it to the litter box. She had feline leukemia, but back then, there was no such diagnosis; the vet thought she had digestive problems. An incontinent kitten can be an issue in a house full of cats, but Scott and Barbara would do anything for their mother. They loved the cats, of course, but that love was mixed up with their pride and admiration for their mom. The passion she felt for the animals, the way she sacrificed to help them, were the defining aspects of their childhood. Everything they experienced was limited by the twin poles of passion and sacrifice; everything they did for their mother was defined by those poles. Was there a little pity, too? Perhaps. Barbara defended her mother. Always. Whenever anyone called her crazy, she told them, "Well, who else is going to do it? Who else, I ask you, is going to help those cats?"

Not once, even as a teenager, did Barbara think, *If it weren't for all these cats, I could have something more.* She helped clip coupons. She went without seconds at dinner. When she was thirteen, she started volunteering at an animal clinic. The Lamberts couldn't afford regular medical care for their cats, but by volunteering, Barbara earned free emergency care when needed.

Since Evelyn Lambert couldn't turn Gracie away — she could never turn away any cat in need — Scott adopted her. He covered the floor and walls of the mudroom with newspaper and brought in a litter box, a food dish, a few toys, and a chair. He sat with Gracie in the mudroom for hours; he even did his homework in there. Whenever Gracie had an accident, Scott threw out the soiled newspaper and brought in a few more sheets. He didn't think of it as a chore. It wasn't something anyone asked him to do. He just loved the little cat.

But Gracie was sick, and without medicine (or even a correct diagnosis), she didn't live long. She died on a freezing February night, and despite the weather, Scott was determined to bury her. He spent the next morning in the wind and ice, crying and banging at the dirt with his shovel, but the ground was frozen solid. He cursed and cried and banged until his hands and face were numb. Finally, out of frustration, he lifted the shovel over his head and slammed it down into the little crevice he had made in the icy dirt . . . and sliced right through the television antennae line.

At that moment, the phone rang. It was Adopt-a-Pet. Someone had thrown a kitten into the Dumpster behind the local pizzeria. She was in surgery because the tops of her ears and half her tail had frozen during the night. Despite the amputations, she was expected to survive. The operation was paid for, but there was no money or space for the hospital to keep the kitten after she woke up from the anesthesia. Barbara's mom didn't hesitate. "We'll take her," she said. "We'll be right over."

That cat was never adopted either. Her name was Amber, and she lived with Barbara's mother for nineteen years. She was stocky and shaped like a sausage, with little cups for ears and hardly any tail, but everybody who knew Amber adored her. Despite the terrible cruelty that led her to the pizzeria Dumpster, she always loved people. She would cuddle on any lap and purr, purr, purr. She was sweet and affectionate, but she was also tough. She was the house's school marm; she didn't let anyone get away with anything. The only female cat who stayed longer than a few weeks, Amber was queen, and everyone knew it. As Barbara recalls, in a house with twelve cats, Amber ate first, drank first, did anything she wanted first. She was the boss, and she had too much respect for Barbara's mother to let any of the other cats misbehave. The house had a large unfinished basement the cats were herded into periodically while the living areas were given a thorough cleaning. Amber made sure all the cats followed orders. She made sure they tried to amuse themselves in the crowded basement. Then, one by one, she sent the boys up the stairs to meow at the door. When Amber came to the door, cleaning time was over. When the queen spoke, even Evelyn Lambert listened.

So there was Harry for Evelyn; Gracie for Scott; Amber for everyone; and for Barbara, of course, there was Smoky. While Evelyn was working, or collecting cans, or just plain exhausted, Smoky was there. No matter what Barbara needed, no matter why, he was always there.

In the end, they were a family, the Lamberts and their cats: a determined mother, a couple of hardworking kids, three permanent cats — Smoky, Harry, and Amber — and a revolving cast of visitors that gave the family an extra reason to pull together. Maybe it wasn't a traditional family, but it was full of love, something that can't be said often enough. There were hard times, of course, especially as the children grew up. In her last year of high school, Barbara grew weary of her mother's complaints about work and her incessant need to be right. (Her mother later admitted she was scared to admit she was wrong about anything because she didn't want Barbara to know she was weak. She thought everything might fall apart.) She was tired of the poverty and the struggle. She didn't understand why her mother didn't just get a better job, why they had to be so different from everyone else, why she had to spend her childhood as the bucktoothed girl with the hand-me-down jeans and the crazy cat-lady mom.

When she graduated from high school and moved to Flint for community college, she didn't speak to her mother for a month. But it didn't take Barbara long to figure out how cruel the world can be and how difficult it is to improve yourself, especially when you were exhausted from the daily struggle to survive. Often, she longed for the comfort of home and her old life: Smoky's head on her arm, Harry's constant purring, Amber's sweet meows. "Normal" life, outside the bounds of cats and poverty, was a little too . . . normal. She craved the company of her cats. But even more, she worried about her mother. She felt obligated to her. Barbara had never known a day in her life when she felt her father loved her. Her mother was the parent who stayed. She was the one who loved her, every minute of every day.

She watched as her mother lost Harry, then Amber. She watched as foster parenting of kittens became so admired, and popular, that Adopt-A-Cat didn't need Evelyn anymore. She went home to her old room and noticed that Smoky, as sweet as ever, had gone completely gray around the muzzle. He still loved her as fervently as before, but he, too, had become old and tired — as tired as Evelyn Lambert had always been. Barbara felt the tears as she held him, remembering their life together. She had by then stopped thinking of her childhood as a curse and had learned to embrace her eccentric mother, her hand-me-down jeans, her buckteeth (which were mostly in her mind anyway), and her outsider status as valuable lessons in perseverance and love. She had never, even in her darkest moments, stopped cherishing the cats. She cherished every moment with Smoky until the day he died and was buried, like all the other kittens who never found love outside the Lambert home, beneath the old apple trees at the back of the yard.

But if the house of cats ultimately took on a patina of charm for Barbara Lajiness, life never got any easier for her mother. On the day Barbara graduated from high school, her mother lost another job. Eleven years later, when Barbara married and settled in Ann Arbor, her mother was still working as a cook in a Flint, Michigan, retirement home. Her car died and she couldn't afford to fix it, so she walked to and from work every day. Every weekend, Barbara drove to Flint to take her grocery shopping. It was a struggle, always a struggle. Every day since her divorce was a fight to survive.

When Evelyn retired at age sixty-five, Barbara moved her mother to a small apartment a few blocks from her house in Ann Arbor. Harry, Amber, and Smoky had passed away, and the only cat left from the great Lambert foster home of Fenton, Michigan, was Bonkers, an older cat that had been abandoned by a neighbor a few years before. Bonkers was a fluffy black cat with a white chest and a calm disposition. She preferred lying about, mostly in the sun or on someone's lap. She wouldn't hurt anything, with the possible exception of walls, which she was always running straight into with her head. That's why they called her Bonkers. Sweet, harmless Bonkers.

Unfortunately, the apartment complex didn't allow pets. So Barbara and her husband, James, took in Bonkers, leaving Evelyn Lambert truly alone for the first time in her life. Almost every day, she came over to their house, but it wasn't really to see her, Barbara knew. Evelyn Lambert wanted to spend time with Bonkers. She would sit on the porch or in the big living room chair, petting Bonkers and staring down at his back as if staring into the past. She told her daughter, "I'm sick, sweetie. You know I'm sick," but Barbara figured it was depression. Evelyn missed the house she had struggled to keep through all the tough times. She missed her garden and her cat cemetery and her lifetime of memories. What could she see, when she looked back on her life, but a path carved out by heartbreak and disappointment? What could she possibly find in the future? Evelyn Lambert had moved from a house full of love, as well as struggle, to a lonely apartment in a new city where they wouldn't even let her keep her beloved cat.

"I don't feel well," she said. "You don't understand."

Barbara figured, in time, her mother would adjust. Harry. Amber. Gracie. Smoky. She had always found a way to survive; she had always discovered a purpose. But she called one morning and told Barbara, "I can't take it anymore, sweetie. Death has been sitting in the apartment with me."

Barbara rushed over. Her mother was in

severe pain. She had been awake all night. "Why didn't you call me?" Barbara kept asking as they rushed to the emergency room. "Why didn't you call me in the middle of the night?"

"I didn't want to wake you."

It was breast cancer, untreated for years, and it had metastasized into her spine and legs. There was nothing they could do but ease the pain, which Barbara realized her mother had been secretly carrying for years. The doctors gave her medicine and sent her home, but the suffering was too much, the cancer too ferocious, the damage too severe. Within a month, she was back in the hospital.

"How's Bonkers?" she asked Barbara as she struggled for breath. She was so weak, she could barely form the words.

Barbara swept a piece of her mother's gray hair from her forehead. "Bonkers is fine," she lied, fighting tears. The truth was that Bonkers was gone. Barbara had spent the previous evening looking for her, but the cat was nowhere to be found.

Barbara's mother nodded, smiled weakly, and closed her eyes. "Bonkers," she muttered under her breath. The next day, no longer conscious or able to breathe on her own, she was placed on a ventilator. She had told Barbara repeatedly that she didn't want to survive like that, with a machine keeping her alive. But she didn't have a living will. She hadn't given her written consent. After a vehement argument, which hurt Barbara as much as anything in her life ever had, the doctors agreed to remove the ventilator. The morphine would keep her comfortable, but it wouldn't prolong her life. She had only a few days to live. Barbara sat on the bed for the rest of the day, watching her mother die.

That night, Barbara Lajiness had a dream. Her mother and Bonkers were together, waving at her from the distance. They were in some vague, undefined place, but her mother was mouthing the words, *Everything's fine, don't worry, everything's fine.*

The next morning, Barbara walked onto her porch to retrieve the morning paper and glanced into the neighbor's driveway. There, in the shadow under a pickup truck that never moved, was Bonkers. Barbara didn't need to step any closer to know that Bonkers had gone off to die, and that she had passed away peacefully in her sleep. She stood on her porch in the cold morning sun, looking at Bonkers and bawling, her coffee cup steaming in her hands.

Finally, she called James. They buried Bonkers in the backyard, under a lilac bush

Barbara's mother had helped her return to life with fertilizer and eggshells.

The next day, Evelyn Lambert passed away. She was only sixty-six years old.

It's not easy for Barbara Lajiness to talk about her mother. Even eight years later, with a loving husband and a wonderful daughter and the hilarious companionship of Ninja, now known as Mr. Sir Bob Kittens, she has to stop every sentence or two to wipe away the tears.

"I admire her," Barbara says. "There are a lot of things I could criticize about her life, but having done that, having put other lives ahead of her own, kitty's lives . . . that's pretty admirable. No matter what anyone can say about her and the choices she made, she cared about everyone and everything else to a fault."

"Do you think she cared too much?"

"Sometimes I think so but, you know, I'm not sure if you can ever really care too much. She really cared about everything that didn't have a voice. She really cared. When I was a kid, the town decided to do this mosquito spraying, and these trucks would drive around with orange lights on top and spray something that was supposed to kill the mosquitoes. A few weeks into it, my mom said to me, 'Do you hear that?' And I said, 'No, I don't hear anything.' She said, 'That's because it's killing more than just the mosquitoes. It's killing all the bugs. That's why you don't hear the birds anymore.' "

Barbara pauses to compose herself. "My mom, she was pretty smart, you know?"

Barbara knows she bottles things up, that she doesn't confront her feelings, that she still has an overwhelming fear of those she loves leaving her behind. For two years after her mother and Bonkers died, she couldn't bring herself to adopt another cat. She had a strong marriage, a wonderful daughter, a steady job, and a nice house. The simple things, some people might call them, the things you don't cherish enough unless you've lived without them. The family had several fish, a few hamsters, and a turtle, but they didn't have a cat. Barbara was happy, comfortable, loved, but she didn't want to risk a cat. She didn't want to lose another one. She didn't want to open herself to another cat only to have it die on her. But nine-year-old Amanda really wanted a cat, and how can a mother refuse?

So they adopted a kitten named Max. He was wonderfully loving, with an endearing habit of sleeping on top of the refrigerator with his tail hanging over the side. But two years later, when he was four years old, Max collapsed. He was walking across the kitchen when, suddenly, he fell over and started trembling wildly, racked with the tremors of a grand mal seizure. Barbara saw it happen and started to panic. Max was so young, so healthy, and he was dying in front of her. It was her nightmare come true. As James frantically made telephone calls, Barbara held her writhing cat. His eyes were glazing over, his eyelids fluttering, his heart pounding wildly. Before she thought about what she was doing, she yelled to her daughter.

Amanda came running. She saw Max shaking and bleeding from the mouth. She started to scream and cry. It was a lot for an eleven-year-old, but when James and Barbara came home an hour later with the news that Max had died, Amanda rushed to her mother.

"Thank you, Mom," she said. "I got to say good-bye to Max while he was alive." She was a strong girl, Barbara realized, seeing for the first time in her well-adjusted daughter the frightened little girl she herself had once been, the one who had struggled so long and so quietly in a broken home.

It took only a month, and three protracted visits to see him at the humane society, before Barbara adopted Ninja. She wasn't ready, but her family, especially her husband, was lost without a furry companion. *Maybe,* she thought, *I can just live with him in the house. For Amanda and James. Maybe I can just treat Ninja like so many other people treat their cats: like animals who happen to share their space.*

Her husband, James, was head over heels for Ninja. He would carry him into the kitchen in the morning, cradling him like a baby. He would ask if Barbara wanted to pet him, and she'd say, "No. Not yet. I like him, but we haven't created a bond." She just kept pushing Ninja away, over and over.

When he contracted a virus at twelve weeks old, Barbara rushed him to the vet. She was standing in the office, watching the doctor examine him, when she suddenly broke into tears, just as she had all those years ago when the camper pulled away from her house and she suddenly became convinced her mother would disappear while she was gone.

"I just lost a cat," she sobbed. "I can't lose this one, too. I just can't. You have to help him."

The veterinarian put her arm around Barbara's shoulders. "Don't worry," she said, "it's only a cold."

Barbara had discovered why her cat was named Ninja on the first or second day, when she opened a door and discovered him crouching at the end of the hall. Completely startled, the kitten sprang up onto his hind legs with his front legs straight out in front of him like an off-balance zombie. He stood like that for a few seconds, watching her. Then he started jumping sideways toward her, waving his arms from side to side in a sort of demented karate move. He jumped all the way down the hall, his neck cocked crazily to the side, his front paws never touching the ground. It was the strangest thing she had ever seen, and it was no accident. Ninja, Barbara soon realized, did his bizarre karate dance whenever he was startled . . . or scared . . . or annoyed . . . or excited. Amanda's teenager drama, in particular, got his ninja juices flowing. Whenever Barbara heard her daughter yell, "Oh my god, Ninja," she knew exactly what was happening. The cat was doing his demented jumping moves on her.

Ninja wasn't a fighter, though. He was just weird. He was all swagger, no bite. And that name, after Barbara finally acknowledged the depth of their bond, just didn't seem right. Appropriate, maybe, but not right. Ninja, after all, was his prison name.

So Barbara started thinking about a new name. One night, she and Amanda were watching a nature program about bobcats.

Ninja's face, they realized, kinda sorta resembled a bobcat's face.

"But he can't be a bobcat," Amanda said. "He has to be a bobkitten."

Bob Kitten. Good, but not quite regal enough. So Barbara dubbed him Sir Bob Kittens.

At his next vet's visit, Barbara told the assistant they had changed Ninja's name. It was now Mr. Sir Bob Kittens. And yes, that was official. Put it on the form.

Of course, one name isn't big enough for a cat like Mr. Sir Bob Kittens, even if that name does have four parts. Soon he was also Mr. Pumpkin Pants. Because he's an orange kitten with big furry thighs, of course. Mr. Sparkle Pants followed soon after. Same reason: the thighs. By the time Barbara's husband dubbed him Fluffalicious (fluffy and delicious, I guess), Amanda thought her parents were totally weird. But they didn't mind. They loved Mr. Sparkle Pumpkin Kitten Pants.

The relationship wasn't perfect. As Barbara always said, Mr. Kittens was a character, not a cuddler. He was always in the room with Barbara, but he preferred to lounge in a cozy spot ten feet away, as if it was a mere accident they ended up in the same space together. He only cuddled if he was in the mood, which was not that often and there-fore extra special when it happened. He was a quiet cat, full of twitches and quirks but not much need for vocal communication. He almost never purred or meowed. Only if he really, really needed something would he bother to speak to Mom and Dad. That usu-ally happened when he smelled his favorite treat: bacon. As soon as he smelled bacon, he bounced into the room on his hind legs, swinging his front legs in that demented ninja dance. If the bacon was really crispy, just the way he liked it, he went absolutely nuts. One day, James made the mistake of giving him bacon on the dining room table. After that, he bounced up on the table for his dinner every night. He wouldn't eat any-where else.

He was a good kid, though. Really he was. Yes, he grabbed Barbara's legs and tried to trip her every time she walked up the base-ment stairs. He liked the surprise, the way she yelled when she nearly fell and broke her neck. Yes, he laid on James's laptop when-ever James tried to work. Even if he closed the lid on him, the cat wouldn't move. He'd just lie there, hanging out both ends like a kitten gyro, a big goofy grin on his face. But Mr. Sir Bob Kittens was more than the class clown. Every morning, when Amanda was getting ready for school, he walked around her room, sniffing everything. He was like a big brother, standoffish and proud, not above a few tasteless jokes but always watching out for his little sister.

Or maybe Barbara just liked to imagine that. Maybe the morning sniffathon was just another part of Mr. Sir Bob Kittens's daily routine, because Mr. Sir Bob Kittens was a cat who liked his routines. Every morning, he woke Barbara at exactly 5:00 A.M. for his breakfast. That was fine during the week, when Barbara had to get up for work, but not so nice on the weekends. Especially since she didn't even get a thank-you nuzzle. Mr. Kittens preferred James, who always wandered in as the coffee was perking, for his morning dose of petting. He loved being petted in the morning . . . but only in the morning . . . and only by James, a routine that began in those first weeks when Barbara was trying to keep from loving the new kitten too much.

Yes, he was a handful. Yes, he was wild. But look at it a different way. His mad scramble for bacon, his crazed eyes, his fear of loud noises and aluminum foil, his extra furry pumpkin-pants thighs, and especially his demented karate dancing — they were *hilarious*. Who wouldn't fall in love with a cat like Mr. Kittens? Despite his aversion to cuddling, Mr. Sir Bob Kittens was as close to Barbara as Smoky or Harry or Amber or Max or any of the other cats in her life had ever been. When she felt sick, he looked at her. When she felt weak one morning, he put his front paws on her knees and meowed in concern. When it was Barbara's turn to collapse in the kitchen, falling first into the table, then clinging desperately to a chair, then slumping helplessly to the floor, Mr. Kittens was there to climb on her knees, look her in the eyes as she blacked out, and scream as loudly as he could.

The cause was bleeding ulcers. One had ruptured a blood vessel, and Barbara had lost three pints of blood. A short course of medicine and a new diet cured the problem, but during a follow-up exam, the doctors detected something not as easily treated: breast cancer, the disease that had killed her mom. Barbara's comfortable life, the one she had worked so hard to craft out of a childhood of disappointment, came crashing down around her. She had surgery, followed by radiation. When the doctors told her chemo was recommended, but was her option, she thought of her mother in those terrible last days. Barbara was forty-one; she didn't want to be on a ventilator at forty-five, with her daughter standing beside her hospital bed, watching her die.

She chose the chemo. She's still on it. She has lost her hair, but she figures, hey, that's five months without shaving her legs. And a great excuse for getting out of all that dreadful holiday stuff. Her daughter, a typical teenager, used to tell her she looked embarrassing and needed some makeup, but now, so what? Who cares? Every day could be your last. If it makes you happy, don't regret it. She eats cupcakes, not all the time but sometimes, and she doesn't feel any guilt. She appreciates them instead. She tries to appreciate everything, even Mr. Kittens nudging her out of bed at 5:00 A.M. every morning. She feeds him and pets him — yes, he sometimes lets her pet him now — and sits in the kitchen and marvels at the morning and the coffee and how very cute Mr. Sir Bob Kittens really is.

She has her husband, James. Her marriage, always strong, is stronger now. She has her daughter, Amanda, and the overwhelming desire to see her grow up. She has Mr. Sir Bob Kittens, who has started sleeping at her feet when she's recovering from her treatment and even, occasionally, cuddling up beside her chest. He may not be the world's best cuddler, but through these simple acts, she knows he cares. She knows that life is good.

And when life is bad? Well, Barbara Lajiness still gets to see Mr. Sir Bob Kittens up on his hind legs, swinging his forelegs and hopping down the hall in that wild, wonderful, demented karate dance.

How could anyone, anywhere, not laugh at that?

THREE
SPOOKY

"I had a cat for twenty-one years. . . . He shouldn't have survived . . . yet he did survive to bring so many hours of joy to my life for so many years. And to this day, you can sometimes feel his wet nose touch your leg as he still waits for my spirit to join him."

Bill Bezanson grew up on a family farm outside the small town of Romeo, Michigan.

Even today, Romeo has a population of only three thousand people, a newspaper that costs eighteen dollars for a yearly subscription, and a downtown whose claim to fame is that it has never been destroyed by a major fire, something apparently quite common in the old logging communities of Macomb County. After living for thirty years in Spencer, Iowa, a town whose downtown was destroyed by fire in 1931, I agree this is quite an accomplishment.

I also understand the isolation of the family farm, at least in the 1950s and early 1960s, when both Bill and I were growing up. In those days, you didn't have television or video games or computers to keep you connected to the outside world. You had a radio — and a ham radio, if you were interested in that hobby. You had an old truck, which might have a CB. And you had a telephone. It was a party line, with a local operator, and half the time the connection was so fuzzy you couldn't understand a word. When my family finally bought a television around 1960, my father mentioned it to his cousins in South Dakota. The phone connection was so bad, they thought our family had tuberculosis — TB. They prayed for us for an entire year.

What you also had on the farm in those

days was family and work. Even as a child, you worked from dawn to dusk during the harvest. When the sun went down, you went to sleep. If you couldn't fall asleep, you could look out your bedroom window and see a million stars but only a single house light way off in the distance. That was my experience anyway. Bill Bezanson couldn't see the light on the next farmhouse no matter how dark the night, and as for neighborhood children . . . well, there weren't any other children around. There was nothing outside the town of Romeo, Michigan, for a young farmboy but fields and trees.

And animals.

The Bezanson farm had two barns, so Bill's dad gave him a room in the smaller one — the breeding barn — for his rescued animals. Bill had dozens of them: foxes, possums, dogs, cats, whatever wandered into his path and needed help. Anything that was hurt, Bill Bezanson nursed back to health. He even had a skunk that ran all over his shoulders and played hide-and-seek with him in the hayloft. If anyone else came near the breeding barn, that skunk lifted his tail. But with Bill, he was as playful as a kitten.

Bill's favorite animal, though, was his rescued raccoon. The mother raccoon had been hit by a car, and the babies were huddled in a tree by the side of the road, staring down at her lifeless body. They were tiny, distraught, confused, no doubt cold and hungry, and nearly petrified with fear. Only one survived. Everyone called him Pierre LaPoop, after the love-crazed French skunk Pepé Le Pew on the old Bugs Bunny Saturday morning cartoons. Bill's grandmother named him. The baby raccoon had pooped right on her lap the first time she held it.

Pierre was a good raccoon, loyal and loving. He and Bill would play together in the barn, toss sticks in the yard, walk together through the fields like a stereotype of a sandy-haired Midwestern boy and his loyal dog. Often, Bill even had a fishing pole slung over his shoulder. But raccoons aren't dogs. They are wild creatures, curious and mischievous and, let's face it, more clever than the average pooch. Pierre could catch fish with his bare hands, peel ears of corn, pick carefully through the garbage, and open doors. One day, the family came home and found Pierre sitting on their kitchen counter, casually throwing plates. There were broken plates all over the floor. There had been a run of raccoonlike behavior from Pierre — petty thievery, picking locks, incessant hand-washing in the rain barrels (raccoons are notoriously anal retentive about hand-washing) — so smashing the family's dinnerware was the proverbial straw that broke the farmer's back. No argument was going to save Pierre this time. Bill's dad threw him in the back of the truck, drove him twenty-eight miles away, and dropped him off at an abandoned barn.

Three weeks later, Bill and his dad were fishing at a nearby lake, and a raccoon started chattering at them from a tree. Bill looked up into the branches and said, "Pierre, is that you?"

Pierre came sprinting down the tree, climbed up Bill's leg into his arms, and started licking his face and biting his nose.

"Well, I guess we've got to keep him," Bill's father said. "I can't afford a plane ticket." In truth, the old farmer was touched by the bond between his son and the wild animal. He wouldn't have driven Pierre away again if he'd had his own plane.

Maybe it was Pierre that made Bill want to be a forest ranger, his dream job for most of his childhood. Everyone else thought he should become a veterinarian. He had a talent with and love for animals like no one they had ever seen. But things change. Pierre LaPoop grew up and started thinking about a family. Raccoons are docile when young, but they often become aggressive and nasty when they reach mating age. Not Pierre. He simply left the barn. Found a wife and moved off to a far corner of the farm. One day, Bill and his father were sitting on the back steps of their farmhouse. Bill looked off toward the fields and saw Pierre coming toward him, four little brown bundles waddling at his side. His mate stood at the edge of the cornfield, pacing nervously, while Pierre picked his children up with his mouth, put them on the porch, and introduced them to his lifelong friend. They stayed only long enough for Bill and his father to hold each child. Then they turned back to the cornfield and headed home.

"That's the most amazing thing I ever saw" was all Bill's father said when the raccoons finally disappeared.

That was the last Bill ever saw of Pierre LaPoop. The raccoon moved into the forest with his family and disappeared. He had just come out to say good-bye.

A few years later, Bill graduated from high school and said his own good-byes. He wasn't going to veterinary school or forest ranger training. He wasn't even going to college. It was June 1964, and Bill Bezanson was going into the army, infantry division, full volunteer. By July 1, he was on his way to basic training. Three years later, barely twenty years old, he was in Vietnam.

Bill was assigned to B Company, 123rd Aviation Battalion of the United States Army. The Warlords. Their job: air cavalry reinforcement, snatch and grab, reconnaissance, secret missions behind enemy lines. Twenty-one soldiers in the unit, seven per helicopter, plus two pilots and two gunners. If an infantry unit or bomber crew reported suspected enemy positions in the distant hills, the brass called in the Warlords. Their role was to sweep through the area, laying down as much fire as they could, to see what kind of return fire they would draw. Bill was the tunnel rat. His job was to drop into any nearby tunnels alone, no cover and no radio, to flush out any Vietcong holed up inside.

Needless to say, it was a messy, dangerous, and unpredictable job. The kind of job so dangerous and unpredictable that, after a few months, it made a man feel invincible just because he survived it. Bill had more running firefights in pitch-black Vietcong tunnels than he cared to count. After one mission, he and the guys counted more than a thousand bullet holes in the shell of their helicopter. There had been eight men inside. Several had holes in their uniforms, but not a single man had bled. That was the way it was for the Warlords. Minor wounds, "a little Purple Star and stuff like that," as Bill says of his military decorations, but nothing major. Nothing lethal. For almost a year.

Then September 1968 hit the calendar. It started badly. One of Bill's close friends — everyone in the unit was close, but they were closer — took a bullet to the head. Bill held the boy on his blood-soaked lap in the chopper back to the medical area, but the hole was so big that Bill could see his friend's brain pulsing every time his heart beat. "I thought I'd never see him again," Bill said. "But in 1996, I got a letter from him. He survived. He'd had complications all his life, but he survived."

A few days later, the Warlords were flown up near the demilitarized zone, beyond an area known as the Rock Pile, near Khe Sanh, where earlier that year a Marine base had been pinned down for 122 days by enemy fire. They dropped as usual, but this time it was right at the edge of a major Vietcong encampment. Every Warlords mission had two gunships and a spotter helicopter for support, but when hundreds of guns opened up, the sky cleared in a hurry. The first gunship went down; the pilot of the second was shot through the heel of his foot. He managed to pull out of the spin and limp home, but the men on the ground were left behind. It took the 196th Infantry Brigade to extract them. By then, the Warlords had taken wounded, and Bill Bezanson had lost his best friend, Lurch (Richard Larrick, rest in peace), to a North Vietnamese bullet. He flew back to base, buried the whole month in his head, and went on with the war.

By the time he came home in November 1968, Bill Bezanson didn't want to have anything more to do with the United States Army or the war in Vietnam. He didn't want to be a veterinarian or a forest ranger. The big banner on the Michigan farmhouse said WELCOME HOME, SON, but he didn't feel like he was home. He and his father went out bass fishing in the eight-foot pram the old man had built by hand. They had always talked on the lake. It was their sanctuary. But this time, they didn't have much to say.

Bill wasn't sure what to do. He didn't know where he fit in. On the way home from a relative's house, where he had gone to show them his dress uniform and medals, a cop pulled him over, looked at his uniform, and snarled, "So you're one of those baby killers." He was asked to speak at his high school, the hero returned, and gave an impassioned antiwar speech. When his mother found out, she was mortified. She was such a strict Catholic that she hand washed the church's altar cloths. She loved her son, but he had changed. He was moody. He was sullen. He was drinking. And now he was antiwar. The war was for God and country and everything else America stood for and believed in, at least for his mother and the "silent majority" of American people who stood by their government on principle. After months of tension, Bill's mother literally closed the door in her son's face.

He hit the bottle hard for a while, then he hit the road. As an active member of Vietnam Veterans Against the War, he gave speeches at PTA meetings and churches, anywhere a group would welcome him. The stories of massacres by American troops were piling up, and a large segment of the public was turning against the war. He didn't know whether his audiences would be for the troops or against them, but he told them all the truth: Even while he was killing for his government, he lost his faith in the war. He had seen too many deaths, too much destruction, too many burned-out villages and hollowed-out souls. He told them how he had pointed his M16 at a fellow soldier who had taken a female prisoner and told him, "If you cut that woman, I will kill you." You don't put a gun to a comrade's head. Not ever. But especially not in a war zone, surrounded by the enemy. His fellow soldiers thought the woman knew something important. They had no proof, but they believed torturing her for information might save lives. Bill believed they were losing, day by day, the values they were fighting for, and he refused to blur the line between right and wrong.

"It was easy to cross a line out there," Bill told me. "Good people lost their way." What had Bill lost? I think he lost his faith not just in the war, but in life. He didn't know what it meant anymore. He couldn't tell the good from the bad. He didn't want that to happen to any other good young men. He didn't want any more parents to send their boys to Vietnam.

But beyond a few speeches, what could he really do? He drifted. He drank. He'd get a job, work it for a while, and then one morning he'd light out, hitching mostly, not sure where he was going or why. Often, he didn't even know he was leaving until he was standing on the corner with his thumb in the air. He made friends, but they didn't last long. There were always people moving into and out of his life, mostly with bottles in their hands. Sometimes he moved because he didn't like his new friends; sometimes he moved because he liked them too much. He didn't want to get close to anyone. One summer he found himself in Alaska, so he bought a Harley-Davidson and rode it back to the Lower 48. That was the stupidest thing he ever did, he said, because it was twelve hundred miles of potholed, washboard, washout dirt roads, and his eyes didn't stop bouncing for a month.

But what difference did it all make? Bill Bezanson was twenty-five years old and he was absolutely convinced that he wouldn't live to see thirty. That feeling had started in the war. He had carried it home along with his scars and his medals, but he didn't realize that at the time. It just became normal to feel doomed. A lot of young men came home that way. Set adrift from the normal world, they found each other. It was all they talked about back then, that they were living on borrowed time.

But Bill didn't die. He just kept going through the motions, day after day, until he found himself in his thirties, with the 1970s winding down, and at almost the same place he'd started twelve years before. The war was over and his anger had cooled, or at least retreated somewhere else to hide. He had narrowed his travels mostly to the sprawling suburbs east of Los Angeles, but he was still working odd jobs, still leaving behind his old life every few months, still hitting the bottle or the road whenever the fear closed in. He'd somehow managed a degree in forestry from Chaffey College in Alta Loma, but beyond that, he was free: no friends, no possessions, no place to be. By June 1979, he was living in yet another Los Angeles suburb, working for a small company that manufactured travel trailers and truck beds and whose name he can't even begin to recall. He was waiting at a stoplight on a nameless road on the edge of downtown San Bernardino, watching the early morning light burn off the haze of another California morning, when, out of nowhere, change came crashing into his life.

It hit like a concussion grenade, literally smashing down above his head. He heard the strike, then the echo, and instinctively he ducked. He waited, but the world around him was silent. He looked out over the dashboard. There were buildings along both sides of the street, but it was 5:30 in the morning and nothing moved. The alleys were quiet, the windows in the storefronts black. There wasn't another car on the road. So Bill cracked his door and squeezed out to examine the top of his car. He figured teenagers had thrown something at him. Sure enough, there was a dent, with a black lump in the center. There were impact lines in the metal and liquid running out in several directions.

Then he realized the liquid was blood. And the lump wasn't a bag. It was a kitten. Someone had thrown a kitten at his car. And from the looks of its broken body, it had been a long throw.

Bill scooped up the kitten and cradled it in his hands. It just lay in his palms, its eyes closed, its head collapsed to the side, its legs curled. The only sign of life was the desperate heave of its chest and a bubbling, rasping sound as it struggled for breath. Bill knew what that meant: a puncture through the rib cage and into the lung. He'd seen a lot of sucking chest wounds in Vietnam. The soldiers in his unit had stripped the plastic wrappers off their cigarette packs and kept them in their kits. Put the plastic wrapper over a sucking chest wound, cover it with a bandage, then a body wrap, and it might save a friend's life. Bill Bezanson didn't have a cigarette packet wrapper that morning in San Bernardino, California, so he did the next best thing. He put his thumb over the puncture to close the wound, swiped his other hand downward over the kitten's face to clear the blood from its nose, and started looking for help.

There was a veterinarian's office down the block. There were no lights on, but Bill was pretty sure he'd just seen someone enter the building. He left the car idling at the intersection and started running. When he reached the vet's office, he started kicking the door. The kitten gurgled, covered with blood.

A man opened the door. Bill thrust the bloody kitten toward him. "Call the vet," he said. "Tell him to take care of this animal. I'll pay whatever it costs, but right now I have to get to work."

The man took the kitten. Bill turned and raced back to his car, sped through the intersection, and arrived for his shift on time.

There's a bond that is formed when you save an animal's life. It can happen even with something as typical as rescuing a dog from the pound. For you, it is an exciting afternoon, but that dog knows he was trapped in a bad place, and you set him free. It happens with dogs when you take them off a choke chain or rescue them from a backyard where they have been abandoned without food and water. It happens with cats when you take them in — not just give them food until they refuse to go away but bring them inside when they are sick or starving and make them a part of your life. It certainly happened with Dewey when I pulled him out of the library return box in the winter of 1988. Like Dewey, most rescued animals never forget what you did for them. They cherish it. And unlike so many people who, no matter what you have done, find a way to turn their back on you, animals are forever grateful.

And if that animal is hurt and needs to be nursed back to health? Well, that just makes the bond stronger. Taking care of Dewey's frostbitten footpads in the week after rescuing him was, as much as anything, the act that pinned us together. Dewey learned my kindness wasn't just for a moment. I was committed; I would be there as long as he wanted and needed me. And I got to know him. That sounds trite, I know, but what else is there to say? After only a few days, I knew Dewey: his outgoing personality, his friendliness, his trust. I had seen him vulnerable, so I had seen his true self. I knew he appreciated me — you could almost say loved me, although we had known each other only a few days — and that he would never leave my side. I like to say we had looked into each other's souls. And maybe we had. Maybe that was the hardwire that connected us for the next nineteen years. Or maybe we had just spent enough time together to realize we were both openhearted individuals ready for someone to love.

Something similar happened to Bill Bezanson. He didn't love that kitten the morning he ran with it bleeding in his hands to the veterinarian's office. That was an act of kindness from a softhearted man who always helped a fellow creature in need. It is probably a stretch to say that he loved the kitten when he stopped at the veterinarian's office after work and discovered that, by some miracle, the little guy had survived. After all, Bill Bezanson hadn't developed a deep, meaningful relationship with another living thing since September 1968. In fact, he had spent twelve years running from every meaningful relationship and hardening his heart against the entanglements of life.

It's probably more accurate to say Bill Bezanson *admired* the kitten. He was small — only a few pounds and about six weeks old — but he was a survivor. The puncture wound in his lung was not, as Bill had assumed, the result of abuse or neglect. It was from the talon of a bird of prey. His forehead was badly torn, probably because the bird attacked him with his beak. At 5:30 in the morning, the only bird feeding would have been an owl. An owl doesn't clutch a small animal and kill it later. An owl attack is designed to hit the animal with enough force to break its back. The kitten had survived the strike. It had struggled with the owl — thus the beak marks and torn face — and somehow in that struggle, the owl had lost its grip.

"This cat is very spooky," the veterinarian — who happened to be the man who opened the door that morning — kept saying as he talked Bill through the kitten's injuries. "He fell out of the sky and landed on your car . . . that's very spooky. This cat is very spooky."

"That was his name," Bill would always conclude when telling the story later (and he told it hundreds of times over the years). "From that moment on, he was Spooky."

Spooky stayed at the veterinary office for a week. The vet donated his time; the only charge was for the medicine, but there was a lot of that. Spooky needed serious attention and care. He was battling infection, a stab wound, and major blunt-force trauma. Every inch of his body was scraped and bruised, and he was so torn up inside that he couldn't eat solid food for a month. Bill had to spoon-feed him every meal. Spooky had several stitches in his chest, where the owl talon had pierced his lung, and he wore a protective cone-shaped collar so he couldn't bite them off. There is nothing more pathetic, I can imagine, than a little kitten head poking through the bottom of a big white megaphone-shaped collar.

But even with the collar, Spooky was beautiful. He was tiny, only a pound or two, less than two months old, but you could see the majestic cat he would become: lean and angular, with bony hips that stuck out from a wiry body. His face was long and lean, with an almost pantherlike thrust around the mouth. It was a regal face, calm and sophisticated with big staring eyes, like the cats in ancient Egyptian carvings. In ordinary light, he was black. But the sunlight, which he loved, would bring out a shimmering copper undercoat. He was a practical cat, not prone to fits of scampering, plaintive meowing, or manic bouts of pencil chasing, but that copper coat hinted at his internal heat. Spooky was never going to let anyone or anything beat him.

Did Bill Bezanson love Spooky after a month of spoon-feeding? If pressed, he would say yes, then he loved Spooky. But thirty years later, that's hard to know for sure. At what point, after all, does admiration become love?

But it isn't the right question anyway. The important thing to know is that Spooky the cat loved Bill Bezanson. Immediately and forever. The first thing Bill would do, whenever he moved into a new rental house or apartment, was cut a hole in a screen. That way, Spooky could entertain himself while Bill worked long hours on assembly lines and in fabrication garages. Spooky spent most of his day outside. But as soon as Bill came home, Spooky came running. If he wasn't there at the front door to greet him, all Bill had to do was step outside and yell, "Spooky," and the little cat would come sprinting home. Often, he came running from four yards away. Bill could see him leaping fences at full speed. He'd come skidding right into Bill, weaving in and out between his leg, rubbing against him and almost tripping him. Bill would plop down on the couch with a beer, and Spooky would climb up on his legs, put his front paws on Bill's chest, and lick him on the nose. Then he would stretch out on Bill's lap. He didn't care about getting back outdoors or having his own space; he just wanted to be with his buddy. Some nights, the two of them sat like that for hours.

It wasn't just friendship. There was a kinship, a parallel in their lives that eased Bill's discontent. Like Bill, Spooky had confronted the darkness of the world. Like

Bill, Spooky shouldn't have been alive. But he was. Spooky was alive and healthy and happy and somehow, in some way, that made Bill feel better about his own survival. At night, Spooky climbed into the bed. Bill always slept on his side, and Spooky would climb onto the pillow and lay beside him, his face pressed against Bill's beard. He would wrap his paws around Bill's arm and pull on it until Bill cradled him in the crook of his elbow. Even when he went to sleep without Spooky, Bill would wake up and find the cat curled on the pillow and his arm around its back. And it made a difference. After a decade of thrashing, Spooky's presence calmed the nightmares. Bill knew, both consciously and subconsciously, that he needed to lie still. If he didn't, he might hurt Spooky.

Not every night, of course, was peace and quiet. Like many Vietnam vets, Bill lived a hard-partying life, and as often as not, his house was filled with loud music and people smoking and drinking beer. Call it self-medication, or youth, or what inevitably happens when you feel doomed to an early death, but ultimately it wasn't anything more than a lifestyle. If the party got too rowdy, Spooky would wander into a back room and curl up on Bill's hiking pack or inside his sleeping bag, but most of the time, Spooky didn't mind the noise. He'd sit right on the back of the couch while the party whirled around him. Or he'd sniff the smoke. Or he'd slink along the floor and put his cold nose on someone's exposed calf. That was Spooky's trick. He'd sneak up on people and put his nose on the square of skin between the bottom of their pants and the top of their socks. That nose was like a sudden splash of water. It got their attention. They'd reach down and pet him, and if he sensed they were friendly, he'd hop on their lap. Spooky loved sitting on laps.

The cold nose of Spooky. It was his thing, his announcement of intention, his calling card. No matter what happened the night before, Bill Bezanson could rest assured he would feel his friend Spooky's cold nose the next morning. At exactly 5:30 A.M. Like many cats, Spooky had an internal clock. He knew exactly when his food was supposed to be served, and he wasn't going to wait a minute longer. No matter how badly he felt, Bill would pad out to the dark kitchen at 5:30 A.M. and give Spooky his bowl. "He was attached to me," Bill would say, by way of explanation. *He was attached to me.*

And Bill Bezanson was attached to him, too. He wouldn't go anywhere without Spooky. When Bill was home, Spooky was beside him. If Bill went for a walk, Spooky followed behind him, never more than a few feet away. There was no more hitchhiking alone. When Bill went out on the road, which he still did whenever the anxiety set in, Spooky went with him. A bowl, a bag of food, and they were free. While Bill thumbed, Spooky played in the grass, chasing grasshoppers or shadows or the tops of daffodils waving in the breeze. When a car slowed down, Bill shouted, "Spooky!" just once and Spooky came running, jumped in the car, and off they went.

Whenever Bill rode his Harley — the one he'd bought in Alaska — he tied Spooky's carrier to the rack on the back. One day, he saw a man with a Chihuahua sitting on the gas tank of his bike, just behind the handlebars. *Spooky would love that,* he thought. Bill knew Spooky's paws would slip off the metal tank, so he scrounged a piece of carpet for Spooky to sit on. He attached it with two-way aircraft tape, but when that didn't work, he glued it down. As long as Bill went slower than twenty-five miles an hour, Spooky would squint, lay his ears back, and let the breeze glide through his hair. Once Bill hit twenty-five, Spooky would jump off. He wasn't angry; he just didn't like that much speed. He could ride in the carrier at any speed, but he could only take so much breeze sitting in the open on the tank. One year, Bill took the bike up to the Sturgis Rally in South Dakota — more than a thousand miles — and Spooky rode up front as Bill eased to a crawl down the main drag. People were whooping and hollering, drinking and making crude jokes, but Spooky didn't care. He laid his ears back and cruised Sturgis like the world's coolest pussycat.

Bill and Spooky went other places, too. They camped together in the forests of the west, hunting insects for Bill's collection. They tromped through the Sierra Nevada mountains. They hitchhiked to Quartzsite, Arizona, for the big rock and mineral show. When Bill went to music festivals, Spooky sat beside him on the blanket. When he moved to a new house, which he now did every September, Spooky went along without complaint. Except for the bar and the job, they went everywhere together. Bill and Spooky. Spooky and Bill. They were a pair.

Then, in 1981, another addition joined the family: a woman. The house she had been living in was covered by ash in the explosion of Mount St. Helens, the big volcano in western Washington, and she ended up renting a room from Bill in Southern California. Bill was managing a beer bar; his female boarder was a bartender at a place down the road; they talked often but always through the bottom of a beer glass. Bill and Spooky were still moving every September, living an itinerant life, so when the woman went back to Washington after a fight, they followed her north. Before Bill knew what was happening, they were married. Bill took a job fabricating metal, settled into married life, and started drinking.

"It was all surface," he would say later of his human relationships. Nothing deep. Nothing lasting. "Anything that had any depth of soul had to do with an animal."

They moved again that September. And the next one, too. And the next. He never thought about that terrible September in Vietnam in 1968. It had been fifteen years, so he never made the connection. He just knew that every September he had the overwhelming feeling that he had to move. It was bigger than his wife, bigger than his career, bigger even than his friendship with Spooky. That fear, even all those years later, was the biggest thing in Bill's life.

The marriage, needless to say, didn't last. It was doomed at the wedding, when Bill stood up to say "I do" and thought, *What am I doing here?* It was crashing on the rocks when, about a year later, Bill woke

137

up to his wife screaming. Spooky, who had been spending more nights in the forest, had brought them a present: a big fat garden snake. And it was writhing in the sheets.

"Get rid of that damn cat," Bill's wife demanded. "Just get rid of it."

It was pretty clear how that relationship was going to end. In 1986, after a year apart and then another year back together, Bill and his wife officially divorced. Spooky moved back onto Bill's lap and back onto the pillow on his bed. From then on, it was just the boys.

No, the snake wasn't a message. There was no jealousy or loneliness or anything like that. Spooky didn't need to be underfoot to know he was loved, because a true connection goes both ways. Comfort, that's how I described it with Dewey. A belief in each other's love. The snake? That was just Spooky being Spooky.

He was a quirky cat, the Spookster. He was always cooking up adventure. For a year, Bill and his wife lived in a ground-floor apartment on a lake. Each apartment had a balcony — Bill's was a few feet off the ground — and every afternoon the woman upstairs threw handfuls of corn from her balcony to the resident ducks and Canadian geese. Spooky would stand at the sliding glass door meowing at the birds, his tail quivering with excitement. He was like that. He saw possibilities. He could never pass up an opportunity to play.

One day, Bill slid the door open. Spooky didn't freak out. He didn't charge onto the deck. Instead, he backed up to the far side of the room, ran as fast as he could, and hurled himself over the railing and right into the middle of fifty ducks and geese — all of which panicked, honking and flapping and running into one another as they tried to get away. Spooky stuck his tail up and his head in the air and strutted back to the door. He was so proud of himself. Every time the flock was outside after that, Spooky meowed and rubbed Bill's legs until he opened the door.

Then one day, Spooky ran and jumped . . . and landed right on top of an enormous goose. The terrified goose jumped five feet in the air, squawked, and started running wildly in a rush of feathers, leaping and honking and trying desperately to take flight. Spooky, clinging desperately to the goose's back, glanced back for a moment at Bill. They locked eyes, and Bill could see that Spooky's were as big as saucers. Then the goose took off. He flew about ten feet before crashing and rolling in a pile of feathers, beak, goose feet, and cat fur. The goose immediately got up and started running for the lake. Spooky got up and sprinted to the apartment. He never jumped into the middle of the flock again.

Spooky being Spooky. Figuring out a plan. Pushing himself toward disaster. Rushing back to the safety of home. That was his charm: He was a lover *and* an adventurer. He was a homebody who sat on your lap one hour and hunted snakes the next.

He even welcomed a new cat into the family, a black kitten named Zippo. This was just after Bill met his wife, when he was working and spending a lot of time in bars playing pool, and he thought Spooky needed a companion. Somewhere along the journey, Spooky had contracted FIV, the feline form of AIDS, so Bill put an ad in the newspaper seeking a friendly, FIV-positive cat. A young couple couldn't afford the medication for their sick kitten, so a few days later, Zippo joined the family.

Spooky loved him instantly. From the first moment, he not only adopted the kitten, he treated him like a brother. If ever there was a natural pair, it was Spooky and Zippo. Spooky was the leader, always into something, while Zippo . . . well, Zippo was a fat, jovial butterball. Spooky chased insects; Zippo lounged in the house. Spooky followed Bill down the street; Zippo watched from the window. On the rare occasions he toddled outside, Zippo could never remember to come back when called. He'd get distracted by a blade of grass or a shadow on a fence and not come inside until the food dish was down. One weekend, Zippo was having one of his rare outdoor adventures when he found an enormous wolf spider in the grass. He played with the spider all afternoon. When he was tired of it, he waddled inside. Spooky was napping on the bed. Zippo jumped up and started looking at him. Spooky's head jerked up. He "listened" to the silent message, then sprang off the bed, ran straight to the spider, and started playing with it, too.

How close were the two cats? Bill once snapped three pictures of them in quick succession. In the first, Zippo was licking Spooky's ear. In the second, Zippo had his tongue out and a horrible look on his face, as if he'd just tasted the worst substance of his life. Spooky looked like he was laughing. In the third, Spooky was licking Zippo's ear. *That's okay, brother,* he could have been saying. *I got you that time, but we're still friends.*

They had each other, the three boys. It was a good life. But that didn't mean life was easy. The divorce left Bill hurt and confused, unable to put his finger on exactly what had happened and sure there was something wrong with him. Why couldn't someone love him? Why couldn't he make the marriage work? There had been a wall between them. In five years of marriage, they had never spoken a single word from the heart. He didn't blame his wife. He blamed himself.

"I went through some heavy drinking after the divorce," Bill admits, "and then I went through some heavy working."

When he was a kid on his family's Michigan farm, Bill had dreamed of becoming a forest ranger. He had a forestry degree; he had fought forest fires; he had even worked for the Bureau of Land Management, but his yearly application to the U.S. Forest Service always received a "Thanks, but no, thanks" reply. He always scored high on the aptitude tests, but less qualified people were given the jobs. In despair after his eleventh rejection (not to mention his divorce) and convinced the world was against him, he pulled into the first factory he passed. As he was filling out his application, a foreman walked into the office, threw a bunch of papers on a desk, and said to the secretary, "Write up his last check. He's out of here."

He turned to Bill and said, "Do you know

how to braise?"

"Sure do," Bill fibbed.

"Then you're hired. Bring your application in the morning."

Bill left the office and went straight to the library to look up "braise." He had no idea what the term meant. It turned out braising meant joining copper to copper, like a plumber does when he solders pipes together. There was a metaphor in there somewhere about two like substances (a man and a cat) who came together to form a solid and unbreakable whole. But there was also a career. The factory made jet engine blades; the braising job was an introduction to the airline industry. Bill worked in the industry on and off for twenty-two years, until retiring from Boeing in 2001. For much of that time, he worked as much as he could physically take, sweating out his frustrations and keeping himself busy on the line.

But even on the longest days on the job, and even when those days stretched into months, Spooky and Zippo stuck with him. He might be gone for sixteen hours, or even whole days, but when Bill Bezanson walked through the door dead tired or drunk, Spooky was always there to meet him. Before he sat down to unwind with some television, Bill made sure to put everything he could possibly need within arm's reach: beer, chips, remote control, books, paper towels. He knew Spooky would be on his lap before he hit the sofa, and he didn't want to have to get up and disturb him. When he went to bed, Spooky crawled up next to his face, as he always had, and demanded to be cradled. Bill fell asleep to his purring, breathing in his fur. Zippo snuggled against Bill's back.

By the time he came out of the fog of work and drink, Bill was ready for a change. He was tired of the cycle: the drinking, the succession of cheap apartments, the mind-numbing jobs with only Spooky and Zippo to keep him company. In California, just before his marriage, a friend had contracted AIDS. It was the early 1980s; everyone was terrified. No one would go near her. Only Bill would touch her. So he took care of her: cooked her meals, bathed her, cleaned up her messes. He did everything but give her shots. He was there as she withered, and he was there when she died. It was the closest thing to useful he had felt since 1968.

Ten years later, he cut back on his drinking and looked for a second job, in health care. After his ten-hour shift on the aircraft assembly line, he worked a ten-hour shift as a night guard at a drug rehabilitation center, but you can only survive on three hours' sleep for so long. When a friend contracted brain cancer, he applied for work at a traumatic brain injury center, where he helped people who had suffered serious accidents. He became a hypnotherapist. He helped crime, accident, and rape victims through their struggles with post-traumatic stress disorder without ever realizing he had PTSD himself. It was physically, emotionally, and mentally exhausting work.

Why did he do it?

"I felt I was paying back."

How so?

Silence. "Because of some of the situations I got out of without being killed or maimed." Another pause. "Because somebody helped me then."

During one particularly long airline industry layoff, he took a job in hospice, working for the dying in their homes. For his first assignment, the company sent him to the most difficult patient on the roster. She was a nasty, cussed, constant complainer, and no caretaker had ever lasted for more than a few days. On the second day, she was screaming at Bill as fiercely and as loudly as she could, when he turned to her and said, "You're afraid of dying, aren't you?"

She quieted down. She stared at him. She looked like she wanted to say something, but then she dropped her eyes and stared at her hands. Bill sat on the bed beside her, and they talked about her life, about its past and its end. They talked until she didn't have anything else to say.

A few days later, on his off day, he received a call from the woman's children. "Mom's dying," they said. "She wants to see you."

When he arrived, she ushered her children out of the room. "Tell me what it's like again," she said, a tremble in her voice.

"Picture the most beautiful place you've ever been," Bill told her, "and you will drift there."

She closed her eyes. When she spoke again, it sounded as if she was shouting softly from a long way away. "You were right, Bill," she whispered just before she died.

This is what I was meant to do, Bill thought.

He quit his career as an aircraft mechanic and devoted himself full-time to home care for the terminally ill. He found a nurse he trusted and started a company, each of them working five days on, then five days off, to provide constant care. When he was working, he left Spooky and Zippo alone with the bottom of a five-gallon bucket full of food. There was a hole in the screen so the cats could play outside. Zippo lounged inside, sleeping mostly, but Spooky loved the old logging towns in the northwestern corner of Washington — towns like Darrington and Granite Falls — that were in constant rotation in Bill's yearly migration to a new home. The forests came right down to the houses, and Spooky had never seen such towering trees. He'd chase a squirrel forty feet into their branches without a second thought, then stretch out and relax while the nervous squirrel chattered away on the slender end of a branch. There was nothing Spooky found more entertaining than squirrels. It was as if he thought they had been put on the earth solely for the amusement of cats. The voles — small mouselike creatures that burrowed through the needles on the forest floor — were for eating. Spooky would dig through the pine needles, dance onto his back legs when he found what he was looking for, and pounce down on the helpless creatures. If left to his own devices, Spooky could catch voles all day.

But as soon as Bill arrived home and called, "Spooky! Spooky!" the cat dropped his voles and came bounding. Sometimes, he was in the backyard. Sometimes, he was ten houses away. Bill would yell, "Spooky!" and see him jump in the distance. Wait a few seconds, and there he was, bounding over a fence. Bill never quite knew what Spooky was doing out there on his own, but he always loved the sight of him hurtling those fences. He would come sliding into Bill's feet, often unable to stop and smashing into him headfirst, and they would spend a day curled up together inside, Bill unwinding from the emotions of five days of devotion to a dying person, and Spooky recovering from his five days alone with Zippo.

But nature is fickle: Sometimes, you're the cat; sometimes, you're the vole. One night in Granite Falls, Bill was throwing out the garbage when he heard several coyotes yelping at each other nearby. He saw movement, a coyote's tail in the shadows, and then he saw Spooky. The cat was suspended in the air, sort of dancing on the noses of four coyotes as they snapped their jaws at him. Bill grabbed his ax, yelled, "Spooky!" as loud as he could, and started sprinting toward the fight. Spooky kept dancing, pushing off their faces and leaping out of reach, but just as help arrived, a coyote clamped his jaws firmly around Spooky's face and started to drag him away. Bill lifted his ax and yelled, and the coyote dropped his meal and ran into the forest. Spooky sprang up and ran the other way, into the house. When Bill got inside, Spooky was curled on his favorite pillow in a pool of blood. Bill rushed him to the vet. He had a deep gash and a broken jaw, but after a few weeks of a liquid diet, he recovered completely. Despite the coyote's bite, Spooky still had a lust for life and that gorgeous Egyptian face.

In Darrington, Washington, a shambling lumber town northeast of Seattle on the edge of the Mount Baker-Snoqualmie National Forest, it was a bear. Bill's house that year was right on the Sauk River, and every day, the bear would amble through the yard to the river, catch a salmon, sit down near the bank, and eat it. And every day, Spooky would sneak through the bear's legs, snatch a piece of salmon, and keep running. The bear would take a lazy swipe with his paw but with little conviction. Spooky was always long gone. Then one day, as Bill watched out the kitchen window, the bear caught the fish. Spooky slipped between his legs to steal a bite. The bear took a lazy swing with his paw. But this time the piece of salmon Spooky grabbed was still stuck to the bone. It jerked him to a stop and spun him around. The bear's paw caught him flush in the side and flung him thirty feet through the air, over some bushes and into the neighbor's yard.

Bill was crushed. He thought, *That's it.*

Spooky's done. Once that bear leaves, I'm gonna have to go over there and find his body.

Two minutes later, Spooky came trotting in through the hole in the screen door. He had three broken ribs and a big gash on his side, but he still had that piece of salmon hanging out of the side of his mouth.

That was Spooky. He was a fiercely loyal friend. But he was also the kind of cat that would stalk a squirrel down the branch of a forty-foot tree and risk his life again and again to steal fish from a bear. And he was tough. There seemed to be no wound — self-inflicted or otherwise — that could keep him down. Spooky might try anything — ride a goose, put a snake in the bed, taunt a bear — but Bill could rest assured about one thing: He would always come back.

Until one day, he didn't.

It was the 1990s. The economy was in a funk. After eight years, Bill had given up his job caring for the terminally ill. The emotional toll of saying good-bye to so many people had worn him down. So he went back to his old work as a mechanic, first in the airline industry and then, after another round of layoffs, for a boat hull manufacturer. One Friday, the owner came into the factory and said, "Business is bad. Really bad. As of Monday, everyone with a beard is fired." Absurd. But also serious. The owner hated beards, and in Washington, you apparently can get fired if the boss doesn't like the way you part your hair.

Bill went home and struggled all weekend with his decision. He had been badly wounded in Vietnam. He spent three months in the hospital with an injury he still won't talk about. When the bandages finally came off, he looked in the mirror and saw a full beard. He didn't want anything more to do with the army, and the army didn't want anything more to do with him, but Bill Bezanson loved that beard. For more than twenty years, he had never shaved it off. Not once. And, he decided, he wouldn't start now. Not for a boat braising job. On Monday morning, he was fired. Over his beard! Everyone who had shaved was laid off within the month anyway.

A few nights later, Bill started talking with the bartender at the local Elks club, explaining his situation, and she offered him her house for a few months. She was leaving for the summer and needed someone to feed her goats. Two days later, Bill, Spooky, and Zippo moved into a nice new home in northwestern Washington. Two days after that, the woman was back. She'd gotten into a fight with the man she was going to visit; she wasn't going away for the summer after all; Bill and his cats had to scram.

That wasn't easy, unfortunately, for an unemployed metal fabricator in the middle of a recession. Bill couldn't rent an apartment without a steady paycheck or money in the bank, and his personal housing crisis dragged on and on. For two weeks, Bill hunted for a job while the woman got madder and madder. Finally, he found work as a caretaker for the very ill. It was a good job in a bad economy, and quite a relief. The first thing Bill did when he arrived home from his first day on the job was to call out, "Spooky! Spooky!" He wanted to celebrate.

No Spooky.

No Spooky for dinner.

And no Spooky at bedtime, either.

Bill knew something was wrong. He searched the neighborhood. No sign of Spooky. The woman said the coyotes must have gotten him. Bill didn't think so. He knew what death felt like, and he didn't have the feeling. He just didn't believe Spooky was gone. He figured Spooky must have been accidently locked in a garage or a work shed, and that when he broke free, he'd come home. At dusk, Bill would stand on the porch and listen for Spooky. Every night, he thought he heard Spooky's distant meow. Zippo was out all the time looking for Spooky in his own way, so it could have been Zippo's meow being carried on the wind. But Bill didn't think so. He'd wake up in the middle of the night and swear he heard Spooky. He became convinced Spooky had fallen in an old well or been trapped in a hole, and he searched through the backyards and the forest looking for him. Bill had walked out on so much else in his life. He would never walk out on Spooky.

But the days passed, and there was still no Spooky. The woman wanted Bill and Zippo out. She was convinced the coyotes had gotten Spooky; she didn't care about that lousy old cat anyway; she just wanted her house back. Bill fought her every day. There was no way he was leaving without Spooky. No way.

Three weeks later, he and Zippo were still there. The woman was standing in the doorway, screaming at him to leave. Bill refused. Again. Not without Spooky, he told her. Not while Spooky might still be alive. The woman turned in a rage, looked into the backyard, and turned stone white. She had to grab the door frame to keep from falling over. There, coming across the yard, was Spooky. He was very skinny, and very dirty, but he was alive.

Bill clutched him in his arms. "Spooky. Spooky," he said, burying his face in Spooky's fur. "I knew you'd come home."

They left that night: Bill, Spooky, and chubby-tubby Zippo. Bill didn't even have a place to go. He just took his cats, his few possessions, and left. He and the cats slept in his car until the first paycheck came through.

A year later, he struck up a conversation with a stranger in a bar. After a few drinks, the man said, "Oh, wait a minute, you're that guy. You lived with my mom. She took your cat to the dump, man, and threw him out with her trash. She almost died when that cat came back."

The dump was twenty miles away. Twenty miles! It took three weeks of walking, but Spooky came back. He had survived a strike from an owl. He had outfoxed four coyotes and withstood a swipe from a bear. He had been thrown out with the trash and found his way home. He was a survivor in every sense of the word.

Eventually, though, there comes a point when we can't come back. Zippo reached it first, in June 2001, at the age of eighteen. He had gone into the animal hospital for routine surgery to remove a tumor. Bill called later that morning, all smiles, and asked how Zippo was. The veterinarian, Dr. Call, had been Zippo and Spooky's veterinarian since they first moved to Washington fifteen years before. One morning soon after moving there, Bill had seen a dog hit by a car. He ran into the road, scooped up the dog, and drove it to the nearest vet. The dog was biting itself and screaming; it was in tremendous pain. When Bill reach for him, the dog reared back and bit him on the neck and shoulder. On the examination table, it thrashed and screamed. It was frantic with terror. Dr. Call walked in, touched the dog gently with his bare hand, and it calmed right down.

Bill was so impressed, he brought Spooky to see Dr. Call the next day. Spooky loved him immediately. And Dr. Call loved Spooky. He later nursed him through the coyote attack and the bear attack. He shook his head in amazement when he heard about the owl. He always called Spooky his miracle cat.

But now Dr. Call was sniffling into the telephone, trying to keep his voice from cracking. Zippo, he told Bill, had a reaction to the anesthesia. He had died in the middle of surgery. Big, sweet Zippo. Just the day before, he had seemed so full of life. Now he was gone. Bill was in shock. Spooky was devastated.

Spooky's own health had been in decline for several years. He was almost twenty-one years old, and the feline AIDS was finally getting a grip on him. He had trouble keeping food in his stomach, and he was prone to terrible, body-shaking fevers. Now, without Zippo, he was lethargic and morose. He missed his buddy, his lazy best friend. When Bill came home from work every day, the first thing he did was close all the cabinet doors. Spooky opened them during the day, looking for Zippo.

Bill adopted another cat: a black kitten just like Zippo. He wanted Spooky to have a companion, but Spooky would have nothing do with the new cat. Spooky had never hated anyone or anything in his life (even those poor voles — that was just his hunter nature getting the best of him), but he did not want that little kitten around.

His fevers grew worse. Most days, he couldn't keep food down. His body was failing on him, and he was sick at heart. In August, Bill took Spooky to Dr. Call, who told him Spooky was dying. There wasn't anything he could do. Spooky had only a few days to live. And it was going to be a painful, difficult death.

Spooky was a survivor, a fighter, an adventurer and a lap sitter, a loyal friend and a constant companion for almost twenty-one years. He was the one who was there, by his side, when Bill needed him. He was the constant in Bill's life. For years, he was his only true connection. He was his security, his lifeline on all those nights when the dreams were bad or the fear crept in. He always came back when Bill called him. And even at the end, he didn't want to go. When most cats receive their final shot, they lie down and pass peacefully away. Spooky lunged when the needle touched his skin. He meowed and tried desperately to pull away. Then he turned, looked Bill in the eyes, and roared like a lion. Like he was fighting. Like he wasn't ready to go. Like Bill had made a terrible mistake.

That scream was a hammer blow to Bill Bezanson's heart. It haunted him. Dr. Call swore Bill had done the right thing, that Spooky had less than a week to live and that he was suffering terrible pain. But that scream ate him up inside. Spooky had wanted to live! Even in pain, even though he knew he was dying, he wanted to live.

A few weeks later, on September 11, 2001, the towers crumbled. Bill Bezanson looked up from his line job at Boeing and wondered if more planes were coming, if the helicopters were all shot down, if he was finally left behind. He missed Zippo. He missed Spooky. He missed the connection. He had lost the security of their presence. He felt, this time, that he was truly alone.

Then he received a letter with no return address. (He found out later it had been sent by Dr. Call's office.) When he heard about Dewey's death seven years later, he sent me a copy. "I know how you can mourn for a cat," he wrote, "because I have done it myself." He thought the note might help me because it had helped him. This is what it said:

LAST WILL AND TESTAMENT

I, Spooky Bezanson, being of poor health, do hereby bequeath to my friend and master, my last will and testament, to be recalled fondly whenever he may think of me.

My time on earth has been a happy time, full of joyful memories and carefree hours. I take with me no worldly possessions, because possessions and property have never been my primary concerns. What was important to me was earning your trust and praise, being obedient and always faithful. But the one thing I possessed and will cherish above all else was

158

my master's love, for no one could have loved me more.

When I am gone and you have occasion to think of me, do not feel sad, for I am at peace and no longer feel any discomfort or pain. All the maladies that age and circumstance had thrust upon my physical being are no longer a concern to me. I am free to romp with the wind at my face and the grass tickling my feet. I nap in the warmth of the sun and sleep under a blanket of stars. In this joy I wait for you.

Because we shared so many happy times together, I know you feel like I cannot ever be replaced and that perhaps you should live the remainder of your life without another pet as a faithful companion. My friend, don't try to replace me, for what we shared is irreplaceable. We grew together, through some pretty hairy (and cold) times. But don't deprive yourself of the warmth and love another companion can bring to you. I would not want you to be alone.

Most of all, remember, dear master, I will always be with you, in your heart, in your mind, and in your memories. For what we shared was special, today, tomorrow, and always. And if you should ever feel a cold nose on your skin, and there's no animal around, just know, in your heart of hearts, it's me, saying hello.

Bill Bezanson is better now. The fear and isolation triggered by the events of September 11, 2001, sent him to the local Veterans Affairs (VA) center for counseling, and he finally confronted his memories of Vietnam, and especially of September 1968. He had been experiencing the "fight or flight" syndrome so common with PTSD, a biological response triggered by a subconscious conviction that the world is unsafe, that to survive, you must either run or defend yourself. For more than thirty years, Bill Bezanson had been running.

"What would you have told me about your life before that breakthrough?" I asked him.

"I wouldn't have talked to you."

It was as simple as that.

A few months later, in late 2001, Bill retired. He adopted another kitten so that the cat he brought home when Spooky was sick would never feel alone. After decades of rental houses, he purchased a condominium in northwestern Washington. He no longer felt the urge to flee, but that September he painted his entire condominium. Painting was a good middle ground.

In 2002, he bought a house outside Maple Falls, Washington, a small town near Mount Baker and the Canadian border. He's still not sure he's truly let anyone in, not all the way, but he's found a home for life, and he's made good friends in the neighborhood. Mr. Helpful, they call him. He built a porch for his neighbor, who is battling cancer. He drives another neighbor, a ninety-year-old former schoolteacher with macular degeneration, on her errands. His father died ten years ago after a long battle with cancer, having told only one story to the nurses who cared for him — the story of how a raccoon loved his son Bill so much that it jumped out of a tree to greet him and brought its babies onto the porch to meet him — but Bill has reconnected with his mother. He calls her in Michigan two or three times a week.

Every now and then, he has friends over: fellow retirees, neighbors, people he met on the job or in the past few years. They share a few drinks, laugh, chat. At some point during the evening, someone always reaches down and brushes the back of their leg. "I thought I felt something," they say, when they see Bill watching them. "A cold spot. But there was nothing there."

Bill doesn't say anything, but he knows there was something there. "It might be Zippo," Bill told me, but I could tell he didn't mean it. That's just a kindness to an old friend. In his heart, he knows it was the cold nose of Spooky. The cat has never left him. He still comes around, sometimes, to say hello. He is waiting for Bill to come home.

Four

Tabitha, Boogie, Gail, BJ, Chimilee, Kit, Miss Gray, Maira, Midnight, Blackie, Honey Bunny, Chazzi, Candi, Nikki, Easy, Buffy, Prissy, Taffy . . . and more

"When I was reading your book I had to think of what a great book it would have been if I would have kept a diary of our times here on Sanibel Island, FL. My husband manages a resort on the island and I work reservations and one night we were taking a walk on the grounds and a lovely cat followed us home and so of course I fed her and she of course kept coming back. . . . Well, to make a long story short, we ended up with 28 cats."

I love Sanibel Island, Florida. I've traveled all over the country to library conferences — and enjoyed every dancing, laughing minute of it — but nothing, for me, compares to that special island. Thanks to my brother Mike, who was friends with the former manager, I've been visiting a resort there called Premier Properties of Pointe Santo de Sanibel for more than twenty years. I was there the week after Dewey died, in fact. Brother Mike's daughter was getting married, and I was packing for the trip when I got the call. Dewey wasn't acting like himself.

I immediately rushed to the library to pick him up and take him to the vet. I thought it was constipation, a frequent problem for our elderly cat. I was stunned when the doctor used words like *tumor, cancer, intense pain,* and *no hope*. I felt as if I had been flattened by a hammer blow, but when I looked into Dewey's eyes, I could tell it was true. He had been hiding it from me for weeks, possibly months, but he wasn't hiding it now. He was hurting. And he was asking for my help.

I signed the paperwork. I held him in my arms and against my heart. I watched his eyes close. I arranged for his cremation, numb from the shock. Then, still in a fog, I rushed home to finish packing, picked up my father at his house half a day later than planned, and drove to Omaha. I rushed to my daughter's house, hugged my twin grandchildren, and hustled everyone to the airport. Our bottoms didn't hit our seats, I think, until a second before the airplane took off. And then of course the twins, who were only two, needed juice and crayons and a hug until the plane leveled out and their ears stopped hurting. When I finally caught my breath somewhere in the sky over Missouri, I picked up the ratty old airline magazine. Someone had already filled in the crossword puzzle. In pen. Ugh. On the next page, though, was a picture of a cat. I started crying, and cried all the way to Sanibel Island.

There is no better place to mourn. Sanibel Island, and in particular Premier Properties of Pointe Santo, is the most relaxing spot on earth. The beach is crystal white, and there is hardly anyone on it. Well, except "no-see-ums," evil little creatures that will bite you mercilessly if your bare flesh touches the sand. But, really, that is a small price for a paradise where you can walk (in flip-flops) along the surf, picking up coral-colored seashells, and sit on your balcony, watching mother dolphins and their babies leaping off-shore. In the afternoon, I like to relax to the arguing of the mockingbirds that call back and forth to each other "Whhhaat?" (that's the male, I've decided) and "Uh-uh" (that's the sass-talking female). Even the four-foot alligator on the property is cool. You see him sometimes shuffling lazily across the lawn, completely ignoring the lounge chairs.

Then there are the sunsets. In Iowa, once in a while you get a blast of color at the end of the day, with pinks and oranges and gold. On Sanibel Island, it's always like that, the vivid colors dominating the sky and then sinking slowly into the gorgeous blue gulf waters and bringing out the stars. You look up from the beach, or from the wine you're sipping on your balcony, and feel happy and free, awed by the natural beauty and ready to toast a perfect end to another glorious day.

Or that's usually how it is. With a wedding to attend and long-absent relatives to soothe (and sometimes pretend to ignore), the week after Dewey's death was going to be crazy, even before the emotional bombshell of his passing. Fortunately, my granddaughter Hannah, the flower girl, distracted me in the unique manner of children: She gave me the flu. Along with twenty-seven other people at the rehearsal dinner. I spent most of the week watching cartoons with Hannah on the sofa, and I spent more time on my knees staring into the toilet bowl than I did watching dolphins frolic in the surf. I was too weak for the telephone, television, or e-mail (I was barely strong enough to follow Dora the Explorer's mind-numbing adventures, in fact), so I had no idea that back home, Dewey's popularity was exploding and the library phones were ringing off the hook. I could only look out the window at the ocean and think what a small piece of the world we all were, and how nice it was that the bathroom was only ten feet from the television. Even when you're vomiting five times a day, there is nothing quite like the peace of Sanibel Island.

So I know what Mary Nan Evans meant when she told me that her thought, on seeing Sanibel Island for the first time, was:

"There is no way I could ever afford to live here." Paradise, after all, had been reserved long ago for the rich and powerful, and like me, Mary Nan was a small-town girl from the Midwest. Her husband, Larry, a maintenance man at a hospital in Waverly, Missouri, had won employee of the year for the state's western district, and the prize was four days on this small island off the southwest coast of Florida. Mary Nan had been to Florida many times before — she had an aunt who lived in Fort Myers, just up the coast — but the merging of the brilliant blue sky and the brilliant blue water around the tight green strip of Sanibel Island was like nothing she had ever seen. Even the white buildings visible on the horizon looked like the sharpened edges of clouds. As she crossed the long causeway linking the island to the mainland, she thought to herself, *Remember this, Mary Nan, because you'll never be back.*

Four years later, in 1984, she and Larry were back, at least in Florida. This time, they weren't looking for a four-day break from their ordinary lives; they were looking for a job. With Larry's fifteen years in maintenance, they felt confident he could find work at one of the many resorts that dotted the coast. And the resorts offered accommodations, since being the maintenance director for a large complex of buildings full of tourists who can't survive a busted ice machine for twenty minutes, let alone two hours, was a twenty-four-hour-a-day job full of people making demands and odd requests. But there was one problem. When Larry mentioned that he owned a cat, the resorts turned him down. Sorry, they said. No animals allowed.

Getting rid of Tabitha, their beloved Siamese, was out of the question. Larry and Mary Nan had adopted her fifteen years earlier, in 1969, when Larry was stationed in California at the end of his military service. Just before Thanksgiving, Mary Nan had seen an ad in the base newspaper: newborn kittens available for adoption. They only had twenty dollars, saved by serious scrimping on an enlisted man's pay, but Mary Nan convinced Larry to have a look. As soon as they arrived at the apartment, a bundle of tiny Siamese kittens came tumbling out of a back room. Most of them were wobbling and falling over, but one came straight to Mary Nan and stumbled into her arms. Mary Nan held the kitten to her chest, and it stretched up and nuzzled her chin.

"I really want a girl," she told the woman with the cats.

"Well, you're holding the only one," the

woman replied.

Mary Nan gave the woman ten dollars for her expenses and left with Tabitha. She spent most of the rest of their life's savings on litter and cat food. That Thanksgiving, Mary Nan and Larry Evans sat down at the dinner table and said grace over two aluminum-tray TV dinners. Mary Nan can't exactly recall, but it was probably Swanson's turkey and gravy. With that little cherry pie on the side. After buying cat food, it was the only Thanksgiving dinner they could afford.

But Tabitha was worth it, because she was the sweetest, most loyal cat any couple could ask for. She never wanted anything but her food. She never made more than a polite sound. She never craved the company of anyone but her parents but was never rude to visitors or handymen. As long as she was in the house, Tabitha wasn't worried about anything. She slept. She lounged. She let Larry vacuum her neck and the top of her head — yes, with the hose from the vacuum cleaner — closing her eyes as the blast of air sucked away her loose fur. "She even made friends with a mouse," Larry told me in amazement. More than once, he found her in the living room just staring as an ancient, gray-whiskered mouse (according to Larry, who is apparently an expert on mouse whiskers) tottered off to his hole. I have no idea how Mary Nan put up with that. I would have demanded my cat — or at least Larry — get rid of that mouse. But she never held this act of clemency against Tabitha. Every night, the cat slept in the center of the bed, right between Larry and Mary Nan. If Mary Nan awoke during the night, she'd often find Tabitha sitting on her chest, staring into her face. Completely mouse-free.

Mary Nan wasn't shy about telling herself, Larry, or any of her friends about Tabitha's role in the family. She and Larry weren't able to have children (Tabitha couldn't either, although that was her owner's decision), and Tabitha was like the daughter they'd never have to argue with or beg not to date that "bad boy" all the girls were cooing over. For a while, Mary Nan even carried Tabitha around in a baby blanket her grandmother had crocheted for her.

Of course, cats aren't children, and they also weren't allowed in their military-base apartment, so Mary Nan was careful to keep Tabitha a secret from the neighbors. When she took Tabby to the car for a vet's visit, she carried her not in a cage but in a brown paper bag, like a sack of groceries. Tabitha never complained. Not once. In fact, she loved it. Brown paper bags became her favorite toys, and she'd roll around with her head inside them for what seemed like hours. She also loved the car. Often, she would meow at the apartment door, begging to be taken down to the car. On mild weather days, and there were a lot of those in Southern California, Mary Nan would leave the cat curled up on the hump in the backseat, which Tabby had torn to shreds with her claws. A little food and water, and Tabby would have lived in the car. She loved it that much.

But by the time Mary Nan and Larry visited Sanibel Island, Tabby was getting older. After Larry left the military, the family moved back to his hometown of Carrollton, Missouri, a little community of about four thousand people, where he had seen Mary Nan for the first time at the skating rink when she was almost sixteen and he was barely twenty. In Missouri, Larry worked as a maintenance man; Mary Nan kept the house. They were content. But the cold Missouri winters were hard on Tabby's joints, and after twelve good years, she began slowing down. Mary Nan took a blanket Larry's grandmother had knitted and folded it on the floor in front of the heater vent. Tabby sat on the blanket until she was steaming hot, but the cat sauna didn't help her aching joints. Tabby was the love of their lives, and she was in decline.

There was no way Larry and Mary Nan were leaving her behind. Not for a month, not for a week, not even if it meant the end of Mary Nan's dream of a life in Florida (and it was her dream, not Larry's) and a long trip back to Carrollton, Missouri, in defeat.

"I have one more place to call," Larry told his wife after two weeks of searching. "If this doesn't work out, we'll head home."

He made the call. "I just want to tell you up front," he said, "that I have a cat, and I'm not getting rid of her."

"So what?" the man on the other end of the line replied. "I have two."

A few weeks later, Larry, Mary Nan, and Tabby Evans had moved all of their possessions into a little bungalow across the street from the Colony Resort on Sanibel Island. This time, Mary Nan knew she was in paradise to stay. The resort was on the eastern, residential end of the island, away from the crowded shops and high-rise developments. The individually owned bungalows and condominiums of Colony Resort were scattered around a property filled with palm trees, bushes, and the grassy areas between them. To the east, a boardwalk led across 160 feet of sparsely overgrown sand dunes to a wide white beach and the gorgeous blue waters of the Gulf of Mexico. A short walk down the beach was the tip of the island, with its famous lighthouse. After dark, the sky was black and full of stars since no streetlights have ever been allowed to mar the quiet wonder of a Sanibel Island night.

Even Tabby, fifteen years old and increasingly arthritic, was rejuvenated. Mary Nan donned a pair of khaki casual shorts and a permanent smile, bought a fat-tired bicycle with a basket on the front, and Tabitha rode with her everywhere. While the girls were out on their leisurely errands, Larry used his weekends to screen in the porch on the back of the bungalow, and after a strenuous morning of basket-sitting (that wind can be murder on a cat's fur!), Tabitha would lay out there all afternoon, warmed by the sun and refreshed by the cool island breeze. Mary Nan and Tabby spent hours together on that porch, Mary Nan with her cross-stitch and Tabby with nothing to do but enjoy her old age.

Maybe it was the sight of Tabby luxuriating on her private porch that attracted the little dappled cat. Maybe it was the obvious love (and food) Mary gave her sweet Siamese. Or maybe it was just inevitable. Sanibel Island in the 1980s was crawling with feral cats.

You would see them everywhere: running through the bushes beside the street, poking around backyard barbeques, scrounging through the sea grass–covered empty lots that would, over the years, be turned into oceanfront estates, hotels, and high-rise condominiums. Maybe the dappled cat was just trying to find an easier way to survive in paradise when she followed Mary Nan and Larry home from their walk one night. She couldn't get onto the porch, but she was hanging around the front door every time they came out.

"I'm going to give that kitten some milk," Mary Nan told Larry after a few days of watching the cat watching her. The poor thing was as skinny as a sandpiper and nearly as skittish, but once Mary Nan started feeding her, she never left the yard.

"I figured," Larry muttered, rolling his eyes with a bemused smile.

"What should I name her?" Mary Nan asked the two little boys who lived next door.

"Call her Boogie," they said.

"What's a boogie?"

The boys looked at each other. "I don't know," one of them replied.

"Okay," Mary Nan said with a smile. "Boogie it is."

Two months later, Larry stopped outside the front door on his way to work. "Mary Nan," he called to his wife, the good-natured exasperation evident in his voice, "you better come out and see what you've done."

On the front porch were three gorgeous, wiggly, sop-eared kittens. Boogie's kittens.

"I guess we have five cats now," Mary Nan said, going inside for a jug of milk. Four for the yard, and Tabitha asleep on the porch.

A year later, the resort manager retired. Larry became the manager, Mary Nan took over the front desk, and the whole family moved across the street to a bungalow on the resort property. By then, Tabitha had passed away. Her health had been in serious decline for months, but Mary Nan and Larry couldn't bring themselves to put her down. In her last week, Larry had to go to the mainland for business. Mary Nan and Tabitha went for the car ride. Riding on that torn-up seat hump was still Tabby's favorite activity, even better than the bicycle or the porch. To sneak her into the hotel, Mary Nan had to swaddle her in a blanket and pretend she was their child, just as she had when Tabby was a kitten, but the effort was worth it. While Larry worked, Mary Nan drove Tabitha around Fort Myers and twenty miles up and down the coast.

When they got home, they took Tabby to the vet. "It's time," he said simply. Mary Nan and Larry didn't reply. They knew he was right, and it was the hardest thing they had ever endured. Tabitha had been like a daughter to them. She had comforted them with her presence, her persistent love, and her refusal to date the wrong men. Even though they knew she was suffering, putting her down was like tearing away a piece of their hearts. That afternoon, Larry and Mary Nan sat together on a bench, just staring at the ocean and crying in each other's arms.

But they still had four cats: Boogie, the original dappled kitten that had walked into Mary Nan's heart, and her three babies. They were outdoor cats, of course, but they apparently had no intention of ever wandering out of sight. Since Sanibel Island summer days were often hot, Larry built a cat house outside the bungalow porch. The box was about four feet by four feet, with a wooden roof for shade and mesh walls to let the breeze blow through. It even had a fan with a mesh cover to keep the kittens cool on those rare sweltering days when the ocean winds didn't blow.

From the comfort of her porch, Mary Nan

watched her cats, thinking of those quiet days with Tabitha and wishing she had such a nice fan for her own house. She watched soon after as one of the cats gave birth to a gaggle of moist, hairless kittens on the roof of the cat house. And she watched the next day as one of the mewling babies, still with its eyes shut and too small to walk, rolled right off the roof and out of sight. Mary Nan ran out expecting an injured or dead little kitten, but the baby was alive and unhurt, lying in a bundle on the grass and crying softly for its mother.

I really should get these cats fixed, she thought.

With so many cats to feed — there were now seven — Larry placed a line of bowls outside the bungalow door. Every morning, before his own breakfast, he filled each one with food. The cats came running . . . all to the same bowl. No matter how many options they were given, they all wanted to eat out of the same bowl at the same time. The kittens would crawl over each other, stumbling, falling, getting in fights, while the older cats stuck their snouts in the bowl and gulped down food while trying to ram each other away with the top of their heads. Mary Nan and Larry couldn't help but laugh.

Eventually, the food began to attract more

feral cats. First it was ten. Then twelve. Then . . . where did that cat come from? Larry would wonder. *Do I know that cat? It sure seems eager and entitled.* But . . . *Aww, what the heck,* Larry thought, *give them another handful of food.* Mary Nan was the one who began to name them. It seemed the best way, in conjunction with spaying the cats she considered her own, to keep the colony organized. But the cats refused to cooperate. They kept coming and going, but mostly coming in greater and greater numbers. It wasn't long before you couldn't walk ten steps at Colony Resort without a cat racing across your path. Every time Mary Nan and Larry walked down the boardwalk to the beach — and they walked down to the beach holding hands every single evening after work for two decades — a parade of cats followed them like a herd of ducklings. They could hear the stampede of paws pounding along the boards, the sound mixing finally with the soft crashing of the waves as the little group cleared the last of the dunes. Some of the cats would wander into the dunes — you know how cats are with sand — but most waited on the boardwalk, wrestling each other or chasing invisible-to-the-human-eye "bugs" until Larry and Mary Nan returned from their evening stroll. Then the gaggle would turn back along the boardwalk and head for home.

Chazzi, Taffy, Buffy, Miss Gray.

Maira. Midnight. Blackie. Candi. Nikki. Easy.

"Can you remember any more?" Mary Nan said over her shoulder, with the phone still to her ear.

"I don't know," Larry said in the background. "Did you say Chimilee?"

"Of course I said Chimilee, Larry. He was my favorite."

When he was a kitten, Chimilee's front leg was badly injured, most likely in a fight, and the veterinary bill was $160. After the surgery, Mary Nan told Larry, "That cat is mine. I've got too much invested in him just to let him go." So Chimilee — who Mary Nan *claims* looked like Dewey — moved into the bungalow. He was a big, sweet twenty-two-pound yellow cat who loved lounging on Mary Nan and Larry but never minded sharing them with a growing assortment of furry pals. After Chimilee, Mary Nan reasoned, there was no reason to consider the indoors off-limits to the other cats, so she opened the window every night for the breeze. She figured most of the cats wouldn't bother coming inside, since they had it so cushy outside, but a few nights later, Larry tried to turn over in bed and found himself trapped under a mound of fur.

What in the heck is going on here? he remembered thinking. "There must have been twenty cats in that bed," Larry told me with a laugh.

"No, Larry, come on now," said Mary Nan, "there were only five. But they *were* fat. We slept with more than eighty pounds of cat every night."

After a few days, Mary Nan closed the window, so it really was only five — except on really hot days, when she left the window open and ten or twelve cats wandered in. It was never the ton of cats in the bed that bothered Mary Nan, though. Or the scratched-up sofa and hair-covered chairs. It was the lizards those cats carried into the living room to torture. And that one awful snake.

"It was hard work," Mary Nan admitted, which made Larry laugh. After all, he was the one who cleaned the litter and served the food. He was the one who got up in the middle of the night when the darn cats wouldn't stop banging on the kitchen cabinet where their food was stored. He was the one who took them to the vet when they needed it and built the special cage for BJ, who got himself sliced in a fight. The vet gave him some medicine and a patch called New-Skin to cover the wound. BJ didn't have a tooth in his head — "he had a mouth like a rock crusher," as Larry put it — but he always managed to get into tussles and knock the patch off. Mr. Bandage, Carl the groundskeeper called him, because for six months the New Skin was hanging half off his leg or lying in the grass somewhere. So Larry built a special cage, and BJ was quarantined until his leg healed. Then, with that problem solved, Larry fixed the condo screens the cats had torn. And repaired their cat house. And mended the shredded curtains. And shooed cats away from the fountain in the courtyard, where they were always trying to drink.

One day, Mary Nan passed a ladder and saw two cats sitting on each rung. *Larry needs to put this stuff away,* she thought. A few evenings later, Larry opened his barbeque grill to light it and found a cat inside. He picked up a huge piece of driftwood from the beach so they could sharpen their claws. *That'll keep them busy,* he thought. Within a few years, it was nothing but a nub, and they still had a four-inch patch on each corner of their sofa where the cats had scratched down to the frame. Larry got the vacuum out every night to suck up the shards of driftwood and cloth.

When they overran the food bowls outside the bungalow, Larry decided to scatter more bowls around the property. Every morning, while Mary Nan fixed breakfast, Larry drove around on his golf cart to the various food bowls. There would be cats lounging in the back and cats clinging to the sides of the cart, trying to open the food bags. He worried at first, but after a while he just whizzed around the property with cats occasionally tumbling off and rolling to their feet in the grass. The feeding trip took most of an hour, and when he finally arrived home and sat down for breakfast, he'd look out the window and see five or six cat staring at his toast and jam.

"They're hungry again," he'd mutter to Mary Nan between mouthfuls of the healthy oatmeal she forced on him though he much preferred bacon and eggs.

And they'd laugh. There was never a moment, after all, when a cat wasn't hungry. They'd follow Larry on his golf cart runs around the property, whining for food. They followed Mary Nan to her car, and she'd have to back out *very* slowly to keep from running them down. They'd follow her into the office and trail her in a long line as she went around the sidewalks picking up lizard tails, because when geckos get scared, they lose their tails, and the poor lizards at the Colony Resort lived in constant fear of the cats.

The only time you wouldn't see cats at the Colony Resort was after the bombing run. In those days, Sanibel Island used old military bombers to spray for mosquitoes. They'd fly just above the treetops and drop poisonous spray over every inch of the island. One second, it was silence and clear blue skies; the next, an old airplane would appear with an earth-shaking drone. The cats would jump up and bolt away in a panic. It was a shame to see them so terrified, but Mary Nan had to admit it was amusing to see twenty cats scatter in every direction like a double set of bowling pins.

One day, Mary Nan ran into Carl the groundskeeper at one of the bungalows in the far corner of the property. He was casually raking the lawn, like nothing unusual was going on, but there was a cat hanging off each of his pant legs.

"They're trying to get my treats," Carl told Mary Nan. He had taken to keeping cat treats in his pockets, and apparently it wasn't out of the ordinary for him to have cats hanging off his hips, trying to steal a bite or two.

"It wasn't just time consuming," Larry laughed. "It was expensive." But Larry and Mary Nan didn't want it any other way. Between the cats, the staff, and the resort guests, their childless union was bursting with companionship and love.

A DAY IN THE LIFE OF LARRY

7:30   Wake up. Shove forty pounds of cat off bed. Trudge into kitchen to open bottom cabinet, where cat food is kept. As usual, trapped cat comes waltzing out, licking its lips.

7:40   Start golf cart for morning round . . . of feeding cats. Visit "nine hole course" of bowls scattered around resort. Try not to send hitchhiking cats flying off cart around corners.

8:30   Breakfast of oatmeal instead of eggs. Darn Mary Nan's health fads.

9:00   Workday officially starts. Cats rush out when workshop door opened since they sleep in the shop when the temperature drops below forty degrees. They think that's brutally cold. Reason #103 why Sanibel Island is the best! Buffy asleep in toolbox again.

9:18   Check overnight work orders in office. Kiss Mary Nan at front desk. No cats allowed, but Gail has snuck in as usual.

9:32   Inspect torn screen cited in work order. Notice cat claws stuck in mesh.

9:45   Open garage to retrieve new screen material. No cats! Whoops, there was one asleep on the ladder.

11:18   Finish installing screen. Notice young boy and cat watching. Both look disappointed.

11:38   Check chemical level in pool. Notice a cat drinking out of the shallow end. Then notice it isn't a cat. It's a raccoon. It stops to sample cat food before waddling off.

12:02   Lunch with Mary Nan in the office. Gail watches, but no handouts.

12:32   Shoo cats out from under the car, walk around twice to make sure they have all left, then back up *very* slowly and proceed to town to pick up mail.

1:13   Take golf cart around resort to inspect grounds. Cats are sleeping in pile on the rack. How many? Maybe four, but too tightly packed to be sure. Cats along route look up briefly, then fall back to sleep. They know this isn't the food run.

1:40   Prune trees with Carl the groundskeeper. Cats crowd around to watch. Cat starts gagging, then throws up a lizard tail. Clean up lizard tail.

5:00   Workday officially ends, but tree branches still need to be hauled away.

5:35   Evening meal run. Gail in the back of the golf cart, munching food from the bag.

6:23   Walk to beach with Mary Nan. Pretend cats aren't following.

7:28   Late dinner. Cats staring in window, begging for food. Where are the curtains?

7:31   Rehang rod that collapsed when cats tried to climb curtains. Pretend there are still eight scratches in the fabric, like yesterday, not thirteen.

7:42   Back to dinner and big staring cat eyes. Oh, what the heck, throw them a few handfuls of food.

8:15   Inspection of bungalow for minor cat damage. Nothing but shards of driftwood. Find three cats, as usual, crammed in the little space between the headboard and the mattress of the bed.

9:00   Kick Maira and Chimi out of the big lounge chair. Watch some TV.

9:36   Almost tell Chimi not to sharpen his claws on the sofa, then remember that both front corners of the sofa have four-inch-square patches where cats have shredded them down to the wooden frame. Decide to sip soda instead. Wish it was soda. It's water. Darn health fads.

11:30   End of local news. Time for bed. Settle onto mattress in typical cat, Mary Nan, cat, cat, Larry, cat order.

11:35   Turn off light, reposition cats three times, find comfortable position, and go to sleep.

12:34   Wake up to bang, bang, bang from the kitchen. Cats are trying to open the cabinet again. Realize this will go on for fifteen minutes until they finally succeed. Contemplate getting up but decide instead to just let the darn cat out, no doubt licking its lips, first thing in the morning. Fall back asleep with a smile.

One evening, no doubt while Mary Nan and Larry were being eyeballed in their scratched-up chairs by several lethargic cats, there was a knock at the bungalow door. Standing outside was a small boy, about eleven years old, whose family had been coming to the resort for several years. In his arms was a beautiful tan kitten.

"Can I have this cat?" the little boy asked, with big pleading eyes. "I love this cat."

Mary Nan was hesitant. She knew the family and liked them, but she didn't have any idea how well they would care for a cat. And, truth be told, she wasn't sure where that little tan cat had come from. Had she even seen it before? Was it really hers to give? Apparently, it had been staying in the family's rented condo, against resort regulations, so Mary Nan figured the cat was a regular resort resident. And since the parents were as enthusiastic to adopt it as the boy, and since the tan kitten really seemed to have taken to the family, she agreed to let it return with them to north Florida.

For several weeks, she was nervous. What had she done? What might have befallen that poor cat? What did she think she was, an adoption agency? Then, just as she was beginning to drive herself crazy, she received a thank-you note with a snapshot of the kitten. Every few months, the family sent her another photograph of the cat in his new home, surrounded by love and lapping up the attention like a forgotten glass of milk left sitting on the kitchen table. Every year, when the family returned to the Colony Resort, they shared more pictures and stories of the cat that had, truly, become a member of their family.

A frequent visitor from Miami was more direct. Connie simply told Mary Nan, "I'm taking these two cats." She already had five cats at home, but she couldn't leave without the two friends she'd made over a series of visits. *As long as the cats are happy,* Mary Nan thought, as ten other cats watched her from the rungs of a ladder. Larry, it seemed, was always leaving that ladder around.

It wasn't as if Mary Nan didn't know these people. The Colony was a family-oriented resort, and most of the renters had been coming for years. Some were second generation, following the path of their parents; some viewed the visit as an opportunity to bring together three or even four generations under the Sanibel sun. A vast majority had a standing reservation and came for the same week or two every year, and by the second or third visit, most came expecting cats. They asked about the cats when confirming reservations, and their ridiculous antics — falling off the towel bin while wrestling, taking naps in beach bags, snacking on lizard tails — were the talk of the poolside lounge chairs. The children, especially, loved chasing, feeding, hugging, and petting the most pampered crowd of feral kittens north of Ernest Hemingway's twelve-toed heirs in Key West. (He'd promised all his cats' descendants permanent residence at his house in his will, and they'd taken to inbreeding like mad.) Every visitor to the Colony, it seemed, had a favorite cat or two.

But no matter how many cats found homes, or how many guests spoke fondly of different kittens, the star of the resort was always Gail, the lone female in Boogie's original litter. Gail was pure white, with soft fluffy fur and an endearing pink nose. In the sunlight, she absolutely shone. Nobody could miss seeing her amid the swirl of fur; everyone felt compelled to comment on her unique beauty and regal bearing. And like Dewey, she had a warm, calm, generous personality to match that outward charm.

One regular guest, Dr. Niki Kimling, a psychologist from Stamford, Connecticut, was particularly smitten. Dr. Kimling loved the Colony cats, and always brought them exotic toys and playthings. One year, she left twenty-five cans of expensive cat food for their Christmas feast — much preferred to their regular fare of dry kibble. But no matter how much Dr. Kimling pampered the other cats, Gail was her favorite. Every year, she called a few weeks before her visit and requested the company of Gail. The cats weren't supposed to stay inside the condominiums, but for eight days every year, Gail lived with Dr. Kimling, who would buy her expensive cat food, brush her, sleep with her, and basically spoil her rotten. If Gail could have been spoiled rotten, that is. Gail never let popularity change her easygoing personality (like Dewey; so cats can manage to control that feline ego), and she never insisted on being an indoor cat at any other time of the year. But she remembered Dr. Kimling, and she loved with complete abandon her eight days a year as the doctor's "rented" cat.

Renter, adopter, or merely a petter, if you were a cat lover, the Colony was for you. In the decade since Mary Nan took Boogie into

her heart, the resort had become, quite by accident, a little patch of cat heaven in the paradise of Sanibel. You couldn't walk five feet without seeing cats hiding under the bushes, strolling across your path, or chasing each other across the lawns. Every day, it seemed, Mary Nan spotted cats lounging on closed screened porches and coming out of bungalows with happy guests, even though they weren't allowed in the rental units.

And it wasn't just cats. One afternoon, Mary Nan looked out her window and saw eight cats and two raccoons lying on a bench in the warm winter Sanibel sun. Another time, a guest spotted a raccoon washing its hands in the pool. The wild animals, she realized, had moved right onto the grounds and mixed with the feral cats. Neither group seemed to mind. The cats, in fact, didn't seem to mind any other animals. Except for the palm rats. Sanibel Island's least popular guests (with the exception of the big tropical roaches known as palmetto bugs) were the rats that liked to hide in the leaves of the island's ever-present palm trees. Mary Nan might not have been able to open her eyes without seeing a cat, but she never, not once, saw a palm rat on the grounds of the Colony Resort. Not when there were twenty-eight cats roaming the few acres of ground. And

that was just the cats Mary Nan had identified and named.

Of course, as I know from my adventures with Dewey, there are always people uncomfortable with attempts at fostering feline-human friendship. I'm sure the resort's board of directors heard plenty of complaints, although I'm also sure they kept them from Mary Nan. They were supportive, perhaps beyond the bounds of rationality, but eventually even the directors had enough. They weren't opposed to cats on the property, but the current population was way beyond their comfort zone. Despite the protests of some guests, Mary Nan and Larry agreed the cat colony at the Colony Resort would have to be trimmed. It was time. Larry was spending hours every day filling food bowls, inspecting the cats for signs of illness or injury, and repairing cat-damaged items. The outdoor cats, although well cared for, were less healthy than house cats, and leukemia and FIV, the cat form of AIDS, spread widely through the population. The average life expectancy at Colony Resort was only eight or nine years, and putting down so many cats took an emotional toll on Larry and Mary Nan.

It was hardest on Larry, who always took

them for their final shots. Putting down Easy, Carl the groundskeeper's favorite cat, was especially difficult. She was so old and weak, her circulatory system had collapsed, and Larry had to hold her down while the veterinarian poked repeatedly at her backside. She cried, and stared into Larry's eyes with fear and accusation, until Larry felt like the lowest heel in the world. Then she shut her eyes and died. He left the office crying, with her limp body in his arms, and brought her home to be buried. He was in such an emotional fog, he forgot to pay the veterinary bill.

Through natural death and the occasional adoption, Mary Nan began to slowly pare down the number of cats living at the resort. With the help of a donation from Gail's friend and benefactor Dr. Kimling, and with vouchers donated by the South Trail Animal Hospital in Fort Myers, she started to spay and neuter the rest of the colony. A nonprofit organization called PAWS Rescue had recently been formed to neuter and find homes for the feral cats of Sanibel, so all over the island the cat population was being contained. Mary Nan once mentioned to a member of the organization, "I wish I could do more to help you."

"Don't worry," the woman replied. "You're

running your own PAWS organization out there."

Most of the cats at Colony Resort came in quietly for their trip to the vet, either because of their trust in Mary Nan and Larry or through blissful ignorance of what awaited them. Some cats resisted. Some, more feral than the others, were simply hard to catch. It took weeks for Mary to capture Prissy, a huge, muscular male cat that was completely misnamed. She managed to struggle him into a carrier for his trip to the vet, but then made the mistake of reaching in to adjust the blanket she used to make the trip more comfortable. Prissy lashed out and scratched her from her elbow to her wrist. The cut was so bad, and so full of blood, that she rushed to the emergency room. Since Mary was diabetic, and a claw wound was prone to infection, the doctors decided to cut out the torn tissue. The operation cost eight thousand dollars and caught the attention of local animal control officials, but Mary insisted it wasn't Prissy's fault. He had never been in a cage; he was scared; he must have, secretly, been angry about that name. A few weeks later, Larry caught Prissy and was scratched so badly, he contemplated going to the hospital, too. But they were sure, as a repeat offender, Prissy would be doomed.

So the next day, they put sleeping pills in his food. Somehow, Prissy managed to wander off and hide in the bushes. He must have gotten a fantastic sleep, because Mary Nan and Larry didn't see him for two days. In the end, twenty-five cats were neutered at Colony Resort. Prissy wasn't one of them.

With most of the cats neutered, and, thanks to PAWS, fewer feral cats roaming the gorgeous palm-lined streets and sea grass–covered dunes of Sanibel Island, the cat colony at the Colony Resort began to dwindle. Mary Nan's favorite cat, Chimilee, died of leukemia and was buried beside the screened porch next to Tabitha, the beloved Siamese that had started it all. A striped cat with lips so black they looked drawn on with Magic Marker was buried outside their bathroom window, where he often sat. Two cats were buried by the fountain in the center of the courtyard, which they had always treated as their personal water bowl. Dr. Kimling stopped visiting in the late 1990s, after the death of her husband. Her beloved Gail died soon after, at the age of twelve. She was buried outside the door of number 34, the unit Dr. Kimling had rented every year.

The last cat to live at the Colony Resort was Maira, a direct descendant of Boogie, the dappled gray that Mary Nan had so innocently given a dish of milk almost twenty years before. Maira was always a loner, and even when the cat colony was at its height, she had gravitated to Mary Nan and Larry. Now, with the others gone, Maira moved into the bungalow and deeper into the daily routine of their lives. She wasn't an overly sentimental cat, but she was always there on the fringes, a shadow that followed them through their busy days. As the years went by, she became quieter, but also sweeter, as if she knew she was the last link to precious days, and that it was her obligation to slowly wind to a close those two decades spent in a joyous, laughing, whirlwind community of fur. She died in 2004, having spent five years in Mary Nan and Larry's home as the last living member of the beloved cat community of Colony Resort.

Mary Nan and Larry Evans still manage the Colony Resort on the eastern end of Sanibel Island. Most of the longtime guests still come back for their week in paradise, and many of them still talk about the cats that once filled their vacations with such amusement and joy. They are a community, the guests and staff at the Colony Resort, and like any community, they share a catalogue of common experiences. Gail, Boogie, Chimilee, Maira, and the others are still with them, like ancestors or favorite television shows, kept alive in conversations on quiet nights spent under the spell of the star-filled Sanibel Island sky.

It's not just the Colony Resort. Across Sanibel Island, once overrun with feral felines, the stray cats are gone, like those terrible bombers and their poisonous insect spray. Twenty years ago, when I first started visiting, you couldn't walk a block without seeing the cats munching on lizards or scrounging scraps at the sidewalk cafés. Now I can drive the length of the island without seeing a single one. Mary Nan knows this is for the best. It's better for the feral cats, many of whom were ill, scrawny, and struggling for survival. It's better for the pet cats, who are no longer exposed to the diseases the feral community carried. It's better for the other animals on Sanibel Island, especially the native animals and birds, so often the victims of a cat's natural urge to hunt and kill. And if, unfortunately, one of those safer animals is the palm rat, that is a small price to pay to restore the balance of life in paradise.

But still, in her heart, Mary Nan misses them. She misses the eighty pounds of cat that used to sleep on her bed at night. She misses the ritual of feeding and grooming and petting. She misses looking out the window and seeing lounging cats sprawled all the way to the top of a ladder, or lying on the benches in the sunlight with their raccoon friends. She misses seeing them scatter in every direction when the bomber roared overhead. She misses the sight of a door opening and a cat strolling out in violation of all the rules of hygiene and property management. Most of all she misses the comradeship, the sense of being a part of something special as people mixed with cats, and cats mixed with people, and they all enjoyed themselves right down to their bones.

There won't be any more cats. At least not at the Colony Resort. But Mary Nan and Larry are thinking about retiring and moving back to the mainland, and they're pretty sure that when they do, they'll adopt another cat. Larry had always been a dog person, cocker spaniels to be precise, but sharing that Thanksgiving TV dinner with Tabitha in 1969 had changed his opinion of cats forever. He loved Tabitha, and he loved every one of those twenty-eight cats at the Colony Resort every bit as much as Mary Nan had loved them. And like her, he knows that he would enjoy nothing more than to live the last decades of his life in the Florida sun, lounging with a furry friend and remembering those hectic but happy days when the world seemed little more than palm trees and friendship and cats.

FIVE
CHRISTMAS CAT

"While I stood there holding him in my hands and talking to the owner as to what to do, the kitten coughed. Or more accurately, he sputtered. That little sputter took us into a chapter of life that still brings tears to my eyes and a smile to my face."

Vicki Kluever never liked cats. Didn't grow up owning one, never had a friend who owned one, but she'd been around them enough to know they weren't for her. Cats were always rubbing against you. They always wanted to sit in your lap. They always wanted to be petted or given some kind of attention. Vicki was born and raised on Kodiak, a large, mountainous island off the harsh southwest coast of Alaska, where the only milk was powdered and the only affordable meat was the fish you pulled from the freezing sea. She considered herself a strong and independent woman, from a long line of independent women, and if she had an animal, she wanted that animal to be strong and independent, too. Cats? They were soft.

But her daughter, Sweetie, was four years old, and Sweetie really wanted a pet. Vicki suggested a dog. After all, she had grown up with dogs. One of her favorite childhood pictures was of herself with two black eyes, one for each time the enthusiastically playful family dog had knocked her off the front porch with its tail. But her landlord was adamant: no dogs. He had no problem with a cat. If the little girl wanted, he said, they could even adopt two, which sounded good to Vicki because two cats could keep each other company, and she might not have to bother with them. So when a coworker's cat had kittens in November, Vicki Kluever thought she'd found the perfect Christmas present. Or at least the best present allowed at her third-rate fourplex apartment building in Anchorage, Alaska.

Two weeks before Christmas, just as the kittens were being weaned, she drove over to meet them. They were pathetically cute, of course, tiny and uncoordinated and nestling energetically against their mother. There was one little guy that stood out, though, the one that kept biting his siblings' tails and stepping on their heads when they tried to suckle their mother. He was a live wire, a real spunky personality. The independent type. So Vicki picked him. Then she chose his exact opposite: a cute little female that looked Siamese and seemed like the most docile kitten in the bunch.

She planned the adoption for Christmas Eve. She and her daughter were having dinner with their friend Michael, so she asked him to pick up Sweetie from day care. (The girl's real name was Adrienna, by the way, but Vicki has called her Sweetie since she was a few weeks old.) Vicki would pick up the kittens. Her daughter was always asleep by seven, so by the time dinner was over and it was time to drive home, she'd be so dead to the world, she wouldn't notice the box in the backseat. Sweetie wouldn't know about the kittens until she woke up Christmas morning and found them under the tree.

It was a perfect plan, Vicki thought. The ideal surprise. But when she went to pick up the kittens, she couldn't find them. Any of them. Her coworker had left on a vacation the day before, and in the twenty-four hours she'd been gone, the kittens had managed to escape from their box. The woman's sister, who had met Vicki at the house with the key, didn't seem too pleased with this development, but she helped search for them. After half an hour, they'd found all but one. The pure black one, the live wire, was gone. Vicki didn't know what to do, but she knew she needed to make a decision because she was expected at Michael's for dinner. Should she adopt just one kitten? Should she choose another?

Thinking back, she was never sure how or why it happened — she had to use the facilities, I suppose — but she wound up in the bathroom. She turned on the lights, looked into the toilet, and her heart collapsed through the floor. The pure black kitten was lying in the bottom of the bowl.

She reached in and pulled him out. He was no bigger than a tennis ball, and she held him easily in one hand. He lay on her palm, as lifeless and cold as a wet dishrag. There was no pulse or breathing, and his eyelids were peeled back just enough to see that he was gone. He had been such an energetic kitten. Vicki knew he was the one who had led the charge over the edge of the box. He had been jumping and swatting at it the first time she saw him; who else could it have been? He must have been peering over the edge of the toilet rim, or maybe stretching for a drink, when he slipped into the bowl. He was so tiny the water was over his head, and trying to scramble up the slick sides must have worn him down. His adventurous spirit, the fearlessness that had drawn her to him, had cost the kitten his life. On Christmas Eve.

"What are you going to do?"

The question shocked her out of her thoughts. She must have shouted when she saw the dead kitten, Vicki realized, because the sister was standing next to her, staring over her shoulder at the lifeless body.

"We should bury him," Vicki said.

"I can't. I'm late for work."

"Well, we can't leave him," Vicki said. "We can't just leave a dead cat lying . . ."

The kitten coughed. Or more accurately, he sputtered. Looking down, Vicki realized that she had been unconsciously rubbing her thumb back and forth over the kitten's

206

stomach and chest. Had she forced water out of his lungs? Was that sputter a sign of life, or just the last gasp of a body settling into death? He wasn't moving. He looked as cold and lifeless as ever. How could he possibly . . . ?

He sputtered again. Not a cough but a small hack that strangled in his throat the moment it began. But this time, the kitten twitched and spat up water.

"He's alive," Vicki said, stroking her thumb down his body. The kitten sputtered, spat up more water, but otherwise didn't move. His eyes were still slightly open in a death stare, his inner flaps drawn inward. "He's alive," Vicki said when he sputtered a fourth time, wetting her hand.

Her friend's sister wasn't impressed. She looked at her watch with a grimace, a not-so-subtle signal that she didn't have time to deal with the possible resurrection of a recently deceased cat. In her defense, she probably thought the sputtering was death throes. There was no way this bedraggled kitten, submerged in water for who knows how long, could possibly be alive.

Vicki wrapped the kitten in a hand towel, still stroking him firmly enough that he kept coughing up water, and called her longtime friend Sharon, who lived nearby. Vicki and

Sharon had helped each other through challenging jobs, dysfunctional families, difficult marriages, and typical babies. When Vicki told her there was an emergency and that she needed to come to her house, Sharon didn't even ask why.

She left the other kitten, the docile one, and rushed to her friend's house. There was no way, Vicki thought, she could give this sickly kitten to her daughter. He was alive, but he looked horrible. Scary almost. And his chances of long-term survival were slim. When you grow up in a fishing town in Alaska, you learn about hypothermia and water in the lungs, and you know the odds aren't good. But this little kitten was a fighter; in spite of her aversion to cats, there was no way Vicki could leave him behind.

Even if her friend was shocked by the sight of the tiny body. "I found him in the toilet," Vicki told her. "Under the water. But he coughed and spit up water."

"He's cold," the friend said. "He needs warmth."

They wrapped a heating pad around the towel, set it on low, and put the kitten on the kitchen counter. As Sharon gently rubbed the top of the kitten's head for comfort, Vicki carefully dried him with a blow-dryer. Halfway through, the kitten started convulsing. His mouth was hanging open; his eyelids were fluttering; he looked like he was having a seizure. He twitched, then started shivering and retching in violent dry heaves. It looked painful, as if his body was being pulled apart like Alaska's pack ice in a spring thaw, but it was an involuntary reaction. The kitten, apart from his spasms, never stirred. More than an hour after his rescue, he still hadn't opened his eyes.

Already late for dinner, Vicki called Michael. "I'm coming," she said. "Tell my daughter I'm coming. I'm just going to be late. And, um . . . Merry Christmas."

Then she called every veterinarian in the phone book. No one answered. Why would they? It was late in the afternoon, and it was Christmas Eve. She couldn't leave the kitten at Sharon's house because her oldest daughter was allergic to cats. Even if she hadn't been, Vicki knew she couldn't abandon the kitten now. Not after all they'd been through. After an hour, when his convulsing slowed, she put him in a shoe box, still wrapped in the towel and heating pad, and drove to Christmas Eve dinner.

"This is Sharon's cat," she told Sweetie when the little girl came to see what her mother had in the box. "He is really sick. But Sharon had to work, so I told her we would

209

watch him through the night." Sweetie was staring at the little black kitten, at his open mouth and his swollen eyes and his lifeless rag of a body, and Vicki could tell she was going to cry.

"He's probably going to die, Sweetie," she said, reaching out to hug her daughter. "I'm sorry. He is very, very sick, and we didn't want him to be alone."

"Okay," Sweetie said, hugging her mother back.

They put his shoe box in the bathroom next to the heat register and sat down to dinner. It was a somber affair, nothing like a typical Christmas Eve filled to bursting with a young child's noisy anticipation. They ate slowly, and their conversation seemed halfhearted. Every few minutes, Vicki and Sweetie tiptoed to the bathroom to check on the little black kitten. He had stopped convulsing and retching, but his panting was so shallow they could barely tell he was alive. He seemed to be struggling for every breath. And four hours after his rescue, he still hadn't opened his eyes.

They left Michael's house just after nine o'clock. Vicki had finally reached a twenty-four-hour emergency veterinary phone service, and they recommended buying some kind of protein, blending it down to liquid, and seeing if the kitten would eat a few drops. So on the way home, they stopped at a convenience store that was just shutting for Christmas. Sweetie, still wide awake, waited with the kitten in the car. "We can't leave him alone, Mommy," she said.

The store had one jar of meat-based baby food. Vicki bought it, along with an eyedropper. She tried to give the kitten a drop of the brown mush, but he gagged. She diluted the baby food again and again, until it was practically water, and finally, about 11:00 P.M., he kept down two drops. That was his limit: two drops of protein water.

"It's time for bed, Sweetie," Vicki said, once the kitten was tucked into his towel.

"But, Mommy . . ." the little girl started to protest, not wanting to leave the kitten, but she was so tired she couldn't fight any longer. She was asleep by the time she reached the bed.

Vicki kissed her good night — *Merry Christmas,* she thought — and made herself a cup of tea. Every hour on the hour, all through the night, she fed the kitten a few drops of diluted baby food. Each time, when she saw him lying motionless on his side, her heart clenched and she feared he was dead. But as she approached, he started to shift his head. He let her push open his mouth (he still hadn't opened his eyes) and squeeze two drops down his throat. Then she went back to the couch, turned on some Christmas music, and tried to stay awake for another hour.

She must have crashed after the 4:00 A.M. feeding, because the next thing she knew, it was Christmas morning. She leapt off the couch and rushed to the bathroom, where she had left the kitten in his blanket in front of the heat register. As soon as she saw him, she gasped. He was standing on four very shaky legs, trying to tip himself over the edge of the shoe box.

"What's wrong, Mommy?" Her daughter trembled in the doorway.

"Oh, Sweetie, look! He's alive. The kitten is alive."

Vicki put her arm around her daughter, and together they watched as the kitten gathered himself on spindly legs and, with great effort, stepped one shaking paw out of the box. He pulled a second leg over, rested for a moment, looked at them with tired eyes. Then he turned back to his task and, with one final shaking lunge, pulled himself free.

Toys and gifts were forgotten. Russian tea (a combination of powdered tea, orange drink mix, and spices that was Vicki's favorite) and hot chocolate were neglected. For the rest of the day, they watched their Christmas miracle. The kitten spent most of the time on his side, since he was so weak, but whenever Sweetie and Vicki brought the eyedropper over, he pushed himself onto his front knees and stretched out his neck. Vicki had never seen a four-year-old child so gentle and careful, or a kitten more determined to succeed. By the afternoon, Christmas Cat, as they named him (or CC, as they called him), was swallowing three or four drops of brown protein water at a time. They were keeping him alive drop by drop, and every hour he was getting stronger. When Sweetie fell asleep that night, her last question was about CC, the Christmas Cat.

"Is he going to be okay?"

"I hope so, Sweetie. You were wonderful."

The girl smiled. Vicki tucked her in, turned off all the lights except the Christmas tree, turned on the radio, and sat on the sofa, rubbing her thumb along the kitten's skinny side. *He's going to live,* she thought, as music floated around them and the tree sparkled in the purple blackness of an eighteen-hour Alaska winter night. *He's really going to live.* She shook her head in wonder, surprised

213

both by his survival and by how much she cared.

The day after Christmas, a Saturday, she finally reached a veterinarian. The next open appointment was three days away, but the veterinarian assured her she was doing everything right. "Just keep up your regimen," she said. "It's worked so far."

On Monday, Vicki went back to work. She had used up her sick days because of some recent health issues, and as a single mother she couldn't afford to take time off. So every few hours, on her morning break, lunch hour, and afternoon break, she rushed home to feed Christmas Cat a few drops of his watery meal. Her coworkers thought it was hysterical. For weeks, she had been complaining nonstop about adopting the cats. "I don't know why I'm doing this," she'd say, shaking her head. "I hope my daughter appreciates this sacrifice," she'd proclaim, as if she were giving her daughter one of her kidneys or something. Now here she was dashing home every few hours so that she could nurse a nearly dead kitten back to health.

"I thought you didn't like cats," her coworkers said, howling with laughter when they saw her tearing off her scarf and jacket.

"I don't," she said. "I really don't. But what can I do?" She was telling the truth:

She still didn't *like* cats. She just happened to like CC. Why? Because helping him had become her project. Because he had proven himself to her. Because he had personality, toughness, and an incredible will to live. As soon as he could stand, even trembling and weak, he had thrown himself over the edge of his box. He wasn't broken; he wasn't giving up. He wasn't . . . soft. And Vicki Kluever admired that.

By the time she visited the veterinarian's office, it had been four days since the accident. Four times she had tried to give CC a bite of food with a little texture, but each time he had thrown up immediately, so she was still feeding him a few diluted drops of baby food at a time. Four drops of liquid was the most he could handle.

"Something's wrong," the veterinarian said. She pressed the kitten's side and his stomach, which was almost nonexistent. There was no way Christmas Cat weighed more than a pound. "He's never going to gain weight on a liquid diet. He can't get enough nutrients. I'm sorry," she said, shaking her head, "but he's starving to death." She made a note on his chart, then looked at Vicki, who was clearly in shock. "Why don't you leave him here with me?"

"Why? What are you going to do?"

"We'll run some tests," she said. "We'll do what's best for him."

Instantly, Vicki snatched CC off the table and wrapped him in her arms. He was trembling, and Vicki might have been, too. "No," she said, turning her shoulder toward the veterinarian in a protective gesture. "No way. We have come this far, and we are going to see this through." She could feel her anger rising, her indignation. This woman didn't believe. This woman wanted to kill her cat!

"No," she said. "We are not giving up." Then, nearly shaking with fury and unable to think of anything else to say, she whirled around and walked out of the office.

She went to a specialty store and found a protein paste for cats. She compared labels. The paste had all the same nutrients as the baby food she had been using, so she started diluting it with water and feeding it to CC through the eyedropper. Sweetie helped, and she was always gentle and caring and enthusiastic, but mostly it was Vicki who squeezed the protein into CC's waiting mouth. He was only ten weeks old, a tiny bundle of bones and fur, so six or seven times a day, she would cradle him in the palm of one hand and lower the dropper tip into his mouth with the other. As she squeezed a single morsel, he would stare up at her, his eyes still glassy, and then close his mouth over his meal with a delicate sigh. She had felt attached to him before — at the moment he sputtered in her hand, as she watched him haul himself over the edge of the shoe box on bandy legs, in the veterinarian's office — but holding him in her hand day after day bonded them in a way Vicki Kluever never thought possible. She had saved his life. But more than that, CC had saved his own.

After another week, he started reaching with his front paws and guiding Vicki's hand toward his mouth. Vicki could see his throat constricting as he swallowed, and she swore she could feel every ounce of weight he gained. His fur became thicker and glossy black, and every day his eyes seemed brighter. She was so confident in his recovery, in fact, that she finally told Sweetie that CC wasn't her friend Sharon's cat, he was her Christmas present. The joy in the girl's eyes! Soon after, Vicki took him to a new veterinarian for his shots. The vet was amazed when he heard the story. "You did everything right," he said.

So did CC, she thought.

"He still can't eat solid food," she told the doctor. "He can't eat anything with texture."

"He may have been born that way," the

veterinarian said, "or his organs may have been damaged when his body shut down. Either way, he appears to be thriving. Just keep doing what you're doing."

Keep doing what you're doing. That was the life that waited for Vicki Kluever with CC. *Keep pampering a sick cat.* Two months before, the thought would have been her worst nightmare. Now it didn't bother her at all. What kind of a cat hater was she?

By March, CC was back to his old self, the adventurous fiend who had bitten the tails of his brothers and sisters and sat on their heads when they tried to suckle their mother. His coat was a gorgeous blue-black, and he had a mischievous gleam in his eye. He was supposed to be Sweetie's cat, but he and Vicki had bonded over those eyedropper dinners, and poor Sweetie was never on his affection radar. It was Vicki he watched, and Vicki he always listened to. But he wasn't one of those sit-on-your-lap, always-underfoot kittens. He remained fearless and independent, undaunted by death and seemingly convinced more than ever that he could survive anything the world threw at him. In short, he was her ideal cat.

But even six months later, when Vicki received the career opportunity of a lifetime to found a new branch office, CC was still eating nothing but liquids from an eyedropper. He would improve over the years, until he could eat small quantities of protein and water mixed in a blender, but Christmas Cat would never fully recover from nearly drowning in a toilet bowl on Christmas Eve.

When Vicki Kluever wrote me, she mentioned how moved she was by the similarities in our lives. And she promised: It wasn't just that we had the same name spelled the same unusual way. After reading about Christmas Cat, I recognized the kinship between CC and Dewey. Both kittens nearly died at a young age — one in a toilet, one in a freezing library book drop. Both were rescued by single mothers who, unbeknownst to themselves, had a gap in their lives a kitten could fill. We weren't looking for cats, or love, or companionship, but they found us. They dedicated their lives to us, and they never seemed to let the tragic events at the start of their lives define them. They kept their personalities. They took advantage of their opportunities. They found their place. They thrived, in the end, not because of the Vickis (although we helped), but because of their own inner strength.

When I talked with her, I realized Vicki and I shared that same inner strength. We both struggled through bad jobs and worse marriages, but we stuck to our moral and professional values, and we found our life's work: I in the library, Vicki in the mortgage business. We succeeded, both of us, because we refused to settle for the ordinary; instead, we reached for a better way.

Although I have never met her in person, I can picture her in her sophisticated business suit the night she accepted the Affiliate of the Year Award from the Matanuska Valley real estate community. She had won the award, ostensibly, for turning around a struggling mortgage lender in the town of Wasilla, Alaska. The office, on the verge of being closed when she took over, was now one of the most profitable in the state. More important for Vicki, she had transformed the morals and attitudes — the very mission — of the office. In a business plunged into corruption by a housing boom (in 1980s Alaska, not 2005 America, but history repeats itself), she had stood on principle. She refused to make loans if unethical side deals had been struck; she told borrowers when a loan was not in their best interest, even if it killed the deal; she threw real estate brokers out of her office for dishonest practice. She chose the twelve most ethical and trustworthy brokers, the ones who truly cared about their clients, and told them she would always stand by them in exchange for their business because she cared about their clients, too. And from that stand, the business had boomed.

She had arrived in Wasilla with nothing but hard-won experience. She had been distrusted by the local real estate community, simply because she had taken over an office they had grown to despise. Now she was a leader of the Rotary club and prominent in fund-raisers and food drives. She was on the board of the Christmas Friendship Dinner, which served a free feast to the needy for the holidays. During the darkest moment of her life, she had lost faith in God, but through her daughter's example she was once again an active and enthusiastic member of a church. It was nice to have the Affiliate of the Year Award because it honored not only her financial acumen — her ability to turn a profit — but her service to the community. And there are few honors greater than the respect and recognition of your peers.

But Vicki never talked about the award. I had to poke and nudge her before I even learned about it. Instead, she talked about the people she helped: the mortgage brokers who lost their values chasing the dollar and who she was able to turn around; the young men and women she mentored; the clients whose dreams she helped fulfill. She worked with one woman, who didn't speak English, for more than two years to help fix her credit and secure an affordable loan. A year later, that woman's son came to see her.

"Do you remember me?" he asked.

"Of course."

"Well, I've gone to college," he said, "and I want you to know that I'm studying finance because I saw what you did for my mother, and it changed our lives."

That's the recognition Vicki cherished. That's the story that brought a tremble to her voice. That's the mission that got her up in the morning and motivated her to work hard every day.

"I believe a house is a stabilizing factor," she told me. "It helps create a healthy family life. That's what I'm doing when I write a loan. I'm giving a family a better chance to succeed."

I feel similarly about libraries. I think they are a stabilizing factor in communities. I think that, at their best, they bring people together like few public institutions can. That was always my focus: to make the library work for Spencer, by making it work for the individuals who lived there. I didn't want money or fame; what librarian has ever gone into the business for that? But I believed, by working the right way and for the right reasons, that I could change my corner of the world. And so did Vicki Kluever. In the end, we both accomplished our goals.

And yet, for all our similarities, I remained skeptical of our sisterhood. We came from such different parts of the world; how much could we really have in common? Northwest Iowa, where I've lived most of my life, is spectacularly flat. The nearest ocean is more than a thousand miles away. We have frigid winters, like Alaska, but they are followed by ninety-degree summers. And while the vast fields of corn and soybeans are beautiful in their way, you are often hard-pressed to find anything more interesting than a few trees on our endless horizon.

Kodiak Island, Vicki Kluever's home for much of her life, is a rugged wilderness, buffeted by the Pacific Ocean and covered with thick, damp plant life. Its mountains rise straight out of the ocean and often plunge straight back into the water on the other side. The shoreline slashes back and forth, marked with tide pools pounded over the centuries into the island's volcanic rock. The landscape is spectacularly varied, ranging from flat and treeless to mountainous and blanketed by towering spruce trees.

The grassy fields and mountain meadows, buried in snow half the year, turn emerald green at the first opportunity, then explode with wildflowers in the summer and locals picking wild berries in the fall. In Iowa, life is slow, defined by the seasonal accumulation and depletion of the soil; in Kodiak, life is dramatic, shaped by the ocean's ferocious storms. In Iowa, the cycle is defined by planting, harvesting, and the rotation of crops; in Kodiak, the cycle begins with the salmon, who are eaten by the bears, who leave scraps for bald eagles and foxes, who leave scales and bones to enrich the soil. In Iowa, the land is tamed, marked out in perfectly straight mile markers and sold to the highest bidder; in Kodiak, it is wild and unforgiving, possessed by the Sitka deer and the Kodiak bear, the largest land mammal in North America and one of the biggest bears in the world. And, I hear, the whole place smells of fish.

And yet . . . Vicki and I were about the same age. We were raised in a similar blue-collar environment where boys were the future and girls were leaned on for emotional support. We were both good daughters from tight-knit extended families. When farm life overwhelmed or bored me, I found comfort in the back fields of corn, where I knew

224

even Sputnik couldn't find me; Vicki found refuge in the forests and on the beach, away from the arguments and chain-smoking of her parents' home. Kodiak and Spencer, three thousand miles apart, were both classic small towns, with tiny schools and party-line telephones. Everybody at least knew of you, which meant they either gossiped about you or helped you, and often both. In Iowa, we lived off the land. In Kodiak, they farmed the ocean. The coming and going of the fishing boats was their traffic; the supply barge from the mainland, frequently delayed by rough seas and carrying only canned or powdered items, was their grocery store; the tide pools and beaches were their playgrounds. Is that so different than life on the farm, where the rumble of traffic meant tractors, and the best food was taken right out of the field?

We were strong by necessity, Vicki and I, proud of our descent from a long line of independent women. My great-aunt Luna Morgan Still founded and taught at the first school in Clay County, a one-room sod-buster constructed of grass and dirt because, even in homesteading days, there were no trees to build with. My grandmother was the rock of my family, holding it together after her husband's early death, with a toughness and generosity that inspired me. My mother ran her family's restaurant when she should have been in elementary school; she raised six kids on a farm with no air-conditioning or washing machine; she battled cancer for thirty years, suffering pain and indignity without complaint. She leaned on me, her eldest daughter. And by doing that, she made me strong.

Vicki Kluever's ancestral line stretches six generations on Kodiak Island, back to the Alutiiq natives who had survived in that harsh land for ten thousand years. She has fond memories of walks in the Kodiak woods with her dog and of late summer outings with her mother and aunts to pick berries, but it was her grandmother who inspired her. Laura Olsen was Alutiiq-Russian-Norwegian, a product of the great melting pot of Kodiak. At sixty-two, already a widow, she moved from the town of Kodiak back to her ancestral land on tiny Larsen Island. The island was named after her father, Anton Larsen, a Norwegian who had immigrated to Kodiak alone on a steamship when he was twelve years old. For Vicki, traveling to Grandma's house meant a long drive over a mountain pass and down a rough dirt road to Anton Larsen Bay, a twenty-minute skiff ride, and a hike up the beach to a steep embankment. Grandma Laura had no telephone, no electricity, no central heat or running water. She had a large garden and a well, washed her clothes in a hand-cranked ringer washer, chopped her own wood, and kept chickens and a goat. She set her own fishing nets, and she maintained her own fishing gear. The door to her tiny house was always open, her rooms were always neat, and Vicki rarely climbed from the skiff without smelling fresh cookies and bread. Grandma Laura had no use for cigarettes or powdered milk or electric lights, the staples of existence in the Kluever home. She subsisted off the land and the ocean, like the Alutiiq and the early settlers, and she was happier than anyone Vicki had ever known.

Old sod schools. Unheated wood homes. Vicki and I never lived that hard, but that didn't mean our lives were easy. Life in farming and fishing country was marked by tragedy. Early death. Accidents. Foreclosure. Financial crisis. The town of Spencer burned to the ground in the 1930s, an event that still defines both the precariousness of rural life and the hardiness of the community that, on pure willpower and muscle, rebuilt itself better than before.

In Kodiak, the defining events were the 1912 eruption of Mount Novarupta, which blanketed the island in ash, and the earthquake of 1964. The tremors from that quake rocked the island, causing the land to heave six feet. But it was the three massive tidal waves on Good Friday that destroyed the town. Vicki's father, who was at work at the power facility, was trapped up to his neck in water for two days. The day after his escape, Easter Sunday, Vicki's cousin roared up to their house in his truck and told them another wave was coming. That's when Vicki saw fear for the first time. She saw it on her grandmother's face. The whole town spent the day on top of Pillar Mountain, watching the ocean. Finally, around dusk, Vicki's mom said, "I need my cigarettes," and hopped in her nephew's truck. The rest of the town followed until, by nightfall, they had all drifted home. The last tidal wave was a false alarm.

The houses were torn down and rebuilt. The boats were scrapped or salvaged, depending on their anchorage. That's when Vicki's grandmother, whose home was wiped out by the waves, built her primitive residence on Anton Larsen Island and moved away from Kodiak. Vicki, all of seven years old, felt her innocence recede with the tide. She had seen the power of nature and the fragility of life.

At eighteen, Vicki and I both left home.

Life was short; opportunities in our home-towns were limited; we wanted to stretch ourselves and see the world. As Vicki put it, "I needed to bruise my knees, skin my face, make mistakes — and not have mom's family watching. I couldn't do anything in Kodiak that my mom didn't know about before I got home."

I wanted to attend college, but my parents didn't have the money. As class valedictorian, Vicki was awarded a scholarship to the University of Alaska, but she preferred to work and support herself instead of living four more years on her parents' tab and under her parents' rules. We both found entry-level jobs in larger cities — I at a box factory in Mankato, Minnesota, Vicki at a bank in Anchorage — and settled into an independent life. A few years later, in our early twenties, we both got married. Were we in love? That's difficult to say. In our day, small-town girls got married young. What else did we know? It wasn't until we were pregnant that we realized how much, for better or worse, your marriage defines your life. Unfortunately for us, it was for the worse.

Shortly after their wedding, Vicki's husband took a security job on the Alaska pipeline and moved his wife one hundred miles east (three hundred miles by the only road) to Valdez, in a mountainous region known as the Alps of Alaska. Their daughter, Adrienna — known as Sweetie — was born there in a vicious Thanksgiving blizzard that dumped four feet of snow in a single day. Two weeks later, Vicki's husband accepted a position as a police officer at the far end of the Aleutians, the long chain of islands that extend almost a thousand miles off the southwest corner of Alaska. Valdez was remote and snowbound, but Unalaska, where they were moving . . . that was beyond the edge of the earth. That was five hundred miles down a spine of rock into the Bering Sea, one of the blackest, angriest, deadliest bodies of water in the world. The Alaska State Ferry service to the island sailed only three times a year, and the trip took seven days. The only airplane that went there was prohibitively expensive, and it only flew twice a week. Your groceries had to be ordered and delivered by mail.

Vicki dreaded the thought of Unalaska, especially with a young child. But her husband had made up his mind. When he left almost immediately for his new job, leaving Vicki in Valdez to care for Sweetie and pack the house, she realized for the first time how much the marriage had uprooted her sense of self. She had already left behind her career, her friends, her family, her home. Now she was losing her independence and freedom of movement, too.

But like a dutiful wife, she lugged her child on the two-week journey to their new home in the Bering Sea. She found the land more harsh and foreboding than she had imagined: rocky, barren, and crosshatched with old trails. A huge military depot, abandoned after World War II, had left the island littered with battered runways, crumbling docks, and rusted artillery pieces. As she drove into her new life, Vicki saw rows of old concertina wire stretched across the horizon. There was beauty there, it was hard to deny. Standing in the howling wind above crashing waves, it felt like the end of the earth, and how many people ever get a chance to stand there? But if the island offered a beautiful loneliness, it was loneliness nonetheless. And isolation. With that concertina wire, Unalaska felt like a prison in the middle of the sea.

That winter, Vicki suffered a miscarriage. It was a dark time, literally, with only a few hours of sunlight a day. Her marriage had been crumbling for years; in that long twilight, it seemed to break and sheer off like tree limbs under ice. When I was married to an alcoholic, I thought of my house as a coffin. Day after day, I was being buried by my husband's neglect. But at least I had friends and family nearby. I had a place I could go for comfort. Vicki Kluever's whole world was a coffin. She had no place to turn. She asked God for help, for a sign, and when she heard nothing but the howling of the wind, she lost her faith, too. By the time winter finally broke, she had made a difficult decision, one that I and many other women have agonized over: She told her husband she was leaving. When the Alaska Ferry Service arrived a month later, she returned to Anchorage with only her daughter and a handful of possessions.

There is a strength that comes from growing up in a small town. That strength is the realization, at a young age, that nothing is ever a given. More often, it is taken by things beyond your control: a flood, a drought, a storm, a pollution bloom, or an unlucky toss of the nets. You can't worry about the bad things. Yes, they hurt. But you move on. You understand, as a life code, that you have no right to money or happiness or even stability. If you want those things, you have to earn them.

Back in Anchorage, Vicki threw herself into earning her happiness. She took an entry-level position in the mortgage industry, where she had worked before her marriage, and began to forge a career. It was the early 1980s, interest rates were plummeting, and Alaska was gripped by a wave of loan refinancing. She often worked seventy hours a week and took files home. Her boss was prone to outbursts of anger, but she was also one of the most accomplished and knowledgeable women in the field. Vicki overlooked the hostility and focused on learning. She progressed quickly from clerk to loan officer, and within a year was familiar with every wrinkle in the Alaska housing authority program, one of the nation's best. She wasn't just living the dream of being self-sufficient; she was helping other people reach their dreams, too.

But it wasn't easy. Her commissions, especially in the first years, were barely enough for basic necessities. She couldn't afford a reliable car, and she often skipped meals in order to feed her daughter. She gave Sweetie as much time as she could, but more often than she preferred, Vicki saw her daughter only long enough to tuck her into bed, kiss her on the cheek, and tell her, *Mommy loves you, Sweetie. Good night.* She took care of herself. She was physically strong. But she was increasingly prone to mood swings, dark thoughts, and fatigue.

I am a firm believer, from personal experience, that stress is a major factor in poor health, and there is nothing quite like the stress of being a single working mother. I know that from experience, too. But stress doesn't cause poor health; it aggravates underlying problems. Perhaps the last hurdle for our generation of women was convincing doctors — most of whom were men — that our indigestion, bloating, headaches, memory loss, and muscle fatigue weren't all in our heads. *Just calm down,* doctors told us. *Relax. It's only water retention. Take a tranquilizer.*

Vicki knew there was something more fundamentally wrong. So instead of giving in, she spent hours at the library (this was before the Internet) studying her condition. After years of reading, researching, and diligently maintaining a daily journal of food intake and physical symptoms, she discovered a physician in London studying female hormone imbalances. One of her protégés happened to work in Anchorage, so Vicki made an appointment. The woman studied Vicki's journals and performed a series of hormone measurements. The problem, the young woman assured her, wasn't in her head. After her miscarriage, her body had failed to restart sufficient hormone production. The recommendation was an ultrahigh dose of hormones administered by a well-known male physician. The procedure, while used in England, was not yet FDA-approved.

Vicki accepted the recommendation. Even today, she vividly remembers signing the waiver form. She was so happy to have her condition taken seriously, after so many years of suffering, that she would have signed practically anything. Her insurance wouldn't cover the treatments, so she went into debt to pay for them.

Luckily, they worked. For three months. Then Vicki began to feel sharp pains in her abdomen. Soon after, she was diagnosed with uterine tumors. She was too stunned and scared to ask questions or seek second opinions. A few days later, at the age of twenty-seven, she was on the operating table, her abdomen cut open, her uterus torn out.

It was a terrible setback, but it was something else, too: freedom. By the spring, despite her surgery, Vicki Kluever felt stronger and more balanced than she had in years. Her symptoms had eased. But more important, her sense of purpose — her vision of the future — had returned. She had made hard decisions. They had cost her dearly, but she had survived them. She was confident she could succeed in her career; she knew she could succeed as a mother. She was ready for her chance.

There was one more step. She enjoyed mortgage lending, but she didn't want to stay in a toxic work environment. And, she realized, she didn't want to raise her daughter in Anchorage. She wanted Sweetie to experience the life she had grown up with: the tight community, the strong women, the beauty and power of the ocean. When she heard the company was opening a branch office, she applied for the manager position. They offered her Kodiak or Ketchikan.

She knew where she wanted to go: home.

It was just before Vicki's surgery, in the summer of 1986, that she and Sweetie had moved into the apartment in Anchorage, where they were allowed to adopt a cat. They had owned an outdoor cat in Unalaska, mainly for catching rats (which were numerous and huge, having traveled to that barren land in the hulls of ships), and perhaps that's why Sweetie was so insistent. Vicki, never having liked that cat (or the rats), was less enthusiastic. But at that point, she would have done almost anything for her daughter. She was still recovering in November when she chose Christmas Cat. And she was still not quite herself, physically or emotionally, when she rescued him from the toilet bowl on Christmas Eve.

It would be hard, then, not to draw a line between Vicki's personal journey and CC's dramatic rescue. People often say love is a matter of luck and timing. The right person (or cat) comes along at the right time and — bang — your life is changed. Many people believe that about Dewey and me, that our love was based on circumstances. After all, I was new to my position as library director, and I was eager to establish myself. I desperately wanted to make the library a more inviting place, and I had been working on that goal for months.

Then Dewey dropped into my arms and, instantly, I knew that he could transform my world. He was friendly. He was confident and outgoing. He tried to include everyone, even when they were leery of his attention. He was loving. He was perceptive. He was dedicated, body and soul, to the Spencer Pubic Library. He was, you might say, the better part of my soul. He inspired and set an example. And not just for me — for an entire town.

Maybe that's what happened with Vicki Kluever and CC. Maybe she saw herself in that cat: adventurous, independent, determined. And when he suffered tragedy and survived? Maybe she saw herself there, too. After all, it's not easy to have your body rebel against you. It's not easy to lose your way, to forget your goals, to have your greatest assets (trust and a desire to explore) lead to your greatest loss. But Christmas Cat didn't quit. As soon as he gained the strength, CC pushed himself to his feet and toppled back into the world. Maybe it was this attitude, this will to succeed, that Vicki admired. Even more than his outgoing personality, even more than his luscious fur and mischievous gold eyes, Vicki saw a kindred spirit in the little black cat. She told me as much numerous times, although she never used quite those words.

It also helped, I'm sure, that CC fit perfectly into her new life in Kodiak. Subsistence, Vicki tells me, is an important concept in Alaska. It conveys both the simplicity of life in the small towns that dot the coast and the internal fortitude needed to survive there. Subsistence, in its purest form, means living from nature and producing with your own hands. It was the way of life for countless generations of the natives of Kodiak and other rugged Alaskan islands. It was the way of life Vicki's great-grandfather Anton Larsen practiced when he homesteaded the island now named for him, and it was the life his daughter, Vicki's grandmother Laura, returned to after the devastating tidal waves of 1964.

Vicki didn't live like her grandmother, but she certainly embraced a simpler lifestyle when she returned to her old hometown. She rented a small house in the woods. She ran the new mortgage office alone, working hard to create a strong foundation before adding staff. She provided her daughter, with the help of her mother (who, unlike Vicki, owned a television, much to Sweetie's delight), a "skinned-knee" kind of childhood, free from the overprotection and overscheduling so common among modern parents. Instead, Sweetie enjoyed long walks in the woods and scavenger hunts along the rocky Kodiak shore.

Christmas Cat, likewise, loved to explore the vast forest beyond the back fence. He hunted mice and spiders and other things he could nose out of the brush, often bringing them home as presents or playthings to be kicked around for an afternoon. He climbed trees with Sweetie and followed Vicki and Sweetie a few hundred yards on their hikes until they disappeared into the woods. There is an enormity and solitude to Alaska, a state more than double the size of Texas with a population of just under 700,000 (about the same as Louisville, Kentucky, and less than half of Columbus, Ohio.) In Kodiak, Vicki loved the way the mountains towered over the river valleys, and the huge eagles soared in an endless sky. But she also appreciated the way the forest closed around her and the familiarity of the shops in town. When she and Sweetie walked the beach, they were drawn to the power of the ocean. But there were also the snails clinging to the sides of the tide pools, the impressions in the rocks, the way the running tide "set the table" by exposing mussel beds and fishing nets. When the salmon were running, Vicki and Sweetie were gone for days, because although Vicki loved fishing for everything, she loved the salmon best, because a hooked salmon would fight. Most of all, she loved to watch Sweetie's face burst into a smile every time the girl caught a fish.

After a year, when she'd saved a little money, Vicki bought a ramshackle house in town. The roof leaked and the walls were noticeably leaning, but she owned it, and that made her feel grounded and whole. The first winter, a pipe burst and the basement flooded. A few days later, a storm knocked three trees through the roof, and she and Sweetie spent a year arranging pots and pans to catch drips when it rained. When she had money, she fixed the house, piece by piece, but she never felt alarmed. After all, Christmas Cat loved drinking out of those rain pans, at least when he wasn't running up and down the stairs. And as long as Sweetie was comfortable, Vicki could happily subsist, like her grandmother, within the limits of her own capabilities.

New house, new forest, owners gone for a few days: Whatever happened, CC never seemed to mind. He wasn't a needy cat. He had his own life and his own habits, and except for his dietary problem — he still ate nothing but paste and, possibly, insects — he could take care of himself. Half the time, Vicki wasn't sure what he was up to, but she always assumed he was doing it with style, even when he was just rummaging for cave crickets in the crawl space under the house. Often when she returned home from the beach, or on lazy Saturday afternoons, she would see CC sitting in his favorite spot on top of the six-foot fence post at the end of the yard, taunting the neighbors' dogs. They would bark and snap, futilely trying to reach him, while he looked out toward the forest, occasionally glancing down at them with confident disregard. CC knew there was no way they could touch him.

But he was loyal, even in his independence.

Almost as soon as Vicki arrived home from the office, CC would appear on the ledge outside the kitchen window. More often than not, his black fur was matted with tree sap or mud or crawl space dust. Vicki brought a towel to the door to wipe him down, but CC always barreled inside, leaving filthy footprints all over the house.

And yet he wouldn't rub against her. Vicki was very conscious of her professional image, and she splurged on her clothes. CC knew she wouldn't tolerate cat hair on her business suits, much less muddy paw prints. So he waited until she changed into her sweater and jeans, then stood on his hind legs, with his front paws on her upper leg, waiting for her to pick him up. When she did, he put a paw lightly on each of her cheeks, as if to hold her steady, and looked into her eyes.

"Hi, CC," she whispered. "How are you?"

He put his cheek against her chin, then bent forward and nuzzled her neck. She pushed him to her shoulder, where he lay against her neck and purred, and that is how they spent the first five minutes of every evening. He wasn't a lap cat by nature, but if Vicki wanted company, she simply sat in her bentwood rocker, purchased when she learned she was pregnant with Sweetie, and

CC came running to curl up on her lap. They spent many a long winter night in that chair by the woodstove, Vicki reading a book and CC purring lightly in his sleep after Sweetie had gone off to bed.

"It was his unconditional love," Vicki said, when asked what made the relationship special. "He was always there. But he let me be the boss."

Eventually, she started dating a man named Ted (not his real name). He was charming and attractive and, to be honest, she enjoyed his attention. It made her feel wanted, I suppose, in a way other things never had. Her friends weren't sure about Ted, and his relationship with Sweetie was rocky at times, but Vicki didn't worry. Even Christmas Cat's obvious dislike of him didn't deter her. Later, she learned to trust the cat's instincts. If her cat didn't like a man, or vice versa, that man was out the door. But at the time, still relatively new to this whole cat thing, she considered CC's attitude nothing more than jealousy. For three years, he had been the man in her life. He had been the one to make her feel wanted. Now he had to share.

A few months later, when Ted started opening her mail and reading her appointment calendar, Vicki made excuses. When he started showing up at restaurants where she was having business meetings, she dumped him. Twice. But each time he begged for forgiveness, saying he just worried about her safety because he loved her so much, that he had learned his lesson, that he wouldn't do it again. She didn't realize she was losing control until he started verbally abusing her. But by then it was too late.

"A bad relationship is like a funnel," Vicki says. "It's easy to slide into, but very hard to climb out of. And it's always pulling you down. The more I struggled for independence, the more he tried to control me."

To the outside world, Vicki was thriving. Her mortgage office was booming, adding staff and quietly becoming one of the best producers in the state. She had harbored some fears about returning to her family, where bad memories crowded the good, but Sweetie grew so close to her grandmother that they spent all their afternoons together, freeing Vicki from worry about her long work hours and giving her daughter a link to her past. She bowled on Wednesdays; she joined a softball team. After two years of work, even her ramshackle residence, once a tilting, leaking mess, was on the verge of becoming the house of her dreams. But her love life was shaking those solid foundations.

"I can run a million-dollar business," she often muttered to Christmas Cat when he jumped on the edge of the bathtub where she soaked away the day's fatigue, "but I can't figure out my love life. What's wrong with me?"

Christmas Cat always leaned over to sniff her, and more often than not, Vicki could see the crawl space dust still powdered in his jet-black fur.

"Do you want to come in?"

He just stared at her. He wasn't coming in, but he also didn't appear to be afraid of the water.

"Suit yourself." She laughed, closing her eyes so that she didn't have to look at the bruises on her arms and feeling her worries about Ted float away on a kitten's soft purr.

Then, in April, her brother committed suicide. I know that pain, because my brother committed suicide, too. There is the horror of suddenly losing someone you love. There is the terror of the details; the memory, in my case, of driving to his apartment and seeing the blood. And there is the nagging belief that you could have done something more, that you had the power to prevent it. I remember the day, ten years before his death, when my brother walked four miles in the cold, in the dead of night, without a jacket in subfreezing temperature, to knock on my door and tell me, "There's something wrong with me, Vicki. Don't tell Mom and Dad." I was only nineteen. I didn't say a word. I wish I had.

For Vicki Kluever, the months after Johnny's suicide were a fog. She has almost no memory of that summer, no recall of anything but a terrible darkness, despite twenty hours of daily sunshine. She had been in Hawaii with Sweetie, the first real vacation of their lives, when her brother died. He had called to say he loved her, to take care of herself. She had felt a terrible premonition, but what could she do? She was a thousand miles away. A few hours later, he was dead by his own hand.

The weight was crushing. She was drowning in grief. And she had no way to comfort her daughter or mother. Sweetie had loved her uncle Johnny. He rode a motorcycle; he wore a leather jacket; he was cool. She couldn't fathom his death. Her mother couldn't handle the loss of her child. She leaned on Vicki for support, as she always had. I remember that as well, the obligation of the good daughter, the need to be strong. When I arrived after my brother's suicide, the first words my mother said to me were,

"You can't cry. Because if you start crying, then I'll start crying, and I don't know if I will ever stop."

So Vicki Kluever held it together, as she always did. Through a terrible summer, as four more suicides rocked the small Kodiak community, she held it together for her daughter and mother. She leaned on whatever she could: work, friends, even Ted. But especially her cat.

And then, in August, Christmas Cat disappeared. He was gone three days before Vicki found his body, battered and lying in the thick undergrowth ten feet beyond her fence. She knew immediately what had happened: CC was sitting on his favorite fence post, taunting the neighbors' dogs, when an eagle struck. The bald eagles of Kodiak had wingspans of eight feet or more; it was nothing for such a bird to pluck a twelve-pound fish from the ocean . . . or a nine-pound cat from a fence. She looked at the sky, so limitless and empty, but didn't know what she was looking for. She remembered the sight of CC on Christmas Eve so long ago, his sputtering cough, his brave attempt to throw himself over the edge of the box. She was Vicki Kluever, strong and independent businesswoman. *She* didn't cry. She definitely didn't cry over cats. But she was crying now. She was crying so hard, and from so deep within, that she would physically ache the next day. Perhaps that seems too much, to cry so hard over a cat, but if you've ever belonged to an animal, you understand the grief. She had lost another family member. She had lost the friend that comforted her. What was she supposed to do now?

Noticing her despair, Ted brought her a new cat. Vicki, perhaps justifying, says he found Shadow outside his office; Sweetie, who, like CC, never cared for Ted, claims he found her outside a bar. Either way, the truth was that, only a month after CC's death, Vicki was in no mood to adopt another cat. Not any cat. Not from anywhere. Believe it or not, there was still a part of her that didn't like the idea of cats, and she certainly didn't think she could just replace CC. But she accepted the tainted gift, the wedge Ted was using to push back into her life. She was too worn out and lonely to refuse.

So she was surprised to realize, when she started to come out of her fog a few months later, that she had grown quite fond of the little girl. Shadow was enough like CC, especially in her love of adventure and her mischievous eyes, to remind Vicki of what she had loved about him. But she was also very much her own cat. Unlike CC, Shadow didn't have much interest in the outdoors. She didn't have his cool dignity. She didn't, if truth be told, let Vicki be the boss. And Vicki loved to be the boss. Instead, Shadow had a racing, jumping, wall-banging energy that completely disrupted, in the best possible way, Vicki's life. She was always around, in other words, but never underfoot. Her favorite game wasn't lap sitting; it was tag. If Vicki was in her casual clothes — there was still a prohibition against fur on the business suits — Shadow would sneak up and touch her on the heel. Then she'd take off running. Usually, Vicki tracked her down and tweaked her tail or tickled her belly, then ran away as Shadow chased after her. Sometimes, though, Shadow sprinted up the stairs. She had numerous places to hide up there, and Vicki could never find her. Shadow had no problem waiting for an hour. Then she'd come prancing out for a congratulatory hug. It was just a silly game, but Vicki liked it. It made her laugh. First Christmas Cat had touched her . . . now Shadow, too? *Maybe,* Vicki thought, *I'm a crazy cat lady after all.*

The next part, in hindsight, was inevitable. Ted slowly became more controlling and abusive, and Vicki, finally, summoned the courage to break it off with him completely. He took it well at first, but then started drinking heavily. He began showing up at her office around closing time. When she went for business lunches, she often noticed him watching her. He always happened to be at the softball field or in the alley at the end of her weekly bowling league. When she refused to come back, his harassment turned to threats. She applied for a restraining order. Her application was refused until he pulled her from the table where she was eating dinner with friends and dragged her across the restaurant in front of a dozen witnesses. The restraining order was approved the next day.

For a while, he stopped coming around. The mortgage business boomed; the boats chugged; the mountains iced over and the bears took to their dens. On the coast, the ocean pounded the tide pools of Kodiak. Vicki settled in with Sweetie and Shadow, relieved by the prospect of long, slow, peaceful winter nights. Then she came home after work to find her front door open. She searched the house. A jacket Ted had given her was missing from her closet. She changed the locks, but things he had given her kept going missing, one at a time.

Just before Christmas, she and Sweetie made the journey by car, skiff, and foot to Grandma Laura's cabin on Larsen Island.

Grandma Laura had been diagnosed with cancer, but whatever was destroying her was hidden deep inside. That day, she was as strong as she had always been. She baked bread; she poured drinks; she fed logs to the fire like she had every winter for almost thirty years. Her only wish, she told her family, was to die as she had lived, on Larsen Island. When Vicki mentioned her problems with Ted, her grandmother shook her head and said, "Love isn't blind, but it sure is cockeyed."

Then she turned to Vicki's cousin, who was also having relationship difficulties, and told them both, "You don't need a man. You may want a man, but you don't need a man. Remember that."

The party lasted two days, and by the time Vicki arrived home late on Christmas Eve, she felt energized by her grandmother's wisdom and energy. In a happy fog, she tucked her nine-year-old daughter, already fast asleep, into bed. She smiled as she turned off the lights, remembering how, exactly six years before, Sweetie had stayed up late for Christmas Cat. *We can't leave him alone, Mommy,* she had said, *even if he's going to die.* When she came down the stairs, still warm from the memories, Ted was standing in her living room.

"You've ruined my life," he said. "Now I'm going to ruin yours. I'm going to burn this house to the ground, and I hope you die in it."

She called the police. The state trooper who had helped her get a restraining order answered. By the time he arrived, Ted had disappeared.

"I know his type," the trooper said. "I know his history. I'm sorry, but this is not going to get better."

For two months, the trooper checked Vicki's house twice a day, varying his routine and time of arrival. Around April, when the ice was just starting to split in the streams, he sat down with her. Ted had been visiting her neighborhood, he told her, almost every day.

"This guy knows how to pick locks," he said. "You could change the locks every hour, and he could still get in. A restraining order is only good if someone is standing here waiting for him." The trooper stopped. Then he said something Vicki never forgot.

"Do you have a gun?"

"Yes."

"Do you know how to use it?"

"Yes."

"Can you shoot to kill?"

Vicki stared at him. She could feel her

heart pounding. "What are you saying?"

"He is dangerous."

"You are asking me to shoot and kill the man I spent two years of my life with?"

"I'm saying that if he's in the house, and you have a gun in your hand, you better shoot to kill."

That night, Vicki slept with her pistol under her pillow. Shadow slept beside her, Sweetie down the hall. The next night, she stopped fooling herself. She couldn't do it. She couldn't shoot to kill.

She called her boss in Anchorage. "I hate to do this," she said, "but I have to leave." She told him the reason. They discussed options and, a few weeks later, he arranged for her to transfer to Wasilla, which, contrary to popular perception, is not a small, off-the-beaten track town like Kodiak but a bedroom community of Anchorage. The company had been planning to close the Wasilla office, which was losing money. Vicki, as the new manager, would have one year to turn it around.

She rented an apartment in Wasilla and started packing. She wanted to leave quickly, but she had to talk to her clients, finish her remaining work, sell her house, say good-bye to her family and friends, and make arrangements for her daughter. Five days before they were scheduled to leave, Sweetie woke up screaming in the middle of the night.

"There's something wrong with Shadow," she said when Vicki came running into her room.

The kitten was lying on her side on Sweetie's pillow, panting heavily. Blood was smeared on her fur and the pillow case. For some reason, when Ted gave her the kitten, Vicki assumed she was fixed. By the time she took Shadow to the vet, it was too late, and in the last few frantic, terrifying months that fact had slipped her mind. Now her cat was giving birth on her daughter's pillow.

"It's fine," Vicki said. "It's just the babies, Sweetie. Shadow's having babies."

She got a packing box. Carefully, she placed Shadow on a blanket in the box and carried her to the empty walk-in closet. Vicki and Sweetie grabbed pillows and lay quietly on the floor beside her. They assisted Shadow with the breaking of the sac on one of the kittens and, despite the chaos of their lives, felt renewed by the five new lives that wiggled on the floor beside them when morning finally came.

A few days later, when Vicki flew to Anchorage, she left Sweetie in Kodiak with her mother but took Shadow and her kittens with her. She had rented her new apartment sight unseen. She had no furniture. She had no child care lined up. She didn't know if she even wanted to live in Wasilla. She knew, at least for the moment, Sweetie would be better off in Kodiak. But Shadow? She didn't trust anyone else to care for her kittens.

The apartment was awful. It had ratty carpet, unscreened windows, a broken stove, and holes in the walls. She had packed only one suitcase, so there were no plates to eat from or cups for water. The ferry from Kodiak was grounded for repairs, so she had flown with Shadow and her kittens tucked in a carrier under her seat. Now, without her car, she had no good way to get around Wasilla. (The six of them would fly back and forth to Kodiak four times to visit Sweetie and complete the move; Vicki always joked that it would have been a lot easier if the cats had qualified for frequent flyer miles.) She went to her new office and realized the only hope was to lay off half the staff and hope the rest could turn the branch around. That afternoon, a severe Alaska summer storm blew in and plunged the world into twilight. She sat in her empty apartment, without dinner, and listened to the rain. She missed the old house in Kodiak. The one she had bought and remodeled and cared for on her own. She missed her old job and her comfortable community. Most of all, she missed her daughter.

Thunder ripped and rain, mixed with summer hail, pounded the window. The suitcase lay in the corner, her two business suits hidden from cat hair in the closet. She reached out and stroked Shadow, who was lying nearby. Her kittens were tottering around her on the dirty carpet, knocking each other over and nuzzling for milk. The runt was black and orange, but the others were jet black like Shadow and Christmas Cat. She stuck her finger near one of them; he rolled over and sniffed it. His paws were like tissue paper, delicate and almost soft. She started to cry. She hadn't known she was going to until the tears were on her cheeks.

How could she have made the same mistake twice? How could she have allowed another man control over her? She had been raised by a difficult father, and she had fallen into the same pattern again and again. Her husband. Ted. She was strong, independent, smart, hardworking, successful, and yet bad relationships had left her sitting on the floor in a dingy apartment, without a stick of furniture, in a town she didn't know. How could she have been so stupid? How could she have been so . . . weak? The rain beat against the window. She sniffled, then wiped the tears from her face. The kittens wrestled on the floor, content and playful, completely oblivious to the situation around them. Shadow looked at her, her eyes half open in a sleepy expression, then turned back to her babies.

And for some reason, that made Vicki smile. And then, because she was smiling, she started to laugh. Here she was, an avowed cat hater — or at least cat ignorer — for most of her life, and she had chosen to bring her kittens instead of her daughter on a life-changing five-hundred-mile trip. Instead of Sweetie, she was sitting on the floor of an empty apartment with a cat and her kittens for company. And not just any cat — the cat her stalker had used to win her back. A cat that, in a way, represented the worst betrayal of her life. But a cat she loved just the same.

Some people say loving a cat is about circumstance. The right cat, the right time, the right story. It's about projecting our desires; it's about having a crisis big enough to create a need. But that's not true. That's not true of Christmas Cat, the first cat Vicki loved. That's not true of Dewey, who won me over not by launching my career but with a playfully obstinate disposition and a sweet and abiding love. That's certainly not true of

Shadow, who had appeared in Vicki's life at the wrong time and, more important, for the wrong reason.

We don't love cats out of need. We don't love them as symbols or projections. We love them individually, in the complex manner of all human love, because cats are living creatures. They have personalities and quirks, good traits and flaws. Sometimes they fit us, and they make us laugh in our darkest moments. And then we love them. It's really as simple as that.

All her adult life, Vicki hadn't wanted to own a cat. She was divorced; she was a single mother; she didn't want to be *that* lady. But leaving her daughter behind to make room for her cats . . . sitting in an empty apartment and laughing at their antics . . . she was clearly *that cat lady* now.

And it was okay. She wasn't beaten. Sitting in that dark apartment, with the rain slamming the window, and the kittens mewling on the floor, she knew she was going to make it. As she wiped the tears from her cheeks, there was no doubt in her mind. She would move out of the dumpy apartment. She would go to the office and fire the smallest number of people possible and then sit down with the others and lead them to success. At the end of the summer, when everything was in order, she would bring Sweetie to Wasilla and raise her as a proud single mother. Nothing is ever a given; Vicki Kluever had always known that. She had learned, more than once, that things could be taken away. But things don't matter. The importance stuff — your faith, your dignity, your will to succeed, your ability to love — those are yours until you choose to let them go.

The next day, she found a better apartment. She fired two employees but managed to keep four. Within five months, the Wasilla office was turning a profit. Eighteen months later, she was standing in front of an audience of her peers, accepting her award for affiliate of the year. And even now, eighteen years later and two thousand miles away, I am proud of her, because I know how hard she worked for that honor and how far she had come.

The next three years, from a professional standpoint, were the best of Vicki's life. Sweetie, at first reluctant to move, soon met two lifelong friends and learned to love Wasilla. Ted called a few times, but Vicki ignored him. He couldn't get to her now, not even emotionally, and eventually he stopped trying. She kept two of the kittens from Shadow's litter, the black and orange runt and a jet-black kitten who looked just like his mother, and when Shadow died of cancer at the age of nine, Rosco and Abbey kept Vicki company. She had owned several cats by then, most of them pure black, and although none moved her like CC the Christmas Cat, she loved every one. Ten years after leaving Kodiak, she broke the pattern and married the right man: one her cats and Sweetie loved, and who loved them all in return.

"Please don't see nor portray me as a victim or some poverty-stricken person," she begged me after our initial conversation. "Yes, there were lots of tough times, but doesn't everyone have tough times? Based on some of the people I worked with during my career, I see my life as a cakewalk!"

A cakewalk? Not really. A successful life well lived? Absolutely. By 2005, when she retired because she no longer believed in the practices of the mortgage industry she had spent twenty-two years championing, Vicki Kluever was one of the most accomplished Alaskan women in her field. She had coauthored and implemented a statewide program to help disabled adults secure discounted financing; she had managed several offices to unprecedented success; she had mentored a generation of female mortgage officers; she had spent her career, she felt, helping thousands of families make their dreams come true.

She lives with her husband now in Palmer, Alaska, another bedroom community of Anchorage. She is happy. She has the marriage she always wanted: the kind that strengthens instead of maims. She has the freedom to spend as much time as she needs in Kodiak, where the salt air, the heartbeat of life in a fishing town, and the sight of boats in the morning sailing off to the deep waters continue to energize and inspire her. Her daughter Adrienna lives two thousand miles away, in Minnesota, but mother and daughter talk all the time. After some rough years when she was a teenager, they are now the best of friends.

And through it all, there have been the animals: eleven cats for this former cat hater, and even a couple of dogs. They were always there whenever Vicki needed them, just as Christmas Cat had always been. Until 2006, that is, when Shadow's kittens Rosco and Abbey both passed away within months of each other at the age of sixteen. Nine months later, Choco, a dog Vicki had nursed through severe injuries after he was hit by a car and who had remained devoted to her for the rest of his life, died at the age of twelve. For the first time since she pulled CC from the water almost twenty-five years before, Vicki had no critters around her. It was an empty feeling, especially with her daughter in Minnesota and her husband often away on long business trips, but one she felt ready to endure. Perhaps even enjoy. Then, on a trip to Kodiak to care for her aging mother, a friend introduced her to an elderly dog whose owners had recently died. Bandit, a loving and energetic Border collie mix, now sleeps in her bed every night. In her heart, she knows, she couldn't possibly love a dog more.

And yet, on those dark Alaska nights, when Vicki Kluever sits in her bentwood rocking chair with the woodstove lit against the long cold hours, a cup of Russian tea in her hand, her husband reading a book on the couch with Bandit at his side, it is the memory of CC the Christmas Cat to which she returns. His lush black fur. His mischievous eyes. The way he would disappear into the forest behind the back fence. The way he would run to her and hold her cheeks and nuzzle his head against her chin. You never forget your first love, I suppose. Especially when his personality embodied everything you believe in. Especially when he taught you to love, when so much of your previous love, outside of family, had been misplaced and flawed. Especially when you saved his life on a quiet Christmas Eve.

SIX
COOKIE

"I have never been loved by anyone, not even my daughter or my parents, the way I have been loved by my Cookie."

This is a New York City story, which may make you think it's as far from Spencer, Iowa, as you can possibly get. But it's not. In a way, it's right next door. Because this is not the kind of New York City story you're used to hearing. It's not the kind with famous people, crazy prices, arrogant financial tycoons, or glitzy signs for Broadway shows. I admit, there's nothing quite like standing in Times Square, looking at those glitzy signs. And there's nothing like walking into Grand Central Station, standing on the upper deck, and seeing the night-sky constellations painted on the ceiling. I was standing near the MetLife Building, just outside Grand Central, when my friend turned to me and said, "You know, before this, I'd never seen a building more than twelve stories tall." I looked up and the building, which seemed to be tipping over on us, was bigger than the sky. There's nothing like New York City to make you feel small — or a part of something enormous and splendid, whichever you prefer.

But that's not New York City. That's Manhattan. New York City has about eight million people, and apparently only about 20 percent of them live in Manhattan. That's what this story is about: the other New York. The city over the bridges and past the waterfronts of Brooklyn and Queens, past LaGuardia Airport and the baseball stadium and the site of the 1964 World's Fair, past even the last stop on the subway lines. This story is about Bayside, a middle-class community near the Long Island Sound, where the traffic is relentless and the houses are crowded thirty to a block, though they still have porches and little front yards. It's the kind of place a librarian might live in a room of her own, with her cat curled up in a window and sunlight falling on the floor. Which makes Bayside the perfect place for this New York story.

Or at least the perfect place to start, because Bayside is where Lynda Caira's grandparents settled when they emigrated from Italy to the United States in the first decades of the twentieth century. In 1927, they bought a piece of land in what was essentially farm country and built a house. There weren't many people in Bayside, Queens, then, but anyone who came by was welcome at the Caira table. When the WPA built the Long Island Expressway on the edge of their land, Lynda's grandmother gave the men free coffee every morning — then paid off the cost of the land and house through the tips she made on her free hot breakfasts. When the expressway was complete, she cooked breakfast for the truckers who stopped by when they saw her light on at 4:00 A.M. Even in the 1950s, when Lynda was born, the house was often full of bags of corn and onions the truckers gave her in exchange for a meal. Often, when Lynda came down for breakfast, she would find a stranger or two at the table. It just wasn't in her grandmother's heart to turn anyone away.

When the city divided Bayside into urban lots, her grandmother (who ran the house after her husband's early death) kept four plots just off a highway exit in the heart of the community. Lynda called it the Farm, because there were a hundred tomato plants, a vegetable garden, a grape arbor, and a small grove of peach, apple, and fig trees. Lynda's family lived on the ground floor with her grandmother, who made wine and tomato sauce and still got up every morning at 4:00 A.M. to cook. Lynda's aunt and uncle lived upstairs. Other relatives were constantly around for a visit. In the case of some relatives from Italy, the visit lasted five years, but her grandmother never considered doing anything other than rising early to cook for them all. Lynda's father's parents, also Italian immigrants, lived a short walk away. Other relatives were scattered on neighboring blocks. Bayside was filling up with houses, most bought by young families, so the backyard barbeques were always smoking and the streets were full of kids. The neighbors watched out for one another; the shopkeepers greeted the children by name. But the defining characteristics of Bayside, at least for Lynda Caira, were her family events: the large Italian meals, the communion dresses, and the week set aside every August for canning tomatoes.

At fourteen, Lynda went to work down the road at Gertz department store. After high school, she trained to become a medical technician. She got married, moved to a tiny four-room town house in the Bell Boulevard section of Bayside, about a mile from her grandmother's house, and worked for a local pediatrician. Two years into the marriage, she gave birth to a daughter and gave her the most popular American name of the 1970s: Jennifer.

After seven years of marriage, Lynda Caira got divorced. The divorce was the right thing to do, and she never questioned her decision. Her parents took the news hard at first, but her grandmother, then in her eighties, told her simply, "If this is what you need, then I support you." With her grandmother's blessing, Lynda's "sin" was absolved and, in time, her parents came around. She even kept two of her best friends: her former mother-in-law and sister-in-law, who sided with her in the divorce.

But that didn't mean the divorce was easy

for Lynda's five-year-old daughter, who was old enough to know her life was changing but too young to understand why. Lynda's neighbor suggested she adopt a cat to help Jennifer with the transition. The neighbor worked in a bakery, and the bakery cat — despite the health code, cats live in many of the small neighborhood bakeries in New York City to keep the mice away — had just given birth to kittens. There was a runt in the litter, and the mother cat refused to take care of her. If she didn't find a home, the kitten was going to die.

"Sure," Lynda told the neighbor. "Bring her home for me."

The next day, the neighbor arrived with a tiny gray dust ball of a kitten. She was tennis ball–size and fuzzy, with little ears and big green eyes. She even trembled a bit as she stared around the unfamiliar room, her eyes wide with fear. How could anyone push this baby away? Lynda wondered. How could her own mother leave her to die?

They took the kitten. Jennifer, who was over the moon, named her Snuggles. The kitten was too young to be weaned, so Lynda and Jennifer fed her formula from a bottle several times a day. When she got a little older, they spoon-fed her liquids and soft food. Jennifer gave her constant attention. Perhaps a little too much attention, and certainly too much grabbing — she was only five — but Snuggles was nurtured with care and love from the moment she entered Lynda and Jennifer's home.

She didn't return the affection. She wasn't a bad cat; she just wasn't much of a . . . Snuggles. Some people have preconceived notions about cats: They are aloof and arrogant; they are self-centered; they are loners. Unfortunately, Snuggles fit the stereotype. It wasn't that she was mean. She never scratched or hissed. She just wasn't a social animal. She didn't want to play; she didn't want to be touched; she wasn't emotionally invested in Lynda and Jennifer and, quite frankly, didn't care whether they were home or away. Snuggles preferred her own space.

Jennifer was disappointed. Adults may appreciate the refined dignity (and quiet!) of a cat staring motionless out a sunny window, completely ignoring the world around them, but what kind of child wants a cat like that?

"I want to go to the baby orphanage!" she told her mother.

"We can go," Lynda told her, "but you can't bring anything home. We are already blessed with Snuggles."

Tight-lipped consideration — is it worth protesting? — and then, "Okay, okay, okay,

Mommy. We won't bring anything home."

The baby orphanage was the North Shore Animal League, the nation's largest no-kill animal shelter. Located in Port Washington, New York, in the western section of Long Island, the sanctuary was only six miles from the Caira home in Bayside. Three or four times a year, Lynda and Jennifer would drive out to the sanctuary to ooh and aah over the baby kittens. They were cute, so playful and full of energy, but Lynda always managed to usher Jennifer from the building after an hour without adoption papers in her hand or a kitten in tow.

Until August 31, 1990. Just another summer day in outer Queens. Just another mother-daughter visit to the "baby orphanage" they so enjoyed. Jennifer was twelve that summer, so the two of them had visited the North Shore Animal League for seven years without giving in to the staring eyes, pink noses, and batting paws of the needy animals. But this time . . . a kitten meowed.

Immediately. As soon as they walked in the door. And she wasn't just meowing. This kitten was stretching her front leg through the bars and screaming for attention. She was gray and black tiger-striped, with a white chest, a mostly white face, and huge bat ears that made her head seem tiny underneath them. She was undeniably cute, so cute, in fact, that Lynda made an effort to ignore her. But Jennifer was captivated.

"Oh, Mommy, look at this one," she said.

Lynda kept walking, putting her finger into a few cages to play with the kittens.

"Oh, please come back and look at this baby," Jennifer pleaded. "Please, Mommy. Look how she's screaming. She really wants me to hold her."

Lynda turned back and stared at the thin little kitten trying desperately to escape her big cage. A card on the front said: COOKIE. FEMALE. DOMESTIC SHORTHAIR.

"Okay," Lynda said to the volunteer. "Take her out. Jennifer, you can hold her. For a minute. Then back she goes."

Cookie had something else in mind. As soon as she was out of the cage, she leapt from Jennifer's hands to Lynda's shirt and, after a desperate scramble, wrapped her arms tightly around Lynda's neck. Then she leaned back, peered up with her big green eyes, and howled into Lynda's face. A volunteer came over to help, but the kitten clasped its paws together and wouldn't let go. She was begging and pleading — for attention? For love? For a home? Whatever it was, the kitten was adamant. She knew what she wanted, and she wanted Lynda. It took two volunteers to pry the two-pound cat off her chest.

"Oh, Mommy," Jennifer pleaded. "We have to take her home. We have to."

"No, Jennifer," Lynda said. "We are not taking her home. We have Snuggles. We cannot have another cat." She wasn't really worried about Snuggles. Snuggles didn't care about anything, so why would she care about another kitten in the house? But their town house was small. It just didn't seem big enough for another pet.

She was turning to tell the volunteers to put the kitten back in its cage when she noticed that it had on several colorful collars, each with a few tags.

"Why is she wearing all those?" Lynda asked.

"Those are for her medications," the volunteer said. And then he told her the story of Cookie.

When she was five weeks old, Cookie was hit by a car. She was found bleeding in the road and brought in terrible pain to the animal league, which performed two surgeries on her broken shoulder. One set of medicine was for the pain in her shoulder, which hadn't yet healed. Beneath the injuries were the affects of a hard life on the street with no mother to teach or protect her: malnutrition and bleeding gums, worms in both ears, parasites in her digestive tract, a left eye (now mostly healed) so swollen from conjunctivitis she could barely open it. They all needed treating. Then there was the gash in her hip. She had been sliced open when the car hit her, and the damage was so severe the veterinarian wasn't able to fully close the wound. She had to be cleaned and bandaged several times a day, and much of her medication was to prevent infection. It had taken several weeks of intensive care, in fact, just to get her well enough for the adoption area, and even now she was relegated to the "solitary confinement" of her private, well-scrubbed cage. The poor cat was lonely, traumatized, and wounded. And she was only nine weeks old.

Lynda looked at Cookie again. This time, she noticed the encrusted eye and the awkward hunch of her shoulder. Her hip wasn't bandaged, but she could see the matting of salve in her fur. She glanced at her infected ears, her poor backside. But what Lynda really saw was the hunger in her eyes. Cookie wasn't Snuggles. In fact, she was the exact opposite of Snuggles. This cat wanted someone to care about her. She was desperate for it. When she reached a paw through the bars this time, Lynda was sure that Cookie had chosen her. *Love me,* she was saying, *and I will love you in return.*

The volunteer placed a hand gently on Lynda's shoulder and said, "She's never acted like that with anyone else."

Lynda believes that to this day. *Cookie chose her.* But I admit I'm skeptical. After all, Cookie was probably reaching for everyone who passed her cage. I tend to think Lynda was the one who acted differently that day, the one who opened her heart to a wounded animal. It was Lynda who thought, *I have to help her. I don't know if she'll live. But she's coming home with me.*

It really was a commitment, too, because Cookie really was sick. Her adoption papers came with a carload of medicine and a box of bandages bigger than she was. The animal league even told Lynda that if she couldn't heal the gash in Cookie's hip, or any of her other major ailments, they would take her back and let her live out her (probably short) life at the shelter. But Lynda wasn't deterred. In fact, she was energized. Every day, she forced five or six pills down Cookie's throat. Twice a day, she applied a salve to Cookie's wound. Then she put a bandage over it and wrapped another bigger bandage around the kitten's furry little bottom to hold everything in place. Then she gave her a hug, and a pet, and told her that she was loved. After a few months, Cookie healed. No more conjunctivitis, no more worms in her intestines, no more ear infections, and no more wound. When you looked at her, it was as if the car accident and illnesses had never happened; she was simply a beautiful cat.

Jennifer really, really, really wanted Cookie to be her cat. Snuggles was supposed to be her cat, but Snuggles wasn't anyone's cat. Cookie was her second chance. Every night, Jennifer took Cookie into her bed to sleep with her. She even closed her door so Cookie couldn't get away. But on the fourth night, when Jennifer forgot to close her door, Cookie scampered out of the room, climbed onto Lynda's bed, and lay down on one of Lynda's pillows. Jennifer couldn't keep Cookie a prisoner every night, and when she left her door open again, the cat ran to Mommy's bed. I've said it before, and I'll say it again: When you give your heart to an injured animal, they never forget it. So when Lynda finally offered her the spare pillow, Cookie climbed onto that pillow and slept in Lynda's bed every night for the rest of her life. She wasn't Jennifer's cat; she was Mommy's cat. The poor little girl had been thwarted again.

Not that it wasn't partially Jennifer's fault.

After all, she did dress Cookie up from time to time in doll dresses. Cabbage Patch Kid dresses, to be exact, since those fit best. And had the nicest accessories. The sole remaining picture of those humiliations shows Cookie on the sofa in a light blue shirt with white fringe and a comically small cowboy hat. Cookie's facial expression can't be mistaken: *I am mortified.*

Don't blame Jennifer, though. She was only twelve. And Cookie may have been humiliated, but she was never harmed. She never protested. She never fought back. She wore the dresses; she played tea party; she was a good friend. She loved Jennifer despite the cowboy hats. But she worshipped Lynda. From the moment Cookie saw Lynda walk into the North Shore Animal League, she was Lynda's cat. Or more accurately, Lynda was Cookie's human. As Lynda always said: Cookie knew a sucker when she saw one.

But that wasn't true, and Lynda knew it. She wasn't being played for a sucker any more than Dewey played me for a sucker all those years. Yes, we were doting parents, but there was a genuine bond. It wasn't a Snuggles situation; it wasn't "give me the food and beat it." Cats like Dewey and Cookie give as much as they get. The only difference? Dewey gave to a community; Cookie gave to Lynda Caira.

She gave Lynda love. She gave Lynda attention. She wanted to be nearby, to be underfoot, to be touched. No, she insisted on being touched. If Lynda left a room, Cookie followed her and brushed against her leg. She sat on her foot. She jumped on her lap. If she wasn't getting enough petting, she nudged Lynda's arm with her head, then twisted around to show exactly the spot where she wanted to be scratched. She loved to climb on Lynda's chest and give her a kiss. That's right, a kiss. Every few hours, Cookie would stretch up and put her lips to Lynda's lips, like a young daughter shyly giving her mother a good-night peck.

Even when Lynda went outside, Cookie sometimes slipped out with her. Lynda tried to stop her, of course, but Cookie was smart. She hid behind the door, then rushed out as Lynda walked through, usually with a garbage bag in her hand. Once outside, Cookie would run. Lynda would drop her bag and chase after her, yelling for her to stop. Halfway down the block, Cookie would decide she'd gone far enough. She'd stop, turn around, and wait for Lynda to snatch her up. Then they'd walk slowly back to the house, Lynda telling her baby to never, never, ever do that again, and Cookie rubbing against

Lynda's chin as if to assure her, *Don't worry, Mom, I would never go too far from you.*

For some people, it might have all been too much. But Lynda's life was busy. After her divorce, she became the general manager of her family's catering business. The business was embedded in the community of Bayside, supporting and being supported by the family and the friends who had sustained Lynda over the years. She worked fifty hours a week, even before an administrator at St. Mary's Hospital for Children asked if she would donate a catered Christmas party for the nurses. She was so impressed with the hospital that the next year, in addition to the nurse's party, she organized and catered a forty-dollar-a-plate fund-raiser. The first year, she raised more than twelve thousand. The next year, she convinced a soap opera star to attend — many of the soaps filmed a few miles away in an industrial part of Queens — and doubled the attendance and donation. Soon, she was raising more than fifty thousand dollars a year with her February fund-raisers and being written up in *Soap Opera Digest* as a favorite charitable event for daytime stars.

When she wasn't working, she was at home preparing dinner, cleaning up, helping with homework, and trundling her young teen off to bed. Her parents would bring her armfuls of homemade spaghetti; her friends would take her out for movies and shows; but most of her time was devoted to Jennifer.

"You know how it is," she told me. "It was all for my daughter. Everything I did was for her."

I did know. When Lynda Caira talked about her life as a single mother, I remembered my own days of working fifty hours a week at the library. I remembered the weekends with my friends and the warm embrace of my family, how sheltered and supported I felt. I was happy. I had my own life. But that life, in a real way, was devoted to my daughter, Jodi. When I was working, it was to give her a better life. When I went to school to qualify for my director position, it was with the goal of making enough money to send her to college. Every moment, whether I was pounding away on a term paper alone in the library or trying to convince Jodi to clean up her filthy bedroom, I was thinking of my daughter.

And I know what Lynda means when she says that Cookie was there for her, because Dewey was there for me, too. Whenever I felt tired or frustrated, Dewey jumped on my lap. Whenever I wondered if the effort was worth it, or if I was making the right choices, Dewey forced me out of my funk and into a game of chase. Every morning, Dewey stood by the front door of the library and waited for me. When he saw me coming, he waved — and whatever was bothering me flew away. Dewey was here. He was waving. The world was good.

Cookie did that for Lynda. Whenever she came home, whether it was from a long day of work or a night out with her friends, Cookie was waiting on the ottoman near the front door. Every time, she followed on Lynda's heel like a dog, waiting for her to put down her bags, straighten her things, and bend down to pet her. Lynda couldn't resist. No matter how often it was given, she always enjoyed Cookie's attention. She never held it against Snuggles, who continued to be standoffish. She never expected it from another cat. This devotion was something special, she realized, something that was Cookie's alone.

Cookie loved fresh laundry, warm from the dryer. Lynda let her curl up in the basket at every opportunity. She couldn't bear to kick Cookie out, so she often washed each load of laundry two or three times. (That's what she told me the first time, anyway. Later she admitted, with a laugh, that she never rewashed.) Cookie was picky about pillowcases. Every time Lynda changed a pillowcase, Cookie jumped onto the bed to test it with a nap. If she didn't like the new fabric, she'd whine and step off, waiting for Lynda to change it. Which, of course, she always did.

Cookie also loved to be in the kitchen when Lynda was cooking. She had a habit, in particular, of sitting on Lynda's foot while she cooked at the stove. She loved Irish soda bread and pumpkin bread, and Lynda knew to cut Cookie a piece whenever she sliced one for herself. She also loved broccoli rabe, an Italian vegetable that connected Lynda with her childhood, her family, and those summers of homemade wine and kitchen-canned tomatoes in her grandmother's house. Broccoli rabe looks like stringy broccoli, and its bitter taste is something most Americans choke down and endure. Even many Italian Americans don't like the bitterness, although broccoli rabe is a staple of Italian cuisine. Cookie loved it. As soon as she smelled broccoli rabe cooking, she ran to the kitchen, stood on Lynda's feet, and meowed until she was given a bite. Or two. Or three. Lynda never cared. She wasn't lonely. Far from it. But Jennifer was having more meals out with her friends, as well as court-ordered weekends with her father, and it was nice to have someone to eat with every night.

It got to the point that Lynda noticed not when Cookie was with her but when she wasn't. If Cookie disappeared for a while, Lynda often walked the town house looking for her. Cookie almost always trotted out after the first few times Lynda called her, but one evening she went missing for hours. That wasn't like Cookie. It took Lynda a few tours of the house before she noticed the screen pushed out in the master bedroom. She looked out the window and there was filthy, disheveled Cookie trying frantically to climb the wall. She must have accidently pushed open the screen and somersaulted out the window. Fortunately, it was the first floor. Cookie had only fallen five feet. Still, by the time Lynda found her, her claws were broken and her paws were bloody from scrabbling at the rough brick wall.

A few years later, Lynda decided to finish her basement. Jennifer was now in high school, and without the basement, there wasn't enough room in the little town house for her friends to hang out. The job would take a few days, and the workmen would be going in and out of the house, so Lynda made sure to lock Cookie and Snuggles in her bedroom before leaving for work. On the second day, after the workmen had left, she unlocked the door to let the cats out. Snuggles was sitting on the windowsill, disdainful as usual. But Cookie didn't come running. And she wasn't anywhere in the room. As she searched the closet and under the bed, it dawned on Lynda that sly, sneaky Cookie must have slipped out the door when she was closing it that morning.

She called to Jennifer. They immediately began searching the house, calling for Cookie. They looked in the closets, under the sofa, in the kitchen cabinets. No Cookie. Lynda checked the television cabinet and under her quilting supplies. She scoured the construction debris stacked in the basement. She examined the windows, but all the screens were locked. There wasn't a single place she didn't search, then search again, then search one final time.

"Ohmygod," she told me, "I was absolutely hysterical."

Jennifer was crying. Lynda was worse. Her Cookie had gotten out. The workmen had propped open the outside doors; they had rummaged around all day with drywall and saws and wooden studs. They had clomped and banged. With no way back into the locked bedroom, Cookie would have been terrified. Of course she ran. Why wouldn't she run? And once she was outside . . .

Ohmygod, she was gone. She was such a baby and Lynda had cured her of all those terrible ailments and she had loved her and they had loved each other and ohmygod, how could she be gone? How could her baby disappear?

"Search one more time," Lynda told Jennifer.

Twenty minutes later, hysterical and tired and desperately pushing pieces of drywall around the basement, Lynda heard it. At first, she thought it was her imagination. Then she heard it again. The faint sound of feet. Then a meow, very soft and far away. She scrambled through the construction debris, yelling, "Cookie! Cookie!" She heard the meow, still far away, like it was coming from the first floor. But how could that be? She had searched and searched and . . . she looked up and there, above her, was a fresh layer of drywall.

"Ohmygod, ohmygod," she yelled to Jennifer. "Ohmygod, she's in the ceiling!"

She climbed up on a small stepladder. "Cookie," she called, banging her hand against the drywall. "Cookie!" She heard the sound of feet running toward her, then a faint meow. Every time she called Cookie's name, she was answered with a meow from just above her head.

She called one of the workmen. "The ceiling," she yelled into the telephone. "In the ceiling!"

"What's in the ceiling?"

"My Cookie."

"Your what?"

"My cat. She's trapped in the ceiling."

She was so hysterical, the contractor came straight over. Sure enough, Cookie had jumped into the partially completed ceiling and been sealed between the joists when the men applied the last of the drywall. The workman cut a hole above the window where the drywall hadn't been sealed, and together he and Lynda, by banging the ceiling and calling Cookie's name, managed to coax the kitten to the hole. Suddenly, there she was, Lynda's little Cookie, peeking over the edge of the drywall. She looked around, as if seeing the basement for the first time, and then leapt down into Lynda's arms, completely covered with dust and construction debris. Lynda was crying and kissing her, overcome with both horror and relief. Cookie didn't care. She jumped down and ran off, as if she'd known all along that Lynda would find her.

Before he left, Lynda made the workman patch the drywall hole and seal every inch of the ceiling. She didn't care that it was the middle of the night. She wasn't taking any more chances.

The first bump in Cookie's life began when Snuggles died. A tumor wrapped suddenly around her heart and lungs, and within forty-eight hours, Snuggles went from seemingly perfectly healthy to gasping for her last breath on the veterinarian's table. It was over before Lynda realized what was happening.

Soon after, she noticed a tiny, stumbling kitten nosing around her front door. The cat was clearly too young to be weaned, but no mother was in sight, so Lynda started feeding her. She fed her on the front porch for nine months, with no intention of ever letting her into the house. She had Cookie. She didn't want or need another cat. But after a while, she realized that Chloe — as she named the little runt — was being terrorized by the big hunting dog next door. Several times a day, he'd come barreling out of his house and chase her across the street, barking and rampaging and scaring her half to death. The neighbor didn't like the situation any more than Lynda did. He worried his precious dog was going to get hit by a car. So he came up with the perfect solution: shoot the kitten with this hunting rifle. Needless to say, Lynda immediately brought Chloe inside and made her a house cat.

Cookie wasn't happy about this at all. She was six years old, and she was used to having the house to herself. She didn't attack Chloe — Cookie was not an aggressive cat — but she turned up her nose at the newcomer and refused to pay her any mind. Chloe was a shy cat, the kind with a habit of lowering her head and staring up at you with big sad eyes, and she readily accepted the role of second cat in the Caira household. She seemed to understand that she could live in the house, but only on Cookie's terms. Cookie ate first. Cookie drank first. And Cookie was not sharing Lynda. That was the line, the one rule that stood above all others. Cookie looked scornfully if Chloe even tried to approach Lynda, and she wasn't above smacking her once to let her know her behavior was not condoned. And if Chloe tried to jump onto Lynda's bed? Unforgivable. One foot on the bedspread, and Cookie arched her back and hissed. She wasn't much of a fighter, but she would have fought to defend that bed because Lynda — Lynda was hers. Lynda was sacrosanct.

Eventually, though, Cookie mellowed. She was a friendly cat at heart, and constant vigilance wasn't in her nature. She was a lover, a happy-go-lucky companion, and once she knew she was still the love of Lynda's life, she began to warm up to sweet, subservient little Chloe. Mind you, it took years. Three years to be exact. But in the end, Cookie and Chloe were wonderful friends.

The second bump came a few years later. Lynda had long since settled into a comfortable life: twenty years in her town house, seventeen years as a divorced mom, sixteen years managing a successful catering business, ten years with her beloved Cookie. After twelve years of fund-raisers, she had donated more than a million dollars to St. Mary's hospital, which used the money to open a traumatic brain injury unit for children — the only such specialized unit on the East Coast. The next year, Lynda organized a fund-raiser for ALS (Lou Gehrig's disease), which had not only killed her aunt but was now affecting one of the soap opera stars who had been instrumental in helping her fund-raisers: Michael Zaslow. He had been fired by *Guiding Light* after his condition was revealed, and, as his health deteriorated rapidly, he told his wife that his biggest regret was not being able to see the friends he had made on that show one last time. Thirty-five of those friends showed up to see him at Lynda's benefit, which raised more than twenty-six thousand dollars. Michael Zaslow died ten days later.

But even as she enlisted the help of her close-knit family and friends, as she always had for a worthy cause, Lynda knew her life was changing. With her father semiretired, the catering business downsized its work space and staff, adding to Lynda's workload and putting an end to her fund-raisers. Her daughter was growing up and would soon be out on her own. Her grandmother died, and the family sold the house where Lynda had spent so many wonderful afternoons with grapevines, canned tomatoes, and a matriarch who never turned anyone away, from WPA highway builders to down-on-their-luck strangers in need of a cup of joe. It was as if her death closed the book on Lynda Caira's Bayside, a community that had long ago paved over most of its orchards and grape arbors, and where nobody talked to strangers anymore — much less invited them inside for a meal. For decades the original immigrants had been leaving, squeezed by newer immigrants and refugees from the City, as the locals called Manhattan, looking for affordable places to live. As the century closed on the old Bayside, Lynda Caira cashed out. She sold her town house for more than ten times what she had paid for it in 1973 and bought a three-bedroom, two-story, stand-alone Victorian in Floral Park.

Floral Park was only seven miles away, but for Lynda Caira, it was another world. Bell Boulevard, the main thoroughfare in her old section of Bayside, was crowded with garish signs, electrical wires, and four lanes of honking traffic. Floral Park's two-lane main thoroughfare, Tulip Avenue, was lined with independent stores fronted by orderly wooden signs: the bakery, the candy shop, the little independent supermarket, the lawyer's office on the second floor. Founded by a flower seed wholesaler in 1874, who named all the streets after flowers, Floral Park was incorporated as a township in 1908, an occasion celebrated by a white-steepled library at one end of Tulip Avenue and the centennial gardens at the other. Every year, the front lawn of Memorial Park featured a Christmas tree, and a crowd always turned out to watch the lights come on, followed by hot chocolate at the Catholic church next door. A Christmas tree on Bell Boulevard in Bayside, Queens? With hot chocolate? Nevah.

For Lynda, Floral Park was heaven, a tree-lined Norman Rockwell town literally one foot across the line from the messy sprawl of outer Queens. Sure, you had to drive thirty miles in any direction to escape the nonstop sprawl of New York City, but here within that maze of highways and apartment blocks was a tiny patch of middle-class, Midwestern Americana. A place with block parties and green lawns, where children rode bikes while the adults ate hot dogs to the sounds of "Light FM" radio. It was a place where she could hang a "Sunny Days" wreath on the door of her gingerbread-trimmed Victorian and tend purple daffodils and black-eyed Susans in her finely turned flower beds. At the end of Floral Boulevard was a grand schoolhouse, straight from the first decade of the twentieth century. On the far side of the neighborhood, behind a thin strip of trees and a bird sanctuary — a bird sanctuary! — sat Belmont Park racetrack, home of one of the three biggest horse races in the world, the Belmont Stakes. On summer weekends, the echo of the race announcer was a pleasant murmur behind the hum of lawn mowers and the bouncing of basketballs.

On the corner of Chestnut and Floral Boulevard, a block from Lynda's house, was the Bellerose station of the Long Island Rail Road. It was only a fifteen-minute train ride to Penn Station, but Lynda never went to the City. Maybe once a year, maybe, if there was a Broadway show she wanted to see. Like most people in Floral Park, her life was not oriented toward Manhattan. Most of her friends — even her best friend, who as a two-year-old had pushed infant Lynda in her baby carriage through Bayside — lived in Floral Park now. They had been raised in outer Queens and then migrated a few miles east to quieter streets and a more suburban neighborhood. In that neighborhood, they re-created for each other what Lynda's family had been in Bayside: a community of support and love. She hadn't moved far. Not geographically, anyway. The ten-mile circle of neighborhoods where Queens meets Long Island, after all, was Lynda's world. She was overjoyed to have found her little plot of Americana right in the center of it.

Jennifer . . . well, not so much. She was twenty-three years old, still living with Mom in the house she had grown up in, and she was adamant that she would not move out of the old neighborhood. She refused to pack so much as a toothbrush; in the end, Lynda was forced to pay the movers to pack her daughter's things.

Chloe and Cookie were worse. Especially Cookie, who was a master communicator. She used pushing, foot sitting, and tripping as a signaling system, and she seemed to have a different meow for every occasion. She had a meow that meant she was annoyed. A meow for when she was happy. A meow that meant *Leave me alone*. A meow that meant *Come here*. A meow that said *I'd like some, please*. A more forceful meow that said *I want* without the *please*. And, of course, a *gimme, gimme, gimme* meow for broccoli rabe. She even had a special high-pitched meow for when she really wanted Lynda's attention, which sounded exactly like *Mom*. Lynda wasn't so delusional to think her cat was really calling her mom. She assumed she was imagining that one. But whenever her friends heard Cookie whining for attention, their jaws dropped.

"Did she say mom?" they all asked.

"It sure sounded like it, didn't it?" Lynda would say, flushing with pride.

Not this time, though. This time, as Lynda packed for the move, Cookie wasn't pleading or questioning or kissing up with her "Mom" meows. This time, she was screaming at Lynda.

When moving day arrived, Cookie stopped screaming and disappeared. She had no intention, absolutely none, of leaving that town house. It took Lynda hours to wrangle both cats and shove them into their carrier. Cookie, in frustration, began to bang her head and rub her face on the bars of the carrier door. By the time they arrived in Floral

Park, only twenty minutes away, Cookie's nose pad was torn and covered with blood. Lynda could barely look at her. She felt so guilty.

When she opened the cage door, Cookie and Chloe didn't even stop to acknowledge her. They ran straight upstairs and hid under the guest bed. Jennifer recovered quickly. Within two days, she met new friends and was right at home in Floral Park. It took Cookie and Chloe a while longer. Except for biological necessity, they refused to come out from under the bed. When Lynda tried to coax them out, Chloe retreated to a corner, and Cookie walked forward a few steps to complain. That was it. For three months.

And then, all was forgiven. Was it a few days after Cookie emerged from under the bed before the complaining stopped? Was it a few months? A year? I'm sure it took Cookie time to adjust, even after giving up her protest, but does it really matter how long? In the end, Cookie loved the new house as much as Lynda did. She loved it so much, in fact, that she couldn't settle on a favorite spot. For a few weeks, it was the ottoman. She sprawled out there every night while Lynda watched television. Then it was the rocking chair. That lasted about six weeks. Then the top of the sofa, a dining room chair, the corner behind a piece of furniture, her little cat bed at the top of the stairs. Lynda was a quilter, and Cookie had several favorite spots in the new quilting room. For a summer, she fell in love with the bottom shelf of the bookcase. Lynda kept the shelf filled with quilts, which she made as presents for her friends and relatives. She made one for Cookie, too, of course. It had a floral pattern in the middle with alternating pictures of kittens and puppies around the edges. Cookie lay on a quilt almost every day, but she never lay on that one. Why dirty her special quilt, after all, when she could leave fur on something everyone else was going to sit on, too?

Eventually, the seasons changed. The leaves along Floral Avenue burst green, turned golden and red, then blew away in the winter wind. The horses raced around Belmont; the commuter train ran back and forth to the City. Jennifer spent more time with her friends and boyfriends until, eventually, she moved into a house three miles away. In her younger years, Lynda had thought about marrying again. She had male companions, but none of the relationships turned out to be what she wanted. She liked the romance, of course, but she never found anyone she wanted to share her life with.

"If a man came along now," Lynda told me, "I'd probably tell him no, thanks."

Younger women (and men) might look on that statement with skepticism — how can a single woman not want a man? — but I understand it perfectly. I've felt it for decades in my own life; I've just put it a little differently. "I only want a man," I've always said, "if I can hang him in my closet, like an old suit I can pull out when I want to dance." Give me the romance. Give me the fun and the dancing. Just don't make me clean some guy's whiskers out of my sink every day for the rest of my life. I'm perfectly happy, thank you very much, the way I am.

So I take Lynda's contentment at face value, because I've experienced that contentment myself. And why wouldn't she be happy? She was confident. She had a great kid. She was accomplished. She had friends and family and companionship from Cookie, who, through years of constant devotion, had come to know just about everything there was to know about her owner and friend. When Lynda was lonely, Cookie nuzzled her on the nose, kissed her on the lips, or sat in her lap. When Lynda was happy, they danced around the house. When she wanted to be alone (rarely), Cookie gave her space. When she was quilting, Cookie sat quietly beside her instead of batting at the thread (usually). It wasn't just her moods; Cookie understood how Lynda was feeling. When Lynda wasn't well, Cookie lay down on whatever part of Lynda's body was hurting. If it was a stomach virus, she lay on Lynda's stomach. If it was a knee ache, she lay on her knee. In her forties, Lynda began to suffer from spinal stenosis, a degeneration of vertebrae in her lower spine. Whenever the pain forced Lynda to lie down, Cookie crawled gingerly onto her back and flattened herself over the spot, a hot compress for the shooting pains.

Even when the problem was sleeplessness, Cookie responded. She sensed Lynda's discomfort with the nighttime silence of Floral Park — not an easy thing to get used to after forty years in the noisy city — even before Lynda realized it. Every time Lynda stirred in her bed, Cookie leapt from her pillow to stand guard. If so much as a fly buzzed at the window, Cookie jumped to attention with her ears laid back against her head.

"Back to sleep, Cookie," Lynda would say with a pet. Cookie would stare in the offending direction — usually the window — then walk around her pillow, curl into a ball, and fall instantly asleep. Lynda would lay awake, wondering, *How can this little kitten love me so much?*

Unfortunately, while her discomfort with silence receded, the pain in her back grew worse. Lynda focused on her exercise and diet. She tried to work less, even though she loved her job. She visited physicians, searching for treatments, but her back continued to deteriorate. When she was in pain, Cookie did everything she could to comfort her. She nuzzled her hand, kissed her nose, and settled onto her back for as long as Lynda needed it. Those eight pounds on her spine, so soft and warm, were like a heat bottle on her sore nerves, but they couldn't stop the slow creep of bone decay. If she didn't have surgery, Lynda's doctor finally told her, she was probably only a year from a wheelchair. A wheelchair! She was only forty-seven years old.

It was a difficult time, although Lynda tried not to show it. She kept her regular routine, entertaining friends, visiting family, and attending her weekly sewing club. She supported Jennifer when she needed her. She worked full-time at the catering business until the day before the surgery. But at night, she often lay awake and worried, even as Cookie jumped to attention at the slightest stirring and nuzzled her side as if to say,

Everything is fine, Mommy, everything is all right.

Then one day, as she absentmindedly stroked Cookie and thought about the surgery, a clump of fur came away in her hand. Lynda stared down at it for a moment, confused. Then she rolled Cookie over and looked at her. The cat's skin was patchy and inflamed, and she was practically hairless on her belly and the inside of her back legs. "Oh no, Cookie," she said. "Oh no." Cookie was fourteen years old, and Lynda had recently been forced to admit that her hearing was beginning to decline. Now the poor cat had developed a skin condition.

Alarmed, Lynda rushed Cookie to the veterinary office. They performed a battery of tests but found nothing wrong. Finally, the veterinarian unhooked his stethoscope and looked at Lynda.

"Are you okay?" he said.

"I'm fine," she replied.

"Are you sick?"

"No, but I'm having trouble with my back. I'm having major surgery in a few days."

The doctor nodded. "How long have you known?"

"Six months."

The doctor put away his instruments. "It's not a physical problem," he said. "It's psychological. Cookie is so worried about you that she is pulling out her own hair to relieve the stress."

Lynda looked at her kitten, at her sweet face and mangy belly and torn-up legs, and began to cry. Cookie had been a wounded animal in a cage. She had watched dozens of people walk past her every day. Out of all those people, Cookie had chosen Lynda. In an instant, it seemed, Cookie had dedicated her life to her. Lynda never understood the reason. What had she done to earn that trust? What had she done to deserve such a fierce and genuine love?

The surgery was over in a few hours, but the recuperation was long and slow. Cookie refused to leave Lynda's bed. Not for a moment. One night, about a week after the surgery, Lynda became intensely ill. The house started spinning so badly that she felt sure she was dying. Terrified, she cried to her daughter for help. Cookie stared at Lynda, then looked at Jennifer, then stared at Lynda. She meowed a new meow — urgent and unsure. Instead of calling the hospital, Jennifer called her grandparents, who rushed over. But as Lynda's mother approached the bed, Cookie jumped up and screamed at her. Lynda's mother sat down on the bed; Cookie hissed and spat until she retreated, afraid Cookie would bite her. Cookie stood where Lynda's mother had been sitting and spat and hissed even more. Her beloved Lynda was in trouble. Nobody was coming near her, Cookie had decided, nobody but her daughter and her cat.

It was only a case of severe vertigo, caused by the manipulation of Lynda's spine during surgery, but it changed Lynda and Cookie's relationship forever. I suppose change isn't the right word, because I don't think Cookie's attitude changed that much. Revealed might be a better word, because for the first time, Lynda understood the depth of Cookie's love. Yes, Cookie knew everything about her and did everything she could to make her happy. Yes, Cookie literally worried herself sick over her friend's health. But that night, Lynda saw sacrifice. She saw that when it came to protecting her, Cookie didn't worry about herself. She would suffer any harm to defend her friend.

After that night, Cookie's love was insatiable. She lay beside her when Lynda was in bed; she sat beside her when Lynda sat up; she walked beside her when Lynda was finally able to stand. As part of the recuperation, Lynda sat in a hip chair, which was tall and straight like a baby's high chair. Cookie learned to climb onto the back of the sofa, then onto the hip chair, then into Lynda's lap. She would sit there all day. Reluctantly, Lynda would have to ask her mother or daughter to take Cookie away because the weight was too much for her recovering spine.

Even after her friend recovered, Cookie didn't relax. Lynda could barely read a book because her cat insisted on sitting on top of it. She couldn't open the door without Cookie running in front of her and trying to prevent her from leaving. Cookie never liked television. When Lynda had watched it before, Cookie wandered in and out of the room, sitting for a moment, then jumping up, agitated. Now she sat on the sofa with Lynda and watched. If Lynda wanted to lie down, she had to make room so Cookie could stretch out on top of her head. At exactly 10:00 P.M., Cookie would get up from the sofa, stand in front of the television, and meow.

The first night, Lynda was shocked. "Cookie," she said, "what's the matter with you?"

Cookie walked out of the room. Thinking something was wrong, Lynda followed. Cookie went straight to the bed. Lynda looked all over, but couldn't find anything wrong. Eventually, she went back to the living room. Cookie came in screaming and led her back to the bed. It took Lynda a while to realize there wasn't anything wrong. Cookie had simply decided it was time for the two of them to go to bed. From that night on, unless there was something special, bedtime in the Caira house was 10:00 P.M. Cookie insisted on it.

Not that there was much sleeping. Cookie was a bundle of nerves in the bed, climbing all over Lynda, playing with her feet, walking around on her pillow. She rubbed her nose on Lynda's lips, her cheek, her nose, anywhere on her face she could reach. When Lynda turned off the light and closed her eyes, Cookie waited a minute and then ran a paw across her face. If Lynda didn't respond, Cookie bent down and pried her eyelid back with her paw.

"Honey, I'm alive," Lynda would tell her softly, closing her eyes.

A few minutes later, Cookie would rub her paw across Lynda's face again. It happened every night, starting with the night after her vertigo. And it didn't stop. Long after Lynda was well, Cookie continued to wake her every night to make sure she was alive. Lynda wasn't annoyed. Instead, she was touched. She loved Cookie. She was dedicated to the little cat. But Cookie . . . Cookie's whole life was defined by her devotion to Lynda. What a humbling and heartwarming experience, to be loved that way. Even if it was "just" the love of a cat.

But while Cookie was worried about Lynda's imminent demise, Lynda was absolutely convinced that Cookie would live forever. She had lost her hearing — a test confirmed that — but otherwise she was as healthy and beautiful as ever into her eighteenth year. If she was slowing down a little, well, that was only natural. A clock could wind down forever, after all, without coming to a stop.

And then Lynda read *Dewey.* Jennifer gave it to her for Christmas, and (surprise!) Cookie even gave her enough space to read it. As she read the last few chapters, she became more and more upset until, she would write in her letter to me, she "became no less than hysterical." Every sign of old age Dewey exhibited in his last year was happening to Cookie!

Like Dewey, Cookie developed hyperthyroidism. And like Dewey, she wasn't very responsible about taking her pills. Lynda would think she had successfully pushed them down her throat, then find them scattered behind the furniture. She developed mats in her hair that were almost impossible to untangle, the result of the barbs on her tongue wearing down and preventing her from cleaning properly. And like Dewey, Cookie had taken a sudden interest in cold cuts, probably because they were loaded with salt. Lynda bought her a half pound of sliced turkey at a time. When she tired of turkey, Lynda switched to chicken, no matter how much turkey was left in the bag. Then Cookie stopped eating cold cuts. She didn't want that old bird. So Lynda tried a whole, fresh-cooked rotisserie chicken. Cookie liked that. So Lynda shared a rotisserie chicken with Cookie every week.

Jennifer thought her mother was spoiling the cat, but Lynda didn't agree. *Dewey* had broken her heart. She had cried every night while reading the last chapters on Dewey's old age and death, thinking not only about my precious library cat but about her precious Cookie. She had seen the future, and she knew the end was near. Cookie was slowing down. She was walking with difficulty. She was struggling with her diet. After nineteen years of Cookie's extraordinary love, there was nothing Lynda wouldn't do for her cat.

That February, Cookie developed kidney and bladder problems. The vet took X-rays and endoscopies, a whole battery of tests. He put her on a strong course of medication, sparing no expense because Lynda would have it no other way, but there was no improvement in Cookie's condition. In April, the vet stopped her treatment. He took her off her hyperthyroid medicine as well, since it was causing rashes on her ears and belly.

"She doesn't need the irritation," the doctor said.

He was telling Lynda to let her go, to give her peace, but Lynda couldn't fully accept that Cookie was dying. The little cat still followed at her heels everywhere she went, eager to love and be loved. She still waited for her on the ottoman by the front door every evening when she arrived home from work. Every morning when she left for work, Cookie looked at her with big pleading eyes, like a young child, as if to say, *How can you leave me, Mommy?*

In July 2009, they celebrated Cookie's nineteenth birthday. Lynda told her she looked forward to celebrating her twentieth the next year, but even she no longer believed it. Cookie had never been big, weighing just ten pounds even as a healthy adult. Now she weighed less than five. She had taken to spending most of her days under the kitchen table. Lynda moved her food and water to the kitchen, and her litter to the adjoining room. She had lost bladder control, but even in her frail state, Cookie would pull herself to the nearest object, a shopping bag, a pair of shoes, even Jennifer's handbag to relieve herself. Cookie would never, no matter how sick, make a mess on the floor.

Lynda's mother was convinced Cookie was staying alive only because she couldn't bear to leave her friend alone. Lynda's heart told her that might be true, that the little cat loved her that much, but she wanted to believe Cookie still enjoyed her life, that her existence wasn't a struggle. She stroked her. She petted her. She fixed her broccoli rabe and rotisserie chicken and talked to her in gentle, loving tones. When Cookie could no longer walk the stairs, Lynda carried her to bed and placed her on the pillow that had been her special place for so long. Every night for nineteen years, Cookie had slept on that pillow. On the third night of carrying her to bed, Lynda realized that as soon as she fell asleep, Cookie was struggling down the steps to the kitchen floor. On the fourth night, she left Cookie under the table.

"Rest here, my little friend," Lynda told her. "You don't have to worry about me."

Cookie never came back to the bed. A few days later, while Lynda was at work, Jennifer called crying. She had found Cookie on the kitchen floor, in a puddle of her own waste.

By the time Lynda arrived home, Cookie was clean, but the energy was gone from her body, the depth and intensity totally absent from her eyes. She lifted her head to look at Lynda, her lifelong companion. Perhaps she even smiled, briefly and weakly, before dropping her head to the floor.

Lynda cradled her in her arms and, as tenderly as she could, eased her into the car. "It's going to be okay," she whispered, as her mind raced and her hands trembled on the steering wheel. "We're going to get some medicine and you're going to be okay." She kept talking, reassuring her, even as her voice was breaking and the tears streamed down her face. She knew it was the end, and she prayed it would be painless and natural. She prayed that, whatever happened, she would be there for her Cookie. Her last obligation, the least she could offer for a lifetime of dedication, was to make these moments as comfortable as possible for her precious girl.

And she did. She made it safely to the vet, although she could barely see through her tears, and she held Cookie in her hands, lightly and lovingly, until her final breath. She held her until the little cat glanced up one last time as if to say, *I love you, I'm sorry,* before she folded under and Lynda felt, with her soul as much as her fingertips, the very last beat of her heart.

I have never been loved by another human being, Lynda wrote in her letter to me, *not even by my daughter or my parents, the way I have been loved by my Cookie.*

I could tell, even from her brief letter, that Lynda wasn't lonely. Her life was filled with happiness and love. I wanted to include a story like this — an ordinary story — because a majority of the letters I received where from ordinary people like Lynda. Why her, you ask? Because of that one beautiful sentence, which celebrated a kitten's extraordinary love without a whisper of despair:

I have never been loved by another human being, not even by my daughter or my parents, the way I have been loved by my Cookie.

"I know that sounds strange," Lynda told me, although after my life with Dewey, it didn't sound strange at all. "It almost sounds sad, I know. But it is absolutely the truth. As much as my daughter loves me, as much as my parents love me, as much as other people have loved me, I have never felt . . . I have never felt what that cat felt for me."

And that love was returned. I'm not saying Lynda loved her cat more than the other people in this book, because love can manifest in myriad ways, but she was the only one who said, "Thank you, Vicki, for doing this *for Cookie*. She was such a good cat. She deserves to have her story told." She was the only one, in other words, who explicitly put her cat before herself, and I admire her for that.

"She was just your typical tabby," Lynda admitted. "She was gray and white, the tiger markings, your little garden-variety kitty. I can't say that she did any extraordinary things. I can't say she was a hero. I can't say she saved somebody from disaster."

Not even Lynda. Cookie, after all, didn't save Lynda Caira from illness . . . or occasional loneliness. This isn't a story of redemption. It isn't a story of need. Lynda Caira has been and will probably always be happy. This is simply a story about being chosen, about being loved so fiercely that it changes your life.

Dewey. Cookie. All the other cats that touch our hearts and change our lives. How can we ever thank them enough? How can we ever explain?

After Cookie's death, Lynda wrote a remembrance of her precious cat. It closed with this: "There is nothing more to say — life will go on, although I will miss her each and every day! Jennifer will get married, I will have precious grandchildren, I will love and lose more pets. But one thing is certain: there will never be another pet who will be my best friend; there will never be another animal who could bring the joy that Cookie brought to my life."

Amen.

SEVEN
MARSHMALLOW

"He was a tough cat. For a cat that was a runt and so weak, he ended up being a pretty strong man. He reminds me of Grizzly Adams a little bit. You know, big heart but you can't see it on the outside. Marshmallow rarely showed his true colors."
"Only to you, huh?"
"Only to me."

I've known Kristie Graham her whole life. I was beside her at her communion. I attended her high school graduation. I did the floral arrangements at her wedding. I even changed her diapers. When she was younger, of course, when she was just a sweet baby girl. When I started college in Minnesota in my thirties, after a bad marriage to an alcoholic that left my life and finances shattered, Kristie's mother, Trudy, was one of my first new friends. While I attended class, she'd often babysit for my daughter, Jodi. When I wasn't working, we'd sit for hours and drink coffee while our children played. That's what Kristie remembers, anyway, that her mother and I drank gallons of coffee. She was only four or five years old at the time, so her memories are pretty scattershot. She remembers that my washing machine didn't spin, so I stirred my laundry with a big wooden spoon (maybe once, for about a week). She remembers that my rusted car never seemed to run (only occasionally); that I bawled my eyes out when Elvis died (not true; it was her mom who cried); and that I was, in her words, "a very hardworking, hard, hardworking woman." (I'll agree with that one. I had to be!)

I simply remember a wonderful girl. Trudy's oldest daughter, Kellie, was Jodi's age.

She was a beautiful, outgoing kid. Kristie, three years younger, was just as beautiful and outgoing, but she never felt she could compare to her sister — even though Kristie was the one who would eventually become homecoming queen. So at the age of three, she went the other way. Kristie became the snot-nosed kid of our little coffee club. Literally. That girl always had something encrusted beneath her nose. If you put her in a clean white dress to have her picture taken at Sears, she walked out of the car covered in dark smudges. It didn't matter how clean the car was. She found a way to ruin the dress. And I'm not making this up. The picture happened. Even Kristie admits (with some pride, I think) that back then, she was always covered with "runny booger dirt." I guess that's why I called her Pigpen. I loved that kid. *Pigpen* was my term of endearment.

But the thing I remember most about Pigpen Kristie wasn't her dirty face and soiled dresses. It was the way we had fun. She and Kellie were the laughing-est, goofing-est, playing-est kids I've ever met. I remember Kristie and a few others convincing (or possibly forcing) Susan, the daughter of another friend, to slide down the laundry chute. Thank goodness there was a pile of laundry at the bottom, because it was a twelve-foot drop. I remember being the "house mom" for big slumber parties of eleven or twelve preteen girls, and always having to come in at 2:00 in the morning to tell them to pipe the heck down. I remember being snowed in during a ferocious blizzard and coaxing Kristie, Kellie, and Jodi to dance and lip-sync to 1970s soft rock songs. Then Trudy and I put on costumes and "sang" a few 1950s girl-group hits. We laughed for years about the Weekend of the Blizzard when, as always, we girls made the best of a tough situation.

I also remember Kristie's cat, Marshmallow. He was a huge, fluffy, off-white fellow who, really and truly, resembled a marshmallow. Not that I saw him much. I usually only glimpsed his tail as he was running away. I liked him, but I'm not sure Marshmallow would have been special to me if it weren't for one thing: He was special to Kristie. If ever a child loved a cat, it was Kristie Graham. She loved her Marshmallow. The girl talked about him all the time.

So when I thought about stories for this book, I thought of Marshmallow. I thought of how much Kristie loved him, how much he was a part of her life, how important it all seemed to her, and how much he loved her in return. Kristie and Marshmallow's relationship was the closest thing I'd ever known to what Dewey and I shared. That is part of Dewey's legacy, of course: the opportunity to tell stories about other special cats and special girls. The opportunity to show the world that those kind of wonderful relationships are happening everywhere, all the time, and that it's okay — in fact, it's perfectly *normal* — for a cat to be your very best friend.

I also knew Kristie could tell a funny story. I expected her to make me laugh. And she did. What I didn't expect was for it to touch me so deeply. I knew Kristie's life hadn't been perfect. She'd had hard times. Who doesn't? That's life. As Kristie told me: "It was an awesome journey. I wouldn't be where I am today without going through all this so I count it as a blessing, obviously." I do, too. I count it a blessing to have known her. I love Kristie and Kellie and their mother to the bottom of my heart. Their presence upgraded my life to first class, even if my washing machine didn't spin and my car broke down. But Kristie's story still surprised me. I expected her to be smart, but I guess I never expected her to be wise. I mean, the girl's only thirty-five. What's she trying to pull?

So, Kristie, let me step aside, for once, and let you tell your tale in your own words. How many stories have been in this book so far? Six? Seven? It's time for my coffee break anyway.

I've been blessed. That's what I always say. I'm so blessed, in fact, that I put a list of my blessings in my Christmas card every year. It looks like this:

I am blessed because all of my kids like mac and cheese, hot dogs, and frozen pizza.

I am blessed that both boys think, talk, and act rough and tough but still sleep with their favorite Teddy.

I am blessed because every day I receive four credit card applications in the mail. Some would call this junk mail; I call it "free envelopes."

I am blessed that my children live on the edge and will do anything if it's a dare and not a sin. Like drinking "Mom's special sauce" for five bucks. Chocolate syrup, ketchup, mustard, and pickle juice.

I am blessed that when Reagan wakes

up, she yells "Lucas, D.J., I'm awake, come get me," and I can get another five minutes of sleep.

I'm blessed that my kids love worms and bugs, since I do, too. I'm blessed that they eat tomatoes and beans straight from my garden, and dig up baby carrots, and bite right into peppers, because I did that, too. I'm blessed that Sioux City is cold enough in the winter for snow forts and hot enough in the summer to throw up a temporary swimming pool in the backyard. I'm blessed that my kids are constantly grass stained and hate to wear shoes, even though my daughter has Fred Flintstone feet just like my husband. (I wonder how that's going to look in high heels.)

I'm blessed that Lucas is the kindest, most empathetic kid I've ever met. I'm blessed that my middle boy, D.J., is so strong-willed that he refused to use his real name, which is Dawson, and everybody said fine. "Why didn't you name me Bruce Wayne or Cowboy D.J.?" he used to whine. He was in a Batman/cowboy phase; he dressed like one or the other every day for three years. I had no trouble pushing Batman through the supermarket in a shopping cart, but I finally had to get his kindergarten teacher to tell him cowboys weren't allowed in school. My three-year-old daughter, Reagan, meanwhile, is a mermaid. She wears orange hair from the dollar store and three-size-too-big tap shoes from the Goodwill and calls my husband Eric (his real name is Steven), since that's the prince from *The Little Mermaid*. "My prince is home!" she yells every evening when he walks in the door. And then they dance. Reagan never dances with me. "Sorry, Mommy," she says, "you're Ursula." (Ursula's the sea witch). But I'm still blessed, because she's eight years younger than D.J., and I thought the next time I heard the patter of baby feet I'd be a grandmother.

I'm blessed with Steven, the man of my dreams. We've been married for thirteen years, and I still get butterflies in my tummy when I am getting ready to go on a date. Alone. With a boy. Hee Hee. And when he takes me out, he lets me order "the usual": a grilled cheese sandwich with crinkle fries. He never tries to change me. He just laughs and says, "You're a cheap date, honey." And I say, "Lucky for you."

I'm blessed because I have a nice house. Because I have a purposeful job, mentoring fifty-two kids with learning disabilities from age sixteen to twenty-four. A job where I can use my experiences to help people I care about, and where their courage and warmth helps me, too. I'm blessed because when my dog Molly died at seventeen, I cried so hard I thought I never wanted another animal. But some of the kids I mentor volunteer at the Siouxland Humane Society, and they introduced me to another dog, and now I have Princess to jog with every morning.

I'm blessed because last fall I ran the Sioux City marathon, and I did it the right way. I even gained weight *on purpose* to compete in the over-150-pound category, where I finished third. Which was amazing! But that wasn't why I was blessed. I was blessed because every two miles my husband, sister, and even my dad were there to hand me water and cheer me on, and each time they were crying because they were so proud of me, because they knew how hard I had worked and how far I had come.

Where did I come from? How did I get here? Those aren't questions I've often asked. I'm blessed by God. Every time I hear my three-year-old pray, I'm reminded of that. But it took hard work, too. I always knew that, because I'm the one who did the work. It wasn't until I started thinking about this book, though, that I realized that maybe Robert Frost was right. Maybe there are two roads that diverge in the yellow woods of our lives, and I . . .

I married my cat.

And that has made all the difference.

If you want an explanation of that, and I hope you do, then we probably need to go back to the beginning, which in this case is 1984, when I was a dirty snot-covered (and proud of it!) nine-year-old kid living in Worthington, Minnesota, a pretty little town on a lake. I was a tomboy, I guess you could say, because I loved gardening with my dad and digging for worms and racing beetles in the palms of my hands. When my mom told me pigtails looked nice, I cut my hair off in the middle of the night and hid it in my jewelry box. I loved sugar, so I would sneak into the pantry and drink all the Hershey's chocolate syrup straight out of the can. Then I'd walk around with chocolate sauce smeared all over my face, denying my crime. You know, that kid. Never worried about a thing.

But in the summer of 1983, Grandpa got sick with colon cancer. He was a big man from a very small town, Whittemore, Iowa, where he owned a meat locker, and to me he was about a hundred feet tall. He was very outspoken, and he had huge raw hands from cutting meat all his life. When my mom and older sister and I moved to Whittemore to take care of him, I was excited because it was like a vacation. And Grandpa was a hero to me. I still remember skating down the street every day to the diner, plopping into my seat, and saying, "I'll have the usual, please" — grilled cheese with crinkle fries, of course — and feeling like I was some kind of grown-up. But the cancer cut Grandpa down so quickly that he started to wither before my eyes. I could see, even as a child, his big hands trembled. They couldn't hold me anymore. My mom was strong-willed. She always said, "I have big shoulders. I can handle anything." When my grandpa stopped fighting, I saw her fear for the first time.

When I got home to Minnesota two weeks later, I found out my cat had died. I'd left Puff at home with my dad in Worthington, but when we came back after the funeral, he told me Puff had died. I looked at him and nodded. Then I went to my room and cried. I was nine years old. What else could I do?

A few days later, another cat showed up at our side door. She was a calico, and she had the wildest mix of colors I have ever seen. No stripes or patterns, just a crazy quilt that made her look like a bunch of parts of different cats stitched together. Her ears were missing, like maybe they had frozen off. Her tail was a stump. She was ugly and beat up and undesirable in every way . . . so obviously I started feeding her. I gave her milk and a name and even a few dinner scraps I managed to slide into my pockets. So of course she kept coming back.

"Kristie," my dad finally said after noticing Bowser hanging around the side door, "why are you feeding that cat?"

"Gwampa sent me dis cat," I told him. I had a little kid lisp back then; I was all "wed woses are pwetty" in those days. But I puffed myself up and said, "Gwampa wants me to have dis cat, Daddy."

Typical for a nine-year-old, right? A little parental manipulation? Maybe, but I believed it to be true. And I still do. If there's a void that someone should fill, but they aren't, God sends an animal. Bowser was sent. And Grandpa had something to do with it.

My dad was a lot like me. Or maybe I was a lot like him, at least when it came to nature. He was a farm boy. He loved to be outside, loved to garden, loved animals. I was the kid who held beetles in her hand and stuck worms up her nose to scare her Care Bears–loving sister. My mom took my sister's side; she was not an animal lover. My dad understood. Plus, he might have been a little guilty about Puff. I don't think he expected me to take the cat's death so hard.

Whatever the reason, it was pretty easy to convince my dad to let me keep Bowser. He put a heat lamp in the garage for her, because the Minnesota winter was brutally cold (the heat lamp was the only way to keep her water from freezing, even in the garage), and Bowser was not, under any circumstances, on Mom's orders, coming into the house. After the heat lamp was in place, Dad moved the old dresser, where he kept his tools, underneath it and put a cardboard box and a blanket on top. A few weeks later, Bowser had kittens, which surprised us both. She gave birth to them outside, right underneath my bedroom window. You aren't supposed to move newborn kittens, but my dad decided to transport them from the window well to the box in the garage. After all, we had a cat condo, penthouse floor. Why would they want to roll in the dirt?

Marshmallow, I must admit, wasn't the best kitten in the litter. In fact, he was probably the worst. He was the runt. He was shy. His hair was poofy, like he was rocking one of the bad perms floating around my small-town Minnesota elementary school in the fall of 1984. He was almost pure white. Almost, I say, because unfortunately his fur had a yellowish undercoat that made him look stained. Think of a sheep. Then think of a sheep floating in a giant ball of static. Or think of a dandelion with its white seed fronds sticking straight out, ready to fly. That was Marshmallow.

As part of the condo project, my dad ran a board from the dresser to the ground. Bowser would stand at the bottom and coax her kittens down one at a time, like a momma bird teaching her babies to fly. Marshmallow was always last. He would stand at the top of the plank with his eyes bugging out, shaking with fear. His mother would meow. His brothers and sisters would get bored and start fighting each other. Marshmallow would just stand there shaking.

"Come on, Mawshmawow," I'd coax him. "Wun down. Just wun down. It's easy."

Finally, he'd take one tiny step, then sort of collapse and slide-tumble in slow motion down the board to the floor. "That's okay, Mawshmawow," I'd tell him. "You'll wun tomowow."

But when it was time to give the kittens away, Marshmallow still wasn't weaned, and he still hadn't worked up the courage to walk (or wun). He was still sliding in slow motion from his drawer to the ground. So my parents let me keep him. I think they figured, in his condition, he wouldn't last long.

"Don't give that cat milk," my dad said,

when he saw me sneaking the carton out of the refrigerator. "He'll get a taste for it, and that stuff is expensive."

So, like a doting mother, I whipped up a substitute: water and flour. It sure looked like milk, but Marshmallow took one sniff and looked at me crooked.

"What's wong, Mawshmawow? You don't wike it? You need to dwink to get stwong, Mawshmawow. I need you."

He never did drink that wet flour, but Marshmallow got strong. When the snow melted in the spring, he started following his mother around the yard. And I followed them. Pretty soon, we were crossing the road to the median near the golf course (in my little kid perspective, it was a forest), where we would turn over leaves and rocks to see what was underneath. "Look at this wowm, Mawshmawow," I'd say, letting the worm crawl along my wrist and down my arm. "Look at this wock. Look at this but-tafwy."

That year, I was finally old enough to walk to school by myself. Marshmallow followed me to the corner, then watched as I disappeared down the block. When I came home, he was always waiting for me at the corner. "Mawshmawow!" I'd yell, running across the last yard. I didn't care who saw me with

Marshmallow. I was proud of him. When my grandmother, who often came for long visits, told me she saw him traipse down to the corner at exactly 2:30 every day, I was even more proud. "Mawshmawow waits faw me aftaw school," I told my friends. I bet they thought that was cool, but I can't remember for sure.

In the fall, I raked the leaves into a big pile and buried Marshmallow underneath them. He'd peak through an opening, wiggle his behind, then spring with his arms outstretched, like he was surprising me. Or hunting me. Marshmallow was a terrific hunter. I'd come careening down the sidewalk on my bike, and whenever I passed the pine tree he'd leap out of the shadows at my tires. I suppose I should have slowed down, since he could have been badly injured under the tires, but instead I just yelled, "Watch out Mawshmawow, coming fwough!!" and pedaled faster. Then I'd throw down my bike, bury my legs in the leaves, wiggle my little toes, and wait for Marshmallow to pounce on them. When we were finally worn out, we'd lay down on the ground next to each other. I'd lay there for a full minute, staring at the sky. The peaceful, quiet sky. Then, all of a sudden, Marshmallow would pounce on my face.

"Why do you have scratches near your eyes?" my teachers asked me.

"That's my cat Mashmawow," I'd say. "He thinks my eyelashes are spidahs."

"Be careful, Kristie," they said. "He could hurt you."

Marshmallow hurt me? No way.

The next year, when Marshmallow was two, his mother, Bowser, was hit by a car. It happened, just like with Puff, when I was out of town. I was distraught. Bowser was my cat. She was Marshmallow's mommy. My grandpa had sent her to me because I was alone. And I loved her. I insisted we bury her underneath my window, where she had given birth to Marshmallow and those other long-forgotten kittens.

After his mother died, Marshmallow changed. I don't know if he was depressed or lonely, but I know that's when he started talking to me. You might find this strange, but I always talked to my cat. I told him about my day, about school, about my toys and my parents arguing, you know, kid stuff. Marshmallow listened, but Marshmallow never talked back. Not until his mother died. Then he started jumping onto my window ledge and talking to me.

Meow, meow, Marshmallow would say to attract my attention.

"Hi, Mawshmawow, how are you?" I'd say, putting down my homework.

Meow.

"Yeah, I'm good, too."

Meow, meow.

"I've been at school. What have you been doing?"

Meow. Meow, meow.

"Yeah, I got my math homework done."

Meow.

"Yeah, I found my socks."

Meow meow meow.

"No, I have my shoes. They still don't fit."

Sometimes, I'd sneak Marshmallow, who Mom never allowed into the house, into my bedroom. My Pigpen tendencies spread to my personal space as well as to my Sears dresses, and my room was . . . well, a pigpen. I mean, you couldn't see the floor. Marshmallow hated walking on that layer of filth, but he loved climbing on top of me. The problem was crossing my lavender bedspread. That bedspread drove Marshmallow bonkers, because his claws would jab through it with each step. Watching Marshmallow walk across my lavender bedspread was like watching someone cross a pool of freshly chewed bubble gum. Every step, the bedspread stuck to his claws and he had to pull away with an exaggerated pop. Even when he reached me, Marshmallow never stayed long. After ten minutes, he always headed back through the bedspread mine-field, meowing to be free. We were both more comfortable down in the "forest" with the worms and the beetles than inside my messy room.

By the third summer, Marshmallow was in his prime. Remember that fragile, timid cat, the poofy runt who tumbled in slow motion — on purpose! — down that scary, three-foot-high board? Well, forget it, because he wasn't like that anymore. Marshmallow was a big old man cat. We'd still go out on our walks in the forest, and I'd show him the beetles and butterflies I found in the yard, but he also had his own sport. Every few days, Marshmallow dragged himself onto the step outside our front door and meowed until I came out. There, at his feet, would be a mangled squirrel. Or bird. Or baby rab-bit. But I knew Marshmallow didn't mean anything by it. He was just a cat, honing his survival skills. So it didn't bother me. It was in his nature, you know?

Our neighbor, a duck hunter, wasn't as tol-erant. He approached me and Marshmallow one day, in full hunting regalia, shotgun on his arm, and pointed to a nest in his yard.

"If your cat ever kills those cardinals," he said, "I'm going to shoot it, because those are beautiful birds."

This was the same man who hung a bird feeder on the edge of our yard, on the lowest branch of a tree, right next to a spot where Marshmallow could hide. I mean, it was practically a baited trap. It was a slaughterhouse over there.

So I put my hands on my hips, stuck out my dirty snot-covered lip, and said, "If you kill ducks, I'm gonna shoot you, because dose are beautiful bodes." What could the poor man do against the righteous indignation of a dirt-encrusted, Elmer Fudd–sounding, cat-adoring fifth-grade girl? He just stared at us, the mangy kid and her mangy cat, and then walked away, shaking his head.

About a week later, Marshmallow killed a duck. He caught it on the golf course, snapped its neck, and laid it on our front step like a chef presenting his prize soufflé. I didn't mind. I had such a blind spot for Marshmallow, I would have let him get away with . . . well, with murder. Of a duck.

My Barbie-loving older sister wasn't as understanding. "Oh my god," she yelled when she saw the carcass. "There's a dead duck at the front door! Oh my god, there's blood on the fence! Dad. Dad! Dad!! DAD!!! There's a dead . . . duck . . . at . . . the . . . door!"

Needless to say, high-fashion, beautiful, girly-girl sister didn't understand mangy, murdering Marshmallow's unique charm. Like my mom, she wasn't an animal lover, and she preferred dressing up to hunting worms and playing in the leaves. But I have to give her credit: She wasn't a fan of my cat, but she more than tolerated him. She even appreciated him at times. She saw our connection, and although she didn't want or need that herself, she was happy for me. She knew Marshmallow was my best friend.

"Hey, Kristie," she'd say. "Your cat is at the window again. I can hear him meowing. Are you sure he's not hungry?"

It wasn't until the seventh grade that the fighting started. And I mean serious fighting. Every day, Kellie and I would scream at each other as loud as we could, with all the windows open so the neighbors could hear. We would literally beat each other with curling irons and hair dryers. We'd have scorch marks on our foreheads and bruises on our arms. Afterward, we'd stand side by side at the mirror, trying to fix ourselves, and she'd say out the side of her mouth, "You're so ugly."

"No, you're so ugly," I'd say. Having gotten over my speech problem, I could spit every letter at her. "You're the ugly one. Not me."

"No I'm not. And you know it."

Meow, Marshmallow would say, scratching at the screen to be let into my bedroom. It's been twenty-five years, but I still get emotional when I see that old screen in my childhood room. That screen, with Marshmallow's claw marks still visible, is a memorial to my youth.

Meow. Me-owww.

"I know, she's an idiot."

Meow meow.

"You're right. I look fine."

Mee-ow, Marshmallow would say, crawling onto my lap. I don't know if your cat does this, but every time he purred, Marshmallow kneaded with his claws, like he was nursing. It was painful, but it also felt good.

"I know, you're right, nobody deserved to be spoken to that way."

Meow, meow. Meow.

"I know, Marshmallow. I hear it, too. They should just get divorced and get it over with."

I suppose it seems odd, talking to my cat that way. No, confiding in my cat that way. Needing my cat that way. Finding comfort in his meows. But Marshmallow was my primary defender, you know? He told me I looked good. He agreed when I said everything was fine.

Even if I was the tallest girl in the sixth grade.

Even if, in seventh grade, a group of older girls stole the new jeans I was so proud of out of my locker. Along with my underwear. And my shoes.

Even if, every time they passed me in the hall, those same girls slammed me against the wall and told me not to even look at some boy they liked. Until my older sister cornered them in the mall, that is, and told them whatever pain they caused me, she would give them double in high school.

She may have beaten me with a curling iron. She may have yelled and cursed me. But my big sister loved me. Even I knew that, even at the time. Those fights were our way of dealing with our fears and frustrations. They were our way of talking about the fact that all Mom seemed to do was yell, and all Dad seemed to do was drink. Starting at ten or eleven years old, I often stayed up past midnight, doing my homework on the living room sofa and waiting for my father to come home drunk. My mother handled it with anger. I was the caregiver. Kellie . . . she took it out on her little sister. But she was there for me, too. Not like Marshmallow, of course. But she was there.

"You really think that cat talks to you, don't you?" my dad asked me once.

"He does, Dad," I said. "I can hear the way he meows. He talks to me."

And he's the only one.

Even when we didn't talk, Marshmallow comforted me. On the nights I was waiting up for my dad, I would watch through the window as Marshmallow sauntered across the front yard and disappeared into the trees across the road. An hour or so later, I'd hear a bump against the glass and there he'd be, sitting on the windowsill. When I was life-guarding at the swimming pool down the road, I'd watch him hunt field mice in the long weeds of the fish hatchery for hours on end. (Yes, we lived in a neighborhood with a golf course, swimming pool, and fish hatchery — but it was perfectly normal and middle class, I swear.) When I broke my leg playing basketball, he'd sharpen his claws on my cast. There were shredded pieces of plaster hanging off in every direction by the time Marshmallow strolled away. How could I feel sorry for myself after that?

He wasn't needy. He never followed me to school anymore, or raced after me when I drove down the street. We never rolled in the leaves or hunted worms either, but whenever I lathered up with tanning oil and sunbathed in the yard, Marshmallow was at my side. And whenever I tried to give myself a pedicure while sunbathing, he was there to sniff my hot-pink toes and shed hair in my wet polish, making the task impossible. More and more, though, he was content to be a spectator in my life. We still talked, mostly about sports (at which I excelled) and boys (at which I also excelled but didn't know it), but he always let me take the lead. He had his own life, out there in the weeds, and I had mine. But when I needed him, Marshmallow was there. My father moved out, then moved back in, then moved out again. In frustration, I took to punishing myself every day with a long run. When I came home, Marshmallow was always waiting for me on the front step. He never let me down.

He also inspected every boy I dated. Every single one. I laugh now because, to me, Marshmallow was and always will be the most beautiful cat in the world. From an outside perspective, though, he was overweight and arthritic. He had a cyst on his face — it looked sort of like a giant blister — that give him an aura of decay and disease. His poofy yellow-white hair, never particularly attractive, was patchy and matted. And I mean really matted. That cat had big, grubby clumps all over his body. Imagine sticking twenty separate pieces of bubble gum on an extra-furry cat. Then twisting the hairs in the gum. Then waiting two weeks for them to get good and dirty. That's what Marshmallow looked like during my high school years. We shaved him every spring, a trauma that made him look like a wounded rat and sent him flying into the garage rafters to hide for days. But Minnesota in the winter was too cold for a shaved cat, so he was always fat, hairy, and clumpy by the time the leaves fell and the homecoming dance arrived. He might have been, even I will admit, the ugliest cat in Worthington, Minnesota.

And every time a boy came for a date, the first thing I did was pick up Marshmallow, kiss him on the nose (right next to that cyst), shove him into my date's face, and say, "This is my cat, Marshmallow. Isn't he the cutest?"

Meee-owwwww, Marshmallow would drone, his breath reeking of contempt and cat food.

The boy would look at my overweight, nicotine-stain-looking, tangle-hair-not-licking, lopsided, lethargic, cyst-on-the-face cat and just . . . stare. Every single one of them must have thought: *What is this? Some kind of test?*

And it was. Sort of. If a boy didn't like my cat, I didn't want to date him.

Or that's what I told myself. I actually ended up dating a boy for two and a half years who did not like my cat. His father was a community leader. My father was a drinker. He was a good-looking charmer. I was the anorexic younger sister of the prettiest girl in school. And I mean rail thin, serious intervention, intensive-therapy anorexic, the kind that pounded her frustrations and insecurities out with long runs and refused to eat more than a mouthful or two. On the outside, I was happy. I loved to laugh (still do). I was gregarious and athletic. I moved easily between social groups and counted almost everyone in the school as a friend. I was the homecoming queen, for goodness' sake! Who is happier in high school than the homecoming queen?

But on the inside, I was tearing myself apart. Anorexia made me feel like it was the first day of school every day. Do you know that feeling when you can't sleep, when you are too busy analyzing everything that might happen the next day? When you are obsessed with the need to look exactly right, with the feeling that everyone can read your thoughts and is watching your every move? The sweaty palms. The heart palpitations.

The horrible moment when you feel yourself falling on the ice or skidding into a car accident. That moment was my life twenty-four hours a day, seven days a week. There was no calm, no resolve, just fear. Always. Fear that someone might see that I was not perfect, that I made mistakes.

Everybody thought my boyfriend was perfect. They said he was good for someone like me. You know, someone with a . . . food problem. My mom loved him. My dad loved him. My sister loved him. They were scared for me, I can see that now. They thought I might die from my disorder. They thought he was saving my life. When I tried to break up with him the first time, even my PE teacher pulled me aside and told me I had to stay with him. For my own good.

My boyfriend knew I had to stay with him, too. "You'll never find anyone as good as me." That was his favorite thing to say to me.

I don't think he meant any harm. He was just a kid, dealing with his own problems. But by then, I had summoned the strength to put myself into therapy. My mother scoffed. She thought I was weak, or at least that's what I thought at the time, when my disease kept telling me everyone thought I was a loser. I found out later she never scoffed;

she was proud of me. My father? He lost his job and had to cancel my health insurance because, he said, the treatments were too expensive. Thankfully, my godmother in Texas cashed in her profit sharing from American Airlines; her retirement money paid for my care. And that care told me I didn't need a boyfriend who said a girl like me should be thankful for a guy like him.

But how does an insecure, anorexic girl cut loose a guy like that? With the help of her cat, of course. Because for two and a half years, I kept telling myself: *He doesn't like Marshmallow. He's not the one. He doesn't like Marshmallow.* Every time he said, "Don't pet that stupid cat. We're going out to eat, in public, and you'll have cat hair on your sweater," it hardened my resolve a little bit more. I mean, I'd been petting Marshmallow since I was in the second grade. I never noticed it, but I must have had cat hair on my clothes every day for ten years. I had been, since second grade, a walking ball of Marshmallow. I was covered in him. He was part of who I was. If a boy didn't like Marshmallow's hair on my sweater, I told myself, then he didn't like me. Finally breaking up with my high school boyfriend *because of cat hair* was the last, most important act of my childhood.

■ ■ ■ ■

I've often wondered why I married my husband. I mean, I love him, I know that. But why him? Steven is one of the quietest men I've ever known. He only speaks when he's spoken to, and then only to relay the appropriate information. Unless he's talking to me. The two of us talk all the time. We have no secrets; I know everything about my husband, and he knows everything about me. But very few other people know him. Not like I do, anyway. They see him. He's the big outdoor type, a serious hunter and excellent athlete. They see that side of him, but they don't know the man. They don't know that he's a snuggler, too. They don't know how he puts his arm around me when I'm upset. They don't know that he goes everywhere with me. He doesn't buy me flowers, but that's fine, because I don't want that. *Don't buy me gifts,* I tell him, *just be there for me. I don't want the jazz. I don't want the huge house. I don't want the big rings. I just want a pal I can walk through life with.*

They say a girl always wants to marry their father. But does she, really? My dad was a drinker. He was very social. He cheated on my mom. Repeatedly. When I was a kid, she went away with Vicki and a few other friends every few months for a woman's weekend. Kellie and I used to joke that they were her man-hating weekends, because she'd always fight with my father when she returned.

"I was with people who loved me this weekend," she'd yell. "I was with people who cared." I joked; I fought with my sister; but only because I was scared. I never wanted to be torn apart like that.

Steven never drinks. He never goes out with the boys, much less any girls. His parents, as far as I know, have never touched a drop of alcohol. They don't yell. When he was growing up, they didn't watch television. Steven and I do watch television (who doesn't?), but we never fight. We've had disagreements, but in fifteen years of marriage, we've never had a yelling argument.

Oh my, Kristie, I said to myself, as I thought about my life, *you married your cat.*

It's so true. I didn't realize it until I started thinking about this book, but it's true. All my life, I was looking for a man like Marshmallow. The other men in my life let me down. They hurt and abandoned me. So I latched on to Marshmallow. Not consciously, of course, not on purpose, but that scraggly runt was my beau ideal. Someone who listened. Someone who talked with me. Someone who was tough and outdoorsy, not soft. Not clingy or needy. Not housebroken. I wanted a man who was comfortable with himself, even if he wasn't the golden boy. A man who built me up instead of tearing me down. Who was confident enough to let me have my space, but in love with me enough to always be there when I needed him. And someone I loved in the exact same way.

Isn't it strange that someone like that existed? Isn't it strange that I found a man as perfect as my cat?

And isn't it strange that Steven was the one person in my life Marshmallow never liked? He wasn't a cat person, for one thing, and cats can sense that. Steven had a man's love for dogs, and particularly his yellow Labrador, Molly, who was two years old when we married and moved to Sioux City, Iowa. But that's not it. My boyfriends all hated my cat. It took me years to realize this, since I had such a soft spot for that lopsided, matted kitten, but it's true. Maybe they were jealous of him. Maybe they thought I was strange for talking about him so much. Maybe they just thought he was ugly or that I had too much cat hair on my prom dress. I guess I thought that was the way relationships worked. I spent my youth saying I wanted a man who loved Marshmallow, and then dating the exact opposite kinds of guys.

But Steven . . . he didn't hate Marshmallow. No way. I'm not saying Steven loved him, but he was more like my sister. He didn't have a connection with Marshmallow, but he was happy that I had such a strong one. He didn't exactly jump for joy, but he didn't argue when I insisted Marshmallow move to Sioux City and share our new lives. He knew how much Marshmallow meant to me.

And besides, Steven thought, just like my parents back in 1984, that Marshmallow wasn't going to live long. He was eleven years old by then, which is not particularly old for a cat, but his hair was so stained and matted, he looked fifty-three. He had degenerative arthritis and sort of shamble-staggered when he walked. His energy was low; his appetite pathetic; his commitment to personal hygiene nonexistent. Worst of all, the cyst on his face had developed an abscess, so the left side of his nose appeared to be collapsing. The vet said he was too weak for surgery; the hole in his face wasn't life-threatening, but the procedure to remove it might kill him. Even I wasn't sure Marshmallow had long to live. But I knew, no matter how many days he had left, I was going to make them as comfortable and pleasurable as possible.

Steven tried. I have to give him that. He

really tried. He got down on the floor every few days and said, "Come here, Marshmallow. Come here, buddy. Let me pet you." Marshmallow would throw him a contemptuous glance — *yeah, whatever, "buddy"* — and walk away.

Being ignored wasn't bad, though, compared to our one and only attempt to groom him. Now that Marshmallow was slowing down, I (foolishly) thought that I might be able to cut a few unsightly tangles out of his fur. I convinced Steven to hold him, while I chopped. Well, Marshmallow may have been old, but his claws were still sharp. He clamped on to Steven's hands with his front claws, pulled his back legs up, and started cutting into his forearms with a series of kicks. He wasn't trying to get away. I want to make that very clear. Marshmallow had been waiting for his chance to pay Steven back — for moving him to Sioux City, for taking me from him, for any number of unknown slights only the cat understood — and he wasn't letting go. He shredded Steven's arms with his back claws, just like he shredded the cast on my broken leg all those years before.

Steven finally tossed Marshmallow off and marched, tight-lipped and bloody, to the basement. He came back a few minutes later in his Carhartt jacket, hockey mask, and hunting gloves. "I'm ready," he said, pounding his pads like a hockey goalie. Steven wasn't going to let Marshmallow beat him.

But he did. Marshmallow won, of course. He wiggled and scratched so ferociously and for so long that we finally gave up and left him alone with his tangles. Marshmallow may have been slow and arthritic, but he was still the boss. That was obvious. When Marshmallow entered a room, Steven's huge Labrador, Molly (a real man's dog most of the time!) would almost bow to him. Molly wasn't scared; it was more an unspoken respect for this wise old cat. After a dozen years of outdoor living, Marshmallow had that aura about him. He was a survivor. A bad boy. A cool cat. He may have been retired, but he was still the Don. He was content to sit all day under a house plant by the front door, hardly moving, but we weren't fooled. Marshmallow knew — and approved — everything that went down in our house.

Like my jogging, for instance. With hard work and a loving husband (and my unbelievable cat, of course!), I had conquered my eating disorder. I had even turned the experience to my advantage, using it to reach and teach my learning-disabled teens and young adults. (Do you understand now why

I felt so blessed to have gained weight, *on purpose,* to compete in a higher division of the marathon? And why my husband — and even my father — had tears in their eyes as they cheered me on? I mean, I might have only finished third, but . . . I *won!* Forever.) I'm not sick anymore, but that doesn't mean I don't take care of my body. I eat well, and I jog every day. Molly learned that last part fast. Every morning, she practically chased me to the front door with her leash jangling in her mouth. While I laced up my shoes and Molly worked herself into a frenzy, complete with flying slobber, Marshmallow lay under his plant watching us. Like the Godfather, he didn't have to talk; everyone knew what he was thinking. *The only reason I'm letting you go out with her, dog, is because I'm too old. One day, dog, you may be called upon to return this favor I now give to you.*

When Molly and I left, Marshmallow hauled himself to the top of the sofa, where he could watch for us out the front window. When we returned, he always lumbered down to the floor and watched me stretch. This time, he would talk, talk, talk. That was a great thing about Marshmallow. No matter how old and tired, he never stopped talking to me.

After two years, he even taught Molly to

find her voice. She started with a whimper, like an old door opening on squeaky hinges. Then she added a rumbling ah-rer, ah-rer, ah-rer, like a weed whacker straining through a pile of thick brush. I came home for lunch every afternoon, and the three of us would sit in my kitchen, chatting away.

"How was your morning, guys?"

Meow.

Ah-rer.

"Yeah, my day's going pretty well, too."

Me-oww.

"It's the usual, peanut butter and jelly."

Ah-rer-rer.

"No, you can't have any."

Meow, meow. Me-oww.

Ah-rrreerrrrr.

"Oh no," my husband said, when he realized what was happening. "Not the dog, too."

A few years later, I got pregnant. "I buy food for that cat," my husband grumbled, when he found out a pregnant woman shouldn't clean a litter box. "I clean up his vomit. Now I scoop his poops. And all he does is ignore me. Why can't he be more like Molly?"

Yeah, whatever, Marshmallow sighed, lifting his head for a moment and then drifting back to sleep under his beloved plant.

I will always cherish, until the moment I die, the night I went into labor with my son Luke. There is an interminable stretch of time, on the edge of motherhood, when it's too soon to go to the hospital and too uncomfortable and exhilarating to relax. So I paced the living room, fighting the tightening in my belly and trying to focus on my breathing. By this time, Marshmallow was sixteen years old. He had lived with Steven and me for four years. He was stiff, arthritic, and nearly deaf. I hadn't seen him move from under his plant, except for food or his litter box, in more than a year. But he got up that evening and walked with me. He always came to my side when I was sick, but this was different. Marshmallow walked with me every step for two hours, meowing the whole time. Molly, hunkered down near the sofa, eventually added her voice, *ah-rer, ah-rer, meow, meow, breathe, breathe, meow,* until the room echoed with sound. And love. Uninhibited, animal love. I was having a conversation with my two pets, while walking in labor on my swollen, calloused feet, and I couldn't have been happier. I couldn't have wished for better support.

When I brought Luke home, Marshmallow surprised me again. He moved out from under his plant and started sleeping under my son's bed. When Luke was in the living room, Marshmallow shambled in and sat by his carrier. People told me, "You have to be careful with a cat. They will pounce on a baby's chest."

I thought, *Marshmallow? Are you kidding me? He wouldn't hurt Luke. And even if he wanted to . . . have you looked at that cat? He's seventeen years old. He can barely walk. He hasn't pounced since I was in high school.*

After Luke's birth, Marshmallow's health continued to decline. Five years after our move to Sioux City, he stopped being able to walk to his litter box. He couldn't climb up or down stairs. Some days, he could barely make it to his food dish, and he suddenly seemed forgetful. There were times when, I was sure, the Godfather had no idea where he was. Arthritis had twisted every joint in his legs. His hearing was gone. His face was a mess. I knew he was in pain. And I didn't need a veterinarian to tell me it was time. It wasn't a hard decision. Not at all. At ten years old, I had watched my grandfather eaten away, in great pain, day after day. Marshmallow was such a good buddy. I couldn't let a friend of mine suffer.

I took a day off from work. I turned off the television. I held my infant son on my hip, so that I could lift Marshmallow into the center of my lap. As I petted him, I watched the loose hair float up into the streaming sunlight and settle over everything, even my sweater. "Mawshmawow," I said to my infant son in baby talk, imitating that little child from so long ago. "This is Mawshmawow. Wemember him."

I looked from my son to my cat to the sunlight shining through the window, still thick with fur. My window. My house. My adult world. The room was quiet, except for a gentle purring. Even at seventeen, Marshmallow was kneading his claws into my leg. I felt the slight pain, and I smiled. A sad day, but a sweet moment, sitting on the sofa with the ones I loved.

I opened my photo album. There I was in a purple zippy wind jacket with my straggly hair, the little girl I used to be. Marshmallow was just a kitten, and I was holding him up to the camera. I was so proud of him. You could see it in my face. I was so proud. It was just a Polaroid, it was starting to fade, but you could see the happiness in my face. We didn't own a Polaroid camera, so our neighbor, Katherine, must have taken the picture. She was an older lady. She loved Marshmallow. She watched us from her window, or when she was gardening, and I'm sure she heard our conversations, too.

I'm sure she heard my parents arguing, and my sister and I beating out our fear on each other. She took the picture and gave it to me, I'm sure, because I was just a little girl, and I was so proud of my cat.

I flipped the pages. There were pictures of me and Marshmallow buried in the leaves. Me and Marshmallow in the backyard. There was a section with nothing but me, in a series of formal dresses, holding Marshmallow. I took a picture with Marshmallow, I remembered, before every school dance I ever attended. Me and Marshmallow lying on our blanket in the sun. Me and Marshmallow when I graduated from high school. Me in my wedding dress, smiling, holding my cat. "Mom," I remembered saying over and over again throughout the years. "Go get the camera, Mom. I want a picture with Marshmallow."

It's hard for me to think about that day. I'm sorry, you probably think I'm weird, but it's hard. I won't talk about his death. I just can't. Because I miss him. Even fifteen years later, I miss my Marshmallow. But there was so much joy in his life. So much joy. He was with me from ten years old to twenty-seven, and it was an awesome journey. I wouldn't be where I am today without it, so I count it as a blessing. Obviously. Even the bad parts were a blessing. I mean, how many people get seventeen years with an animal, you know? How many people ever get to experience that kind of love?

EIGHT
CHURCH CAT

"Words cannot express how much the book Dewey *meant to me. . . . We adopted a stray cat at our church many years ago: 'Church Cat'! She was pregnant and when her babies came, members adopted them. Then a collection of funds got her to the vet to be spayed. She lived in the church until we had major renovations and I took her home."*

Carol Ann Riggs surprised me. Her short

note about Church Cat, a stray cat adopted by the Camden United Methodist Church in Camden, Alabama, had piqued my interest, but after the first ten minutes of our telephone conversation, I must admit, I was completely flummoxed. Not by the things she said, but by the way she said them. Ms. Carol Ann Riggs (as her friends call her) had an extraordinary Southern accent, the kind full of slow, honey-dripping pronunciations, the "sugahs" mixing with the "small-town law-yas" and singing in "the church qui-ah."

I must admit, I liked it immensely. And I liked Carol Ann Riggs, too. She was born in the tiny town of Bragg, Alabama, where the nearest high school was a thirty-mile bus ride away. (Even today, Lowndes County has only two public high schools.) When she married Harris Riggs at nineteen and moved to his hometown of Camden, she thought she was moving to the big city. Camden, after all, had two stoplights, two restaurants, two banks, and almost fifteen hundred people. But it was a wonderfully friendly place, despite the "large" size. There wasn't much money in Camden, but when someone died, not only did all the neighbors bring food, everyone in town attended the funeral. "Almost everybody was kin to everybody,"

Carol Ann told me, and that included her husband Harris's "people," who for several generations had operated the town's hardware store. Carol Ann wasn't a librarian — she worked for that small town "law-ya" I mentioned earlier — but she was a longtime member of the local library board. And despite my misgivings about library boards, I liked that. In fact, I liked everything about her. Especially that accent.

"I know, I know," her friend Kim Knox said. "It's that Southern accent you hear on television, and you say to yourself, *That's not real.*" Kim was born and raised across the border in Laurel, Mississippi, so she knows Southern accents. "But that's a Camden accent. Lots of people in Camden talk that way. People think its old Southern aristocrat, but people in Camden aren't like that. They're very down to earth. Not any kind of attitude or anything."

It's the isolation, Kim figures, that keeps the citizens of Camden so charming. The town is the seat of Wilcox County, a sparsely populated area in the hardpan hill country of southwest Alabama. The county has only thirteen thousand residents, less even than Clay County, Iowa, and the median income is only sixteen thousand dollars, a third of the national median and six thousand dollars below the poverty line. People think of south Alabama as plantation country, with sprawling mansions and fields of cotton. But you don't see large farms in Wilcox County. You see the occasional small family farm, essentially a sharecropper's plot, sandwiched between thousands upon thousands of acres of tall straight southern pines.

"It's a town in the middle of nowhere," Kim Knox said. "It's a picturesque gem." When I heard that, I thought of Spencer, with its wide sidewalks and blocks of locally owned, pleasantly thread-worn shops. I pictured a town where the generations have their own tables at the local diner and a cup of coffee lasted two hours at least.

But Camden didn't work like that, as photographs of their threadbare downtown showed. In Camden, the social life wasn't centered on the commercial strip. There weren't any movie theatres, fancy restaurants, or chain superstores. The center of social life in Camden, Alabama, was the churches. The four largest were located, one after another, on a stretch of Broad Street that was as immaculately maintained as the nearby shopping district was ragged. The biggest was the Baptist church. Across the street, next door to each other, were the two Presbyterian churches. Down the block toward the town's main intersection and next to the Exxon gas station that marked the unofficial entrance to downtown was Camden United Methodist. None of the churches were huge — between them they probably had seven hundred members, or about half the town — but they offered meals, prayer meetings, youth activities, and adult and junior "qui-ahs." And when something important came along, like the yearly Christmas pageant, they all worked together to put on a show.

It was Camden Methodist's newest member and part-time secretary, Kim Knox, who first noticed the cat outside the old parsonage that served as the church's administrative office. The cat was a little gray tabby, and when Kim walked out for a short break, the cat was crouched in the shadow of the nearby bushes. She had an adorable round face with soft eyes, and when Kim looked at her, the cat didn't turn away but kept staring right toward her. Then she started talking. When Kim talked back — "well, hey, kitty cat" — the cat jumped onto the porch, causing Kim to, quite naturally, reach down and pet her. The cat rolled over for a belly rub. When Kim opened the door to return to her office, the cat hopped up and jogged inside.

Hmmm.

Now, Camden United Methodist was not a formal church. It could be formal about some things, like its doxology and its sanctuary, but in general it was a blue-collar, salt-of-the-earth congregation. The administrative offices were, to say the least, not pristine. The old parsonage was a one-story, cottage-style house from the early 1920s, with creaking floorboards and clattering windows, and the small space was overflowing with boxes and files. The pastor was from the laid-back school of liturgy, always sporting an open collar, an absentminded smile, and a joke for his parishioners. Even Kim wasn't the typical fussy church secretary. It seemed to her, after a bit of reflection, that a stray cat might fit right in.

But she wasn't sure. The pastor's office of a small-town church was a community gathering place. People were always dropping by, not just to talk about problems but to gossip and shoot the breeze. What if they didn't feel comfortable with the sweet, moon-faced gray cat now lounging in their secretary's chair? Was it really appropriate for the part-time secretary, who had been in town only a few months, to let a cat live in the church?

Meow, the gray tabby said, right on cue.

Fortunately, the next person to enter the parsonage was Ms. Carol Ann Riggs. Carol

Ann had been a member of Camden Methodist since moving to town in 1961. She was in the choir and on several committees and knew just about everybody, so she often dropped by to say hello and see if anything needed doing. Her daughters had gone to college and then moved away, so Carol Ann had, in a sense, taken to mothering the Camden Methodist congregation. She was also, as Kim discovered, a lifelong cat lover.

"Oh, you have to keep her," Carol Ann said, when the little tabby sauntered over to sniff her hand and meow. "She's just dahlin." She didn't tell Kim that she was pretty sure she'd just adopted a prison cat. There were a gaggle of them that lived in the alley behind the jail, waiting for the prison cook to throw out the scraps. It wouldn't have been any problem for this little kitten to stroll a block down Broad Street, then cross the street to the parsonage door.

Instead, Carol Ann simply said, "Kim, you've got to hold on to this little sugah." And since Carol Ann had been a member of the church for decades, and since her husband's family had been in Camden for generations, that was all the endorsement Kim needed.

The next time Carol Ann dropped by the parsonage — and she suddenly found more excuses to do that than ever — the little gray tabby was sitting in the middle of Kim's chair. Kim was perched hazardously on the front edge.

"She tried to sit on my lap," Kim told her, a little embarrassed, "but she hated how many times I got up and down. So she took the comfortable part of the seat."

Meow, the cat said, as if in agreement, before jumping down to let Carol Ann pet her. She slept most of the day, snuggled behind Kim on the chair, but every time someone came in, she meowed and ran to greet them.

"Well, hey, little girl," most people would say, reaching down to pet her. "Aren't you darling?"

And she was. The little cat was irresistible. Even Carol Ann, who had owned and loved animals all her life, had to admit this kitten was special. Maybe it was her round face, which was so soft and babyish. Or her sweet disposition. Her meow was so peaceful, and her approach so gentle, that you couldn't help being drawn to her. She was spunky. She was friendly. But more than that, she was endearing. That's the word: endearing. You couldn't look at her sauntering across the floor toward you with her sweet eyes up-turned without thinking, *aaawwww.*

Still, the kitten almost certainly elicited smirks from the more starched-collar members of the congregation. They never said anything, at least not to Kim, but nothing that happened around there, neither rude look nor sly remark, ever slipped past Carol Ann.

"They just didn't like animals," she explained. "I can put my finger on each one of them right now, and I know they didn't have animals in their homes. They weren't raised with them, you see, so they never understood them. They didn't think it was appropriate for a church to have an animal."

Any tension, though, was quickly defused by the church's pastor. He was a young man leading his first congregation, but he was good with people and impossible not to like. He had been at Camden Methodist only a few weeks longer than Kim Knox, but if he had any nervousness about his recent promotion to head clergy, he dealt with it through an endless stream of good-natured banter and positive affirmation. He may not have been a cat person, and he may have wanted to please his new parishioners, but he wasn't the kind of man to kick out the less fortunate, no matter how often they shredded the toilet paper in his office bathroom or how much hair they shed on his couch.

Really, his laugh seemed to say whenever Church Cat came up, *what's the harm?*

And even the most reluctant among the congregation had to admit that the children, at least, loved having Church Cat around. The parsonage was across a wide lawn from the main church building, and the lawn served as an informal social area, where the adults hobnobbed after church service and the children ran around pushing, chasing, and staining their clothes. Every Sunday, the little gray cat sat on the edge of the lawn and watched them. She didn't play. She definitely wasn't a fan of being chased. But she loved it when the kids came over to pet her.

"Now move back, children," Carol Ann would say, taking on the role of protector. "Give her some room, she's getting nahvous." The children would take a step back, elbowing and jostling for position until one little girl, who must have been two, since she still toddled, couldn't control her excitement and lunged forward with a squeal. It happened every Sunday, and Kim and Carol Ann couldn't help but laugh. The girl meant to be loving, but there was something about her that terrified the poor gray tabby. As soon as the little girl started squealing, the cat turned and ran for the office, where she had a dozen little holes in which to hide.

"Where's Church Cat?" the kids would scream, searching for her. "Where's Church Cat?"

That's how she got her name. Somehow, one Sunday, she went from That Cat at the Church to Church Cat. "I'm just going to give this little bit to Church Cat," the ladies started saying at Fifth Sunday Potluck, sliding a bite of meat to the side of their plates.

One day, Kim's husband was driving down Broad Street when he noticed an elderly lady sprawled on the ground outside the church office. He immediately pulled over and ran toward her. Halfway there, he recognized her as Carol Ann's mother-in-law, who was in her late eighties. "Ms. Hattie," he yelled, "are you all right?"

A second later, he noticed Church Cat beside her, getting a belly rub. "I was just lovin' on her," Ms. Hattie said, pushing herself to her feet with a smile. And just like that, the little gray tabby from the prison alley was adopted, not just by Kim Knox and Carol Ann Riggs, but by Camden United Methodist Church.

When winter arrived, whispering into south Alabama with a thick layer of frost just before Christmas, Carol Ann and Kim decided Church Cat could start staying indoors overnight. They purchased some litter and food, and Church Cat immediately took to the comforts of a warm, safe place to sleep. She was such an outgoing cat, though, that she got bored during the night. The young pastor was bemused by the sight, every morning, of Kim's papers scattered all over the floor. Kim would hear him talking in his office and think, *I don't remember anyone going in there*. Then she'd hear a meow and rush in to find Church Cat sitting on his desk. She'd apologize, but he'd just laugh, and then Church Cat would start purring in her arms. That's the warmth and companionship a cat provides. When she arrived in the morning, Kim always started smiling when she saw Church Cat peeking through the blinds, ready for another day of greeting congregants . . . by sleeping 90 percent of it away on the seat of Kim's chair.

Keeping Church Cat indoors at night meant other accommodations, too. Carol Ann and Kim were primary caregivers, but if they were away, someone had to feed her and change her litter. When the office was closed for a few days, someone had to let her outside or she'd go wild with cabin fever. And, as always, someone had to watch to make sure she didn't sneak into the sanctuary, which had never been officially designated a cat-free zone but seemed the exact excuse for the cat haters — and there were always some, as Carol Ann knew — to start talking about disrespecting holy ground. Even asking for help with Church Cat's care made Carol Ann nervous, like she was pushing too far. But she didn't need to worry. Church Cat had plenty of fans, and there were more than enough enthusiastic volunteers.

With basic care out of the way, Carol Ann and Kim moved to step two: spaying and vaccination. And that led to the first big surprise of the great Camden Methodist cat experiment. Church Cat was pregnant.

By March, word had spread through the church: A single mother was in their midst. Church Cat, for her part, wasn't hiding it. When she walked, her belly was swinging like a church bell. No doubt there were questions from young kids around the family table that spring, but for the most part, the congregation was excited. If possible, the children followed Church Cat even more than usual. And Church Cat, despite her condition, was accommodating. The day before Palm Sunday, Carol Ann drove by and saw her sprinting happily around the church lawn.

But on Palm Sunday, Church Cat was

gone. The children came out to the lawn after the church service, dressed in their choir robes and waving palm fronds, but there was no cat to meet them. They stopped and looked around, bewildered. Then they started searching: in the bushes, in the Sunday school rooms, in the administrative offices, and even in the sanctuary. But they couldn't find the cat.

"Did she have her baby?" the squealing girl squealed, almost falling down with excitement.

"Probably," Carol Ann told her, "but we don't know for sure."

The next day, Kim went looking for her cat. That year, in addition to adopting a stray cat, Camden United Methodist Church had started a major building project. The primary church building would be expanded; the old parsonage would be hauled away; and a recently acquired abandoned motel next to the property would be torn down for a parking lot. Kim figured the old motel rooms, many with their doors already removed for demolition, afforded an ideal place for a cat to hole up with her kittens. She spent a few hours searching the dilapidated ruin and calling, before Church Cat finally answered. One of the rooms was full of old furniture and mattresses, and Church Cat was using it as a quiet nursery for her four Palm Sunday kittens.

For a week, Kim and Carol Ann took food down to the room, and Kim snuck down to check on her once every day, but for the most part, Church Cat had a week alone with her babies. The next Sunday, after church, the children found her. They were standing around the lawn, talking about Church Cat and her babies, when one of them spotted her slinking around the old motel. About six kids, all younger than six, followed her to the room where her kittens were mewling and stumbling all over one another. Carol Ann arrived quickly enough to make sure the children didn't do anything but ogle and coo, but by the next day, Church Cat had left the motel.

There are times, as I well know, when it's good to have a strong network of friends. When you are being unfairly maligned. When you face a personal challenge. When the board tries to throw your community's beloved cat out of the library. Fortunately, Carol Ann had a strong social network in Camden, and one of her acquaintances lived across the street and a few doors down from the church. This young woman watched from her front porch as Church Cat carried her kittens, one by one by the scruff of the neck, across Broad Street and into the second-floor window of a beat-up old house.

The young woman called Carol Ann. Carol Ann called Kim Knox. Together, they decided they better move those kittens before the owner of the house came back. Nobody had lived in the house for years, but Carol Ann knew the owner was storing stuff inside. He was a fine man, but she wasn't sure how he'd react if he discovered the kittens. With the entire underage congregation of Camden United Methodist Church eagerly anticipating the return of Church Cat, she didn't want to take any chances.

"I don't break the law as a rule," Kim told me, "but there are times when you just have to." So a few days later, Kim Knox found herself crawling through the first-floor window of an abandoned house, on a main street a mere block from downtown Camden, while Carol Ann waited outside, amazed that a fine, upstanding woman like herself was standing watch during a trespass.

There must have been a point, perhaps halfway through the window, as she stretched to find the floor hidden in the darkness, when Kim wondered what she was doing. She was a law-abiding citizen. She was a church secretary. She was wearing her nice work clothes, for goodness' sake. And here she was, breaking and entering a dilapidated and possibly dangerous dwelling. She told herself, no doubt, that she was doing it for the children, who needed to know that Church Cat and her kittens were safe. Perhaps she told herself she was doing it for Church Cat, but she must have known a savvy prison tabby like Church Cat didn't need help raising her family. She was really doing it, she must have realized as she stepped into the dusty darkness, for herself.

She went to the back door and let Carol Ann's friend, the young neighbor, into the house, Carol Ann being convinced she was too advanced (in age) for such a perilous mission. "Church Cat," Kim whispered when her companion was inside, trying to disturb nothing more than cobwebs and grime. "Where are you, Church Cat?" Old furniture was scattered in the downstairs rooms, between piles of boxes filled with junk. Even in full daylight, the arrangement seemed dangerous. *It's a tetanus nightmare,* Kim thought as her feet crunched broken glass. The stairs were even less appealing, but eventually they climbed to the second floor and, in the back bedroom, heard Church Cat meowing. When Kim peaked around the corner, the little gray tabby came running to her friend, as sweet and endearing as always.

Like a good mother, Church Cat had found the most comfortable place in downtown Camden for her brood of kittens, a stack of mattresses and box springs piled in a corner. Modern box springs are hollow, but one of these box springs was the old-fashioned sort stuffed full of cotton. Church Cat had hollowed out the stuffing to create a nest. Inside was her smorgasbord of kittens: a solid white one, a solid black one, a calico, and a gray tabby just like his mother.

Kim and the neighbor found a safe place in the middle of the floor and sat down. They waited, whispering occasional encouragement, hoping the kittens would come to them. The mattress was a perfect place to raise a family, but they wanted the kittens to know and trust them, in case they needed to move them out quickly. The first day, Church Cat was the only one who ventured into the center of the room. As always, she was talkative, sweet and eager for attention. Kim stroked her, feeling that good cat warm, and then, after half an hour, she descended the stairs, locked the back door behind her friend, and climbed back out the window.

She came in through the window again the next day, and every day for the next two weeks. There was something compulsive about her desire to check on the cats, something that must have said more about her needs than theirs. But what did that matter? After a few days, the kittens loved her company, too. Like their mother, they came to sniff her hand and be stroked, to accept her as part of their world. All but the gray tabby, who hissed and snarled and then dove back into the cotton-filled box spring whenever Kim made a move in his direction. He was the only male in the litter; perhaps that made him more cautious than the others. Or perhaps, despite looking just like his mother, he was the only cat that hadn't inherited her endearing personality.

During the second week, a rumor reached Carol Ann that the owner of the house was coming back. He was going to fix the place up and sell it. So, for the last time, Kim Knox climbed through the window of the old house to see the kittens. Carol Ann handed her several cat carriers, then went around the back to wait. Kim took the carriers to the upstairs bedroom and, as always, sat on the floor to coax the kittens out. The first one was easy: She came right up. The next two were wiser. They ran around the room a bit, but with the help of the young neighbor, Kim was able to wrangle them into the carriers.

That left only the gray tabby male. Instead of running, he burrowed into the box spring and spat and hissed every time Kim tried to reach him. Each time she failed, he turned and dug himself deeper into the cotton ticking. He dug himself so deep that, eventually, they had to take the whole stack of mattresses apart to reach him. Then they piled them back up, exactly as they had been before. Finally, after almost an hour, Kim handed the cat carriers out the back door to Carol Ann, then locked the door, straightened anything that had been knocked askew and climbed, for the last time, out the first-floor window of the abandoned house. She dropped to the ground, wiped the dust off her nice blouse and skirt, checked both ways to make sure no one was watching, then walked casually across the street to help Carol Ann throw the cat carriers into the back of her car.

Since the kittens were too young to be weaned, Carol Ann had decided not to bring them back to the church. Carol Ann had a cat at home, so the ladies took the kittens to Kim's house, where Church Cat nourished and raised them in the spare bedroom. A few weeks later, when they were weaned, the amused pastor allowed Kim and Carol Ann to put a notice in the church bulletin that the kittens were available for adoption.

They also asked for help paying for Church Cat's spaying, which started a flood of donations, not just for the procedure but for her food and litter as well. After the notice, Kim and Carol Ann never had to pay for Church Cat's expenses again.

The three female kittens, all cute and social like their mother, were adopted quickly. But the fourth kitten, the male tabby, would never come out when potential owners came by. Instead, he hid under the bed, hissing and spitting. If Kim surprised him, he would rear onto his back legs, puff out his fur, hiss viciously in her direction, then take off running the other way.

After the third kitten was adopted, Carol Ann took Church Cat back to Camden United Methodist. Kim and her husband sat on their porch, tired but happy, wondering what to do with the unadoptable male. After half an hour, Kim decided she better check on him, since he was now alone in the bedroom. This time, when she opened the door, the kitten came running to her, meowing and meowing, like he just realized he'd been left behind.

"Well," she said, "you've certainly changed your tune."

She looked at her husband. He rolled his eyes, then smiled and nodded. Church Cat's little gray tabby kitten stayed. They named him Chi-Chi, and although he grew to be bigger and leaner than his mother, without her endearing baby face, he always reminded Kim of her office friend. He was never warm; in fact, he was quite aloof. "But that was just his personality," Kim said. "He was a good, good cat. Just like his mama."

A town is a series of changes, and to live in a town for long is to incorporate those changes into your life. When Carol Ann moved to Camden, the downtown hardware store run by her father-in-law was the hub of commercial life. They sold everything from shovels and biscuits to nails and dinner plates, but also made crop loans and bartered bales of cotton. For a while, they ran the area's only ambulance service and served as the town's funeral home, even employing an undertaker. When Harris went to college, he decided to pass on the hardware store in favor of the bank, but he quit that job two years later when MacMillan-Bloedel, a conglomerate out of Canada, opened a paper mill near town. By the time his father retired, Harris had earned an MBA and was an executive at the mill. The hardware store was sold and became a True Value franchise, selling standard nails and tools, and slowly became threadbare with the rest of downtown. But if you've lived in Camden long enough, and know where to look, you can still see MATTHEW'S HARDWARE written on the old brick wall.

By the time Church Cat arrived, there wasn't much thought of reviving downtown. There wasn't a Walmart for fifty miles, but most of the residents of Camden found a reason to make it out there at least once a month. "My mom couldn't pass a Walmart," Harris told me with a laugh. "Didn't matter what part of the state we were in, or what we were doing, we had to stop." Religion had always been a major part of life in Camden, and even with the downtown falling on hard times, more and more effort and expense went into the four big churches on Broad Street. By the 1990s, in true modern style, each started a series of major renovations, one after another.

The first thing to go at Camden Methodist was the comfortable old parsonage, with its eighty-year history and creaking floorboards, which was sold to a young couple. When the truck came to lift the building off its foundation and haul it away, there was quite a crowd on the church lawn, and a number of teary eyes, especially from the older generation. It was just a small wooden bungalow, simple and plain, but it was built immaculately, and built to last. It sits now in a neighborhood less than a mile from the church, once again filled with the laughter and tears of a young family growing up together.

The old motel, a long-derelict eyesore without a single redeeming feature, was torn down and paved over for a parking lot. The church left only the former restaurant, converting it to a youth center and temporary offices for the church administration. For almost a year, Church Cat and the children coexisted in that space, something that brought joy to both of them. The cat preferred Kim's company, and especially the seat of her comfy office chair, but she also liked to wander out when the children were in the youth center and meow for attention. When the cooing and stroking became too much — the little girl still squealed at the sight of Church Cat, but now the cavernous former restaurant magnified the sound — Church Cat simply scampered away and hid in the kitchen.

In the year after giving birth to her kittens, in fact, Church Cat only got into trouble one time: at the Methodist Charge Meeting. Kim was out of town, and Carol Ann wasn't sure what to do with Church Cat while she worked at the meeting. It was just after Easter, the perfect time of year in southern Alabama, when the evenings are still damp and cool enough to stamp down the day's heat, so she decided to let Church Cat out for the night. Then she hurried off to greet participants in the Charge Meeting, a major event attended by the district superintendent and representatives from other local Methodist churches. Carol Ann, from her spot at the door, made sure Church Cat didn't sneak into the sanctuary as the crowd arrived, but the little tabby must have slipped in with a latecomer because right in the middle of the assembly, she walked straight down the center aisle, meowing for attention.

Carol Ann was mortified. I wish I could write that like she said it — "MAWT-a-fied" — because no one can express social embarrassment like a proper Southern lady. But suffice it to say that Carol Ann was deeply worried about Church Cat barging into the sanctuary during the biggest meeting of the year.

Oh, that's it, she thought, as she hustled Church Cat out the back door. *That's gonna be the end of Church Cat.*

But instead of anger, she heard, behind her from the dais, the sound of laughter. Then the young pastor saying something, and then other people laughing, until Church Cat's mawt-a-fyin' faux pas became not a tragic error, but a funny story to be told again and again around the big lawn at Camden United Methodist Church.

Soon after, the young pastor left. Carol Ann and Kim and many of the other parishioners were sorry to see him go, but the Methodist church rotates pastors on a regular basis, and it was time (according to the national office) for a change. The building project was nearing completion, and without the young pastor, a few whispers and rumors started to filter through to Carol Ann. One person in particular made it clear to all and sundry that he did not want Church Cat inside any of the new buildings.

So Kim and Carol Ann decided to place a notice in the church bulletin: Church Cat was up for adoption. They expected a flood of responses, but after a week, nobody stepped forward. Some in the congregation, of course, had never wanted her around the church, much less their homes. The people who loved her — and there were many — didn't feel it was their place to claim her. Everyone knew Carol Ann had recently lost her beloved cat Hogan and that she was hoping, in her polite Southern style, that no one would step forward for

Church Cat. So they didn't.

And that's how in 2001, less than four years after she walked onto the porch of the parsonage and followed Kim Knox into the church offices, Church Cat's time at Camden United Methodist Church came to an end. She went home to Carol Ann's house, where she took, with a vengeance, to the lazy life of a spoiled and beloved house cat. Kim Knox visited often, and each time she did, her jaw dropped closer to the floor.

"I know, I know," Carol Ann said. "I don't feed her that much. I really don't. I don't know how she got so heavy."

Soon after, the church christened their new buildings. They have, as far as I know, never been defiled by a single hair from a single cat.

Carol Ann states unequivocally that the building project was a good idea, even if it cost Church Cat her home. The church needed a nicer sanctuary, a larger kitchen for Wednesday prayer dinners and the Fifth Sunday Potlucks, and more classrooms for children's Sunday school. The new buildings were for Camden, not just the church members, Carol Ann said. With them, for instance, they could expand their Lenten dinner to the whole town. "We needed new bathrooms, too," Harris added. "There was a desperate need for bathrooms."

Kim Knox agrees the upgrade was a good idea. And, she wanted everyone to know, the buildings are beautiful. Redbrick with white trim, they are immaculately maintained and large enough to accommodate further growth — if the congregation of Camden United Methodist Church, and the town of Camden in general, ever experiences a growth spurt. They are infinitely better than the horrible motel that was torn down. And they are without a doubt more practical and visually pleasing than the former buildings that stood in their place. They are everything a modern, forward-looking church should be.

But Kim Knox can't help thinking something was lost, too. "It is a more structured environment," she said of the new church. "It is less laid-back and relaxed." The old parsonage, where she had worked with Church Cat, was drafty. The only way to heat it was with space heaters, so all winter it smelled of kerosene. The windows rattled. The doors creaked. But even on the coldest day, Kim felt, it had a warmth that came from its long history and worn-down wood, from the sound of a young pastor's laughter echoing out of his office, from the feeling of a sleeping cat pressed against her back as she tried, sometimes in vain, to balance herself on the edge of her chair. And then there was the door creaking open, Church Cat stirring, a warm "Mornin', Kim" followed by an even warmer "meow."

Yes, the new church is beautiful. It is lovingly maintained. It is something that, rightfully, the citizens of Camden can be proud of. But it is just a building. It doesn't have warmth or history. It can't. Not yet, anyway. The new Camden United Methodist Church, to put it another way, is not the kind of place that could ever adopt a cat.

And that's the conundrum of life, whether you eschew progress or embrace it full force: For everything that is gained, there is also something lost.

In some sense, there's a very short distance to go until the end of this story. The only thing left to say, I suppose, is that Church Cat loved her life with Carol Ann, who spoiled her like the doting grandmother she is, but that her life in that home was tragically short. When Church Cat contracted an infection and died in the summer of 2005, at only eight years old, Carol Ann was so distraught, it took her several weeks to tell the congregation. She was the fattest cat you have ever seen, as both Kim and Carol

Ann told me in separate conversations, but also the happiest, and Carol Ann and her husband, Harris, missed her terribly. They buried her in their family plot, alongside generations of ancestors that had lived and died in Wilcox County, Alabama.

The next year, Carol Ann and Harris Riggs moved away. Ms. Hattie, the woman who had lain on the ground to pet Church Cat, and the last of their living parents, had died, and they had long promised themselves that, when they no longer had family responsibility in Camden, they would move somewhere new. When their daughters were young, they had traveled extensively: to the Western United States, to Canada, to Australia. For their retirement, they moved two and a half hours away to Tuscaloosa, Alabama, home of the University of Alabama, where they can watch plays and attend sporting events without having to drive ninety miles home after dark.

They say that's the reason they left Camden, to experience more of life, but it's clear there were other factors as well. Neither one of their daughters wanted to live in the area. They were married, to a lawyer and a federal emergency response director, respectively, and they were both studying for careers in medicine. There were no jobs for them in

Wilcox County.

Meanwhile, the MacMillan-Bloedel paper mill where Harris had worked most of his life was sold first to Weyerhaeuser, then to International Paper. At its height, the mill had employed almost two thousand people from the area. Now Harris estimates it employs four hundred, although he isn't sure. "You know these international companies," he said. "When you retire, they take your name out of the computer, and you're just gone." *Just gone*. It seemed such a minor end to more than a hundred years of Riggs family history in Camden.

And so one story ends, but of course it is not the only story that can be told about Camden. The town is located in the heart of Civil Rights era unrest — forty miles north is Selma, site of the famous march, and thirty miles east is Lowndes County, known as "Bloody Lowndes" for its staunch refusal to register black voters. So there are at least two sets of circumstances in Camden, two histories, two views of the world. If you asked someone else about Camden, Alabama, especially a longtime black resident, you would no doubt hear a different story from the one you've read today.

But there are always other stories to tell. I haven't set out to provide a history of a town but simply to tell the story of Church Cat, who stayed four cherished years at Camden United Methodist and died as she had always lived, with Ms. Carol Ann Riggs by her side. That seems simple enough, and I have tried my best to tell the story as Ms. Carol Ann told it to me. But even something as seemingly straightforward as the life of Church Cat, as I well know, is filled with personal meanings and interpretations.

Nothing made that more clear than my three conversations, spaced over a series of months, with Carol Ann's good friend Kim Knox. Kim, you see, had a different view of Church Cat. A view not based on Church Cat's actions but on the fact that she was terribly unhappy after her move to Camden, a town she had never even heard of until her husband got a job teaching school there. She loved the town and the people but, as the Bible says, it was a time of trial. Her mother died just after she moved, and without any friends in the area, she had no one to confide in. Even worse, after years of trying, she learned she would never be able to have a child.

This was not like Mary Nan Evans with her twenty-eight cats on Sanibel Island. Mary Nan told me, with no hesitation, that she never regretted not being able to have children. She is older than Kim, and therefore further from the disappointment, but I don't think that was the reason for her lack of regret. Having children, it seemed, was never integral to Mary Nan's life. It wasn't something she ever needed to be happy.

Kim Knox was different. I could hear that clearly in her voice. Kim Knox desperately wanted children. She needed them, and it was a crushing blow when she found out she was unable to have them. She and her husband tried every fertility treatment short of in vitro fertilization, which they couldn't afford. They researched adoption, but after more than a year of phone calls and meetings, they realized that even the cheaper alternatives were beyond their modest means. There was no single moment, Kim said, when the reality hit her. There were no breakdowns in the office; no sobs in the night; no dark mornings when Church Cat's presence lifted her spirits just as her strength collapsed. There were tears with her husband, many thousands of them, but the emotional process was a gradual chipping away of her hopes, a slow and crushing collapse of all her dreams, not a sudden surrender, and Church Cat's contribution was a constant affection, a daily warmth, more than one unforgettable act.

But that affection was important, more than Carol Ann or even I can understand. To Kim, Church Cat wasn't just a cute cat. She was a source of comfort and strength. She was a friend Kim could put her maternal compassion and energy into when she had nowhere else to place it.

Be present. That's the advice for helping people in pain. Be present *for them,* whatever they need. That, in a nutshell, was Church Cat.

And just as important, through that little cat, Kim built a local community of support. Through her, Kim became friends with Carol Ann Riggs and ultimately confided in her. With the help of the strewn papers and torn-up toilet paper, she developed the kind of warm, lighthearted relationship with the young pastor that allowed her to finally, in the quiet of the parsonage with only Church Cat as a witness, unburden her heart.

Does that change the story of Church Cat? Does it explain why a professional woman would spend her lunch break climbing through the window of an abandoned house? I don't know. Kim's husband, who was older, was on his second marriage and second career, as a schoolteacher. He had a son from a previous marriage, but the boy had been seriously ill his whole life. In 1999, as Church Cat was birthing her kittens in an old motel, the boy's doctors recommended a transplant. Kim's husband donated a kidney. He and Kim both understood that the time, physical recovery, and expense meant the end of their last faint hope of ever adopting a child of their own. But it was something they never hesitated to do. I cannot help but believe that when Kim Knox sat in that abandoned bedroom, softly encouraging Church Cat's kittens to trust her, that she was taking a turn at motherhood. That she was being comforted by those soft little lives. That she was grieving, in her way, for what she could never have.

Then, in August 2002, Kim received a call from the young, now former pastor of Camden United Methodist Church. A woman had come to see him, the pastor told her. Her niece knew a young woman who could not afford to keep her baby. She was seven months' pregnant, and she was searching for someone to adopt him.

Eight weeks later, in October 2002, Kim Knox drove five hours to meet the mother. She brought nothing but one change of clothes and a child's car seat, still in the box. She refused to buy anything else. She was terrified, after all those years of struggle, that something would go wrong.

Two days later, she was in the delivery room when her adopted son, Noah, entered the world. The mother spoke no English, but she begged Kim in broken syllables and gestures to stay with her in the recovery room, to let her hold, for a moment, the newborn baby. They saw the mother again when the boy was eleven months old. They drove to Birmingham, a few hours from Camden, to meet her. The woman cried, smiled, thanked them in broken English, hugged her child, and then disappeared. Kim could feel her heartbreak, almost as strongly as she had felt her own. But where she went, or why, Kim has no idea.

"We were so thrilled when we met Noah," Ms. Carol Ann said. "He was the cutest thing. The whole congregation absolutely loved him."

In 2005, Kim and her husband moved back to Laurel, Mississippi, Kim's hometown. They loved Camden, but they had no relatives in the area, and they wanted to raise their boy surrounded by family. They moved just two months before Hurricane Katrina. Although they were a hundred miles from the coast, they watched in horror from their aunt Lee's house as trees shattered and toppled. They clutched their child and hoped that Church Cat's son, Chi-Chi, who they had left in their nearby rental cottage, survived the storm.

He did, but that is yet another story. Suffice it to say, for this story, that Church Cat wasn't just a pretty face, that her love gave Kim Knox, and perhaps others in Camden, a calming presence in times of need. And that Kim Knox, with the help of a gentle cat and a kindly pastor, survived her time of trials and saw her dreams of motherhood come true. And that Church Cat's son, Chi-Chi, although never a friendly cat like his mother, loved his little brother Noah with a ferocity that surprised even Kim, who will forever appreciate the warmth and intelligence of cats.

NINE
DEWEY AND RUSTY

"I was lying upside down on the front seat with my head under the dashboard and I felt something on my chest. I looked up and here's this little orange and white kitty cat. Estimated age six to eight weeks. And he was on my chest meowing. I looked up and said, 'Well, hey, Rusty, how are you?' I petted him, and he laid right down on my

chest, and he just stayed there. He never left."

PART I

For those of us in northwest Iowa, Sioux City is the hub of activity. We go there for Christmas shopping, for theatre and entertainment, for business meetings and dancing and advanced medical care. The big city, we mutter in Spencer, shaking our heads. Railroad town, we say, because you can't drive three miles in Sioux City without crossing a railroad track. Too crowded. Too much traffic.

But that's not entirely true. The truth is that Sioux City is just different from the rest of the world out here on the high plains. Towns here are mostly flat, sunny, and open to the sky. Sioux City is dense, industrial, and tall, full of church steeples and factory towers. It's one of those old towns, like Pittsburgh or Cleveland, that seems to have been carved by brute force out of the ground. Pittsburgh had steel. Cleveland had oil. Sioux City was built for cattle. They came a thousand head at a time down the Missouri River or on overland trails to be penned and fattened and slaughtered in the raw brick factories along the river, then shipped back out on railroad cars.

The Missouri River, the reason for the location of the town, brought other things as well: granite, grain, steel, hides, and the men who raised and built and transported them. Downtown Sioux City featured the best restaurants and hotels in the region. The warehouses of Lower Fourth Street, on the edge of downtown, were the center of vice — mostly the liquid kind — for a hundred miles around. The workingmen's homes stretched into the hills carved by the river and its tributaries, punctuated by Catholic and Orthodox churches for the mainly Eastern European immigrants building the city one stone at a time. On a bluff sat the octagon, an old steamboat captain's house, built so he could watch the river. On the highest hill, Rose Hill, were the mansions of the slaughter bosses and factory owners, built mostly of the rough-hewn Sioux Falls granite that was always being shipped down the river and moved out to the rest of the world.

Glenn Albertson grew up in a working-class neighborhood on the edge of Rose Hill, in the days when the factories were humming, the riverboats were running, and every ten blocks of closely built four-room houses and four-story apartment buildings felt like its own world. Glenn's family moved often, but they always seemed to end up near Pierce Street, where the storefronts were feet from the road and often attached at the back to Victorian-era boardinghouses. In the 1950s, when Glenn was growing up, there were bakeries, barbershops, and locally owned grocery stores on almost every corner. The kids played stickball, rode bikes, and walked to school, even in the brutally cold Sioux City winter. In the summer, they congregated on the sidewalk, watching the big color television in the window of Williams Television & Appliance Store.

They were self-sufficient, the kids of Pierce Street. Their fathers worked in the factories. Most of their mothers worked to support the family in "women's jobs" like waitressing, sewing, and housekeeping that were the secret backbone of Midwestern America. As the family drifted through apartments, Glenn's mother worked for a catering company, cooked for a local restaurant, and waitressed at the coffee shop in the Warrior, the grand old hotel that had been a fixture of downtown Sioux City since 1930. Eventually, she found a permanent position running the kitchen at a retirement home for women. She cooked breakfast, lunch, and dinner, with special requests taken. She started cooking at dawn and rushed home every afternoon, because she knew that as soon as her husband opened the door, he'd boom, "Is there anyone who can cook around here?" Then he'd smile and envelope her in a hug. She always had a meal ready for him, too.

Glenn's father worked at the Albertson Tool Company. The name wasn't a coincidence. Glenn Albertson, Sr., a soldier from the stone-quarry region of southern Indiana, married Christel Mai, a farm girl from the small town of Pierce, Nebraska, at the end of World War II. They tried to make a life in rural Nebraska but soon moved to Sioux City, about seventy miles away, in search of job opportunities. Glenn, Sr., saw a notice about the Albertson Tool Company and decided, with a name like that, the company must be his destiny. He worked at Albertson Tool, manufacturing air and electrical tools, for a few decades before leaving to become the best commercial painter around.

Glenn, Sr., was a "man's man," stern and strong. He worked hard labor, and he worked it hard. He stood six feet tall with two hundred fifty pounds of muscle molded by his hours lifting hammers and steel. Days, he shaped tools at the Albertson company; nights, he was a bartender and bouncer on Lower Fourth Street, the gin-joint district on the edge of downtown. He was a gregarious man with a lot of buddies, and it wasn't uncommon for him to disappear with them for days on end. By the time Glenn, Jr., was nine years old, he knew just about every bartender in the Lower Fourth ward.

"Sit down, kid, and have a strawberry pop," they'd say. "I'll find your dad for you." It wouldn't be long before Glenn's father would walk in and clap his son on the back, bags under his eyes and a rumpled smile on his face, but otherwise hardly worse for wear.

"Let's go home," he'd say. "I'm hungry."

By eighteen, Glenn, Jr., was six feet four and two hundred sixty-five hard pounds. He was even bigger than his father, but everyone called him Tiny. When the school principal introduced him before the big football game, Glenn came out carrying the smallest guy in the school in the palm of his hand. The kid jumped down, slapped him five, and everybody laughed. Glen was a gentle giant, the big man on campus (if by campus you mean Pierce Street), and a friend to all.

Six months later, he was married, a proud (if accidental) papa, not quite graduated from high school but already pumping gas and repairing cars. The gas station where he worked was near the highest point of Court

Street, a few blocks from where he grew up. From the front of the lot, he could see the ten-story buildings downtown. Beyond them, hidden from view, were the Missouri River and Lower Fourth Street, where his father spent his afternoons in the company of other hardworking men. Behind him, less than a mile away, his mother labored over the stoves of Rose Hill. When he left the gas station, he walked the same blocks he had always walked, where the kids still rode their bikes to the corner shops for soda pops and candy even if they didn't congregate on the corner to watch television through the appliance store window anymore. It was the 1960s. Most of them had their own televisions now.

Glenn was content. He wanted nothing more than to be a good father to his boy. He was home every night to tuck him into bed. He read him books and explained how motors worked and told him that he loved him, that he was there for him, whatever he needed. He nearly froze that first winter at the gas station, with the continuous blanket of snow and the cold wind of the Upper Midwest blasting him day after day. He took a second job as a fry cook, for the extra money, but also to keep warm. After a few years, he gave up the gas station for the temperate environment of the assembly line at Sioux Tools, formerly the Albertson company.

In his spare time, he trained to be a cop. There was no police academy in Sioux City in those days. Studying to be a policeman meant experiencing it, strictly volunteer, with a senior officer. Glenn rode in a squad car for a year. He called on domestic disturbances. He was in car chases. He talked angry, drunk, and angry-drunk people out of foolish decisions. He was good. But police work didn't pay. So when his second son was born, he took a job at his father-in-law's insurance office. He was even better at selling insurance, he soon realized, than he had been at police work. He knew how to put people at ease. He was enormous, but he wasn't intimidating. I am reminded of the words used to describe a commander from the Second World War, who also happened to be from Iowa: "[He] was a leader — quiet, unselfish, modest, yet very strong . . . One believed what he said; one wanted to do what he proposed." You wanted to buy, in other words, what Glenn Albertson was selling — whether it was an insurance policy or a Sunday school lesson — because you believed in him. And you knew he believed what he said. Glenn Albertson, people could see right away, was a stand-up guy.

Honesty and openness served him well, and by the time Glenn was thirty, he was making seventy thousand dollars a year selling insurance. He had a house in the suburbs on the far side of Rose Hill, with four bedrooms, a huge deck, and a white fence that ran all the way around the yard. There was peewee football with his oldest son, Indian Guides with his middle boy, and his infant daughter to hold in his arms in the still of the night and wonder at the miracle of life. His wife tended to use the smoke alarm for her cooking timer, so Glenn often prepared the evening meals, too. He took his boys with him everywhere: on errands to the gas station or the grocery store, and almost every Saturday to the garage where he rebuilt the hot rod cars he liked to race. He even had a big happy dog named Maggie. The boys would run around with her in the neatly trimmed backyard while Glenn laughed from his big back porch and turned the burgers on the grill.

On Sunday, they went to church. Not a new-style megachurch but an old-fashioned church in a building that was beautiful for its simplicity and modesty. The services were no-frills, and the community was so small, Glenn became the Sunday school teacher for every kid in the congregation, from toddler to twelfth grade. Only three boys were interested in the basketball team, so Glenn recruited a few kids from the neighborhood, who turned out to be a Sioux City melting pot of Greek, African American, and Native American, and told them they could play basketball as long as they attended church every Sunday. Those boys became Glenn's extended family, too. There was nothing, Glenn Albertson would have said, that hard work and a good attitude and genuine love couldn't solve.

And then his daughter Kari got a fever.

She was only six months old, and the girls in Sunday school loved to hold her. It was a typical bone-cold winter Sunday, all fifteen kids running ragged, when one of the girls came over to Glenn and said, "Kari's hot."

Glenn felt his baby's head. It was burning. "I'm taking her home," he said.

He trundled the boys into the car and started up Rose Hill. It was snowing heavily, and the world was hazy and white. Coming around the last corner, Glenn could barely make out the vehicle blocking his driveway. He pulled around to the front, tucked his daughter deep into a blanket, and ran her up to the door.

He couldn't reach his keys with his daughter in his arms, so he rang the doorbell. His wife was home sick, so she should have been able to let them in, but she didn't answer.

He rang again. The boys were at his side, shivering in their heavy jackets. He pulled the blanket close around his daughter. No answer.

He rang. And rang. And rang.

Finally, the door opened. It wasn't his wife. It was one of his best friends.

"Where's my wife?" he said.

"She's in the shower," his friend said.

The marriage was over at that very moment. The trust — the bedrock of Glenn's existence — was gone. He hung around for a few months, never talked about what had happened, but the white fence and the four-bedroom house and the happy life had all dissolved into the cold of that snowy Sunday morning.

They got divorced. He moved out of the house and into a bachelor apartment, hardly a stick of furniture in the place. Soon after, he arrived early at the insurance office, to discover that his key no longer worked. His former in-laws had changed the locks.

He went back to what he knew. His father-in-law had filed to have Glenn's insurance license revoked, so Glenn spent his days underneath cars, managing the service department at an auto dealership. He spent his nights on Lower Fourth Street, working as a bouncer and a bartender down the block from the place where his dad held court with a bottle in his hand. The second job was for the attorney's fees to fight for custody of his children, but in the early 1970s, in Sioux City, Iowa, fathers weren't considered rightful parents. He lost his kids, except for Sunday visitation. He lost his house. He lost his dog. He had a lot of friends, but he lost most of them in the divorce, too. He hated explaining himself, he said; he'd rather be alone. A stray cat, Chloe, showed up at his apartment and kept him company. She was a bit standoffish, but she'd curl up in his lap sometimes. Not all the time, but every now and then.

About a year later, Glenn's oldest boy called him on a Saturday afternoon. That was rare. His boys didn't talk to him much anymore.

"Mom's drinking," the boy said in his small child's voice. "There are motorcycles in the yard."

Glenn jumped in his car. When he pulled up at his former house, he saw four motorcycles on the lawn and a few more on the sidewalk. A biker stepped out of the front door and said, "Who the hell are you?"

"I'm her ex-husband," Glenn said, standing in the middle of the yard.

"Then you better go."

"I'm just here for my kids."

A couple more bikers stepped onto the porch. Two of them stepped down to the lawn. "I don't want any rash judgments," Glenn said, holding out his empty hands. "There are children in that house, and I just want them safe."

There was a kid's baseball bat lying in the grass. Glenn didn't notice it until one of the bikers picked it up and stepped toward him. When he started to swing, Glenn didn't run. Instead, he stepped in, ripped the bat from the biker's hand, and brought it down on the man's knee. His friends leapt off the porch. If there had been one more of them, or if they'd been sober, Glenn might have been in trouble. But as a bouncer, he knew how to handle drunks. Before he had time to think, a second biker was on the ground with a dislocated elbow, and the other two were kicking their rides into gear. Glenn threw down the baseball bat, walked into his old house, retrieved his children, and drove them back to his apartment.

Three hours later, a policeman knocked on his door. It was an officer Glenn knew from his days in training.

Glenn told him the story. The policeman said, "Well, Glenn, that's fine, but her parents are there now, and you need to take those kids home, because there's a kidnapping charge filed against you."

After that, life in Sioux City became unbearable for Glenn Albertson.

One day, when he was still working for his father-in-law's insurance business, an older man had stopped Glenn on the street. "Just wanted to tell you, young man," he said, checking out Glenn's suit, "that you look pretty sharp. You got a minute?"

"Yes, I do," Glenn said.

They sat down together. The man was filthy and disheveled, wearing a tattered cream-colored suit. His shoes hadn't been shined in a long, long time.

"I used to be a banker," the older man said, handing Glenn a business card. It read VICE PRESIDENT, FIRST NATIONAL BANK OF CHICAGO. "My father was a banker, and his father was a banker before him. Everyone I associated with was a banker. That's all I knew. But when the Depression hit, my bank went under. I lost my job." Glenn nodded and waited.

"What do you do, young man?"

"I sell insurance."

"Well, I'm going to tell you something in case that doesn't work out for you: Learn as much about as many things as you can, because that way you will never have trouble finding a job."

Glenn thanked the man for the advice and handed him back his business card, along with some loose change. He never saw him again, and he never knew if the man had really been a banker or was just an old drunk with a business card, but his words stuck with him. Glenn never went to college, but he became a student of life. When his boys were young, he learned to cut hair at barber school. He knew police work and security. He could sell insurance, tend bar, and fix just about any make or model of car. He knew carpentry, plumbing, and just enough electrical to get out of trouble. "Learn to do." That was his motto. "Learn *and* do" was his creed. But he had been born in a place where it was a short, easy path to the bottom and a long, hard road to the top, and if ever there was a time when he could have taken the lower path, it was after his divorce. He was angry enough, and hurt enough, to throw it away in a bottle of booze. Because it's easy to learn a new trade, but it's hard to learn a new way of life. And when the going got hard, the men of Pierce Street hit the bars. Glenn? He may have worked on Lower Fourth, but he spent his nights in a diner near his apartment instead of on a barstool. Three years later, he married a waitress there and moved with her to St. Petersburg, Florida.

"There were too many ghosts," he said of his decision to leave Sioux City. "Too many people running around thinking they knew something. I just got tired."

In Florida, Glenn worked construction, until the owner of the gym where he worked out, seeing how popular he was, offered him a job. Within a year, he was managing the place: selling memberships, changing pool filters, repairing the hot tub. He went to classes for six months and became a certified massage therapist. He worked seven days a week, not just for the money but because he was a blue-collar guy from Sioux City, Iowa, and he loved hard work.

When the investors pulled out, and the health club shut down, Glenn moved his family to Texas, where a friend had a contract to repaint the Dallas city schools. He was thirty-five years old, and he didn't have a single key on his key ring. No house. No apartment. No bank account. He didn't even own a car. But he had the important things: a wife, a new baby son, and a family dog. It was never about the job for Glenn Anderson. He could be happy doing just about anything. It was about having a family. They were all Glenn needed to feel at home.

But Texas wasn't home. Florida had never been home either. Not really. Home was Sioux City, Iowa, where his parents had eventually purchased a small white house on a busy corner, and his kids from his first marriage were growing up in his old four-bedroom split-level ranch without him. After a few years, when the painting contract expired, Glenn and his new family moved back to northwest Iowa: back to the cold winters, the hard granite, and the questions from old friends. He went back to his old line of work, repairing cars. His wife drove regularly to visit her parents in Michigan, always taking their son along. The trips were a financial hardship, and he missed his boy terribly, but Glenn didn't mind since it kept his wife happy. He was a year away, he figured, from the white picket fence, the big backyard, and the family home.

Her cousin was the one who spilled the beans. "She's seeing her old high school boyfriend, you know," the cousin told him. "She never got over him."

Glenn didn't know. Despite the collapse of his first marriage, Glenn Albertson was still too honest and trusting to consider the possibility that his second wife was cheating on him, too.

At least this time, he was warned. When his wife told him she was moving to Michigan and taking their child, Glenn didn't ask why. He didn't fight for his boy because he knew from experience that was a battle he couldn't win. They just split the sheets and moved on.

He tried one more time. This time he married a friend, a woman he had known for more than ten years. He might have loved her, and she said she loved him, so marrying her seemed like a good thing to do. They weren't young, so they started trying to have a child right away. After a few years of heartache and stress, she got pregnant. Then she lost the baby. For a month, they held each other and cried. Then the doctor told them she wouldn't get another chance; they would never have a child of their own. It was devastating news.

They took in foster children, infants and young kids but also older kids who had been shuffled through the system and were desperate to form attachments to someone. Foster parenting was rewarding, but it was also hard. Glenn would dedicate himself to a child, work to create safety and security and a feeling of family, become strongly bonded and invested in his or her life, and then watch the child ushered away, often for reasons he couldn't comprehend. They fostered eleven children. Eleven stints of joy; eleven heartbreaks. The twelfth, they decided to adopt. She was a full-blood Sioux, born to a young mother unable to care for her, and Glenn was at the hospital the day she entered the world. As soon as he saw her, he knew she was the one. His heart just opened and gobbled her up. His wife knew it, too. This is what she had been waiting for: a daughter of her own. They named her Jenny, and when they held her, it was like the world closed around them and was complete.

Or so Glenn thought. He didn't understand the real state of his marriage until he came home early one day and overheard his wife talking to her mother in the kitchen.

"I don't need him now," he heard his wife say.

"Then get rid of him," her mother replied. "You have your daughter, and you can get his money. What more do you want?"

"Nothing."

With that one word, another door slammed shut on Glenn Albertson, in his life and in his heart. He was fifty years old, he had been married to three women for a total of twenty-four years, and what did he have to show for it? All his life, he had wanted nothing more than love, nothing more than a family. *I'm not going to do it anymore,* he told himself. He was done.

There are a million ways for a man to get knocked down. Not down for the count, but knocked down hard enough that when he gets back up, he isn't the man he was before. Maybe he's better. Maybe he's worse. Maybe he's worse for a while, then he gets better, and he ends up better than he ever would have been. Or maybe he gets up staggering, wounded beyond repair. After all, if there are a million ways to get knocked down, there are at least a thousand ways to get back up.

You think about things like that in northwest Iowa, a region that's been knocked down more than a few times over the years. In my lifetime, the biggest blow was to the family farm. My father was a proud descendant of a line of farmers, but in the 1950s the advent of enormous threshers and reapers changed both the nature and finances of farming. Unable to afford the big machines, our production held steady against falling prices, undercutting our family's foundation. Eventually, my father was forced to sell out to a neighbor, who cut down our trees, knocked down our house, and plowed under our land.

In Sioux City, the same forces — the consolidation and industrialization of farming and ranching — caused changes almost as drastic. When the Missouri River was the primary artery of the Upper Midwest, the town was a major transportation hub, a rough-and-tumble crossroads where cowboys and boat captains met whiskey and women. The stockyards were some of the busiest in the world, and even in a town of 120,000 people, the cows often outnumbered the citizens ten to one. The slaughter-boss mansions on Rose Hill were built of solid granite, but so were the churches. Even Central High School, built of Sioux Falls granite in 1893, was a castle, complete with towers and turrets.

But after World War II, the Missouri River began to lose its pull. Highways replaced railroads and steamboats, decentralizing agricultural production and driving ranchers and farmers closer to their home fields. The town flooded repeatedly, until a major project was finally undertaken to change the flow of the tributaries meeting the Missouri. The slaughter business declined, along with the factories that supported it and, eventually, the population. Sioux City shrank from 120,000 people to 100,000, then down to 90,000. The airport closed a gate, dropping to a few flights a day. In time, the downtown would be revitalized and Lower Fourth Street turned into a high-end shopping and entertainment district, with even the former El Forastero motorcycle clubhouse converted to pricey condominiums. But outside downtown, the ice still cracked the steep roads, no matter how often they were repaved, and the Arctic wind tore through the storefronts on Pierce Street. Most of the Rose Hill mansions were cut up into apartments. Sioux Tools closed down. The bakery on the corner across from Glenn's parents' house became a late-night convenience store, its lights blaring out over the shoddy gas pumps until 3:00 A.M. Glenn's father, a hard-drinking, hard-laughing, hardworking man of old Sioux City, developed an inoperable tumor on his liver.

Years earlier, before Glenn had his own family, his father had moved out. Glenn never knew why; he assumed it had something to do with alcohol. For a while, he thought he'd never see his father again. But when Glenn Albertson, Sr., came back three years later, he was a new man. Still a drinker and a worker, but kinder and more understanding. More appreciative of what he had at home. He romanced his wife into falling in love with him again, remarried her, and they were happy for the rest of his life. He won over his son again — Glenn had always loved his father, no matter what — and now cherished their relationship. Even when he was away in Florida and Texas, Glenn called his father every week. After his third divorce, they started a painting business together, often sharing hotel rooms for weeks at a time. They painted McGuire Air Force Base in Trenton, New Jersey. They painted the high school in Madison, Nebraska, including Glenn's beautiful freehand mural of a dragon, the school's mascot. When he saw Donnelly Marketing in South Sioux City, Glenn thought they'd never finish. The building was a block square and three stories high, without windows. Working side by side, just the two of them, they finished the job in only three months, complete with hand-lettering.

But the most important job Glenn ever worked was painting his father's beloved 1984 Buick LeSabre after a hailstorm. For a week, Glenn banged out every dent while his father leaned against the wall and watched. He painted the car burgundy, slowly and exactly, even removing the gold pinstripe his father hated and replacing it with a metallic maroon. When Glenn was done, his father took the car out and showed it to all his friends. He was so amazed at what his son had done — so proud — that he wanted everyone to see it. Glenn had fought for approval all his life, and he'd finally won it at forty. A few years later, Glenn Albertson, Sr., died.

Shortly thereafter, Glenn moved in with his mother. They were both in transition: Christel Albertson from life as a wife, Glenn from decades of trying to be a husband and father. Glenn ran errands for his mother, made repairs around the house, and occasionally cooked a meal, even though his mother was by far the best cook in the neighborhood. His room was a monk's cell, as he called it: a bed, a dresser, no radio or television, nothing on the walls. At night, he played guitar, fingering the frets for a few minutes while he developed those old calluses, the ones that help you bend the chords. During the day, he worked on New Car Row, the three blocks of Sixth Street between the railroad tracks where all the car dealerships had their showrooms. As the years passed, he worked at almost every dealership on the strip, taking comfort in the routine of inspecting, diagnosing, taking apart, and putting together.

And if a Porsche had to be driven fast every now and then, just to test it for a client, well then, Glenn never complained.

He saw his adopted daughter, Jenny, every Sunday for church, followed by whatever the little girl wanted — ice cream, a walk in the park, a carousel ride. He called his other children, sent them cards on their birthdays, tried to stay in touch, but they rarely returned his calls. He felt the shame of their denial of his love, and he took his share of the blame for failing to be the father he had always meant to be. Eventually, when his guitar didn't give him the answers he was looking for, he started counseling. He became a regular at a support group for divorced fathers, sitting in the smoke of a dozen cigarettes and hearing stories of other fathers who had been thrown out . . . or who had thrown it away. He spoke slowly, in a deep voice, offering comfort more than advice, and rarely discussing his own circumstances. One night, he mentioned that playing music had been one of the great joys of his life, and the nun who ran the group asked him to bring his guitar. He played in front of an audience, a group of misplaced husbands and forgotten fathers, for the first time in years.

Soon after, while jogging with a neighbor's

dog down a country road, he noticed a flat-bed truck edging into a grove of trees.

"What's going on?" he asked the driver.

"Farmer's got an old car in there. We're going to cut down some trees, haul her out, take her to the crusher."

Glenn recognized the rusted shell: a 1953 Studebaker Commander. Seeing those curved lines, even half hidden in the trees, brought back childhood memories. Not of Sioux City, where Glenn spent the school year, but of his grandmother's rural home-town of Pierce, Nebraska, where he had spent his summers. Pierce was a sleepy crossroads town of less than a thousand people, the kind of place where the men drove jalopies, the women baked pies, and the neighbor across the street from his grandmother's house still mowed his lawn with a team of horses. From any room in his grandmother's house, Glenn could hear the whistle of the steam train when it approached the intersection in the center of town, and he would run to watch it pass in a cloud of smoke. As much as he was Sioux City granite, Glenn Albert-son was summers in Pierce: the long ride on his bike to the fishing hole; the rumble of the cars on the cobblestone streets; the town's one big tree; the town's one cop; the close-ness of a people that knew each other (and were often related, if not by blood, then by their German heritage) and pulled through life together, working a neighbor's farm one summer when the man fell sick and never asking for a dime.

His grandmother spent her days in the kitchen, talking to Glenn in a steady patter that mixed German and English the way her hands mixed flour and butter. She was never comfortable with English, so Glenn wrote her letters that she read over and over to study the language. The afternoons were spent waiting for his grandfather. Even in his sixties, the man worked long days as a carpenter, and if the first thing he did when he arrived home was grab a Salem cigarette and water the garden, Glenn knew he was worn out. If he left his 1941 Studebaker in the driveway instead of the garage, Glenn knew they were going fishing. Glenn would hold the poles, the ends sticking out the window and his dog, Spook, barking in the backseat as the gray Studebaker stormed down the dusty country roads.

When Glenn wasn't in his grandmother's kitchen, he was next door at the auto repair shop. Watching the mechanic there dismantle motors, Glenn fell in love with cars. By ten, he was driving his grandfather's Studebaker. By twelve, he knew exactly how the car worked. Across the street from the repair shop was a salvage yard, owned by the mechanic's brother, and Glenn would ride along on trips to tow tractors and trucks out of backfields and break them down for parts. One day, the tow truck passed a car lot and there, shining in the sun, was a 1953 Studebaker Commander. *Someday I'm gonna get one of those,* Glenn promised himself.

It wasn't just the idea of owning a sporty car, something that said "I'm a man" to every right-minded American boy. It was the idea of making it, of being successful, of living a life a boy would be proud of. But it was also, all those years later on a country road outside Sioux City, the idea of home. There was something about a 1953 Studebaker Commander that was tied up with memories of apple strudel and fishing holes and Spook the dog in his little wagon being pulled behind a young boy's bike.

"I want that car," Glenn told the driver of the flatbed truck.

"I don't think so, friend," the driver said. "That car is rusted through. Hasn't run in years."

"I still want it," Glenn said. A few hours later, the Commander was sitting in a garage just down the street from Glenn's mother's house. That afternoon, Glenn must have circled it twenty times, just following the lines with his eyes. It was as bad as the flat-bed driver had said. Maybe worse. Glenn knew he'd found the project of a lifetime.

The first thing he did was sand off the rust. There's nothing like an outer layer of ne-glect, that old dead skin, to make a car seem beyond repair. Chip away the rust, and you know what you have left. Holes can be fixed easier than people imagine. You just have to take the time to figure out where they are and how deep they go. Glenn took the time. He ground every spot of rust, until he was staring at the metal below. Then he repaired the holes. The 1953 Studebaker Commander is a mid-century sportster, reminiscent of the cars Sean Connery drove in the old James Bond movies, and Glenn bonded and sanded the car until the body was smoothly curved and secret-agent sleek.

He removed the engine. Then he disman-tled the block so that the bent, broken, and rusted pieces could be inspected and thrown out if need be. He worked slowly, attending his divorced-fathers meetings in the eve-nings, fingering his guitar at night, saving his money for parts. He bought intake valves from an old Ford; exhaust valves from an Oldsmobile; pistons from a vintage Chevro-let. He'd walk out of the garage, light a cigarette, and stare into the night sky, thinking of his grandmother's kitchen and his father's beloved Buick. After a while, he'd snuff his butt and head back to work, grinding down fenders or scrubbing out cylinders. He worked every crevice, checked every flap and valve. It took more than a year, but when the engine block went back into the Studebaker, it was completely rebuilt and spotless.

His next task was to hook it all up. The drive shaft, crank shaft, wheel axles, steering column, everything had to work together. Glenn scrubbed out and rebuilt the connections bolt by bolt and joint by joint. Two years into the project, the key turned in the ignition, the engine revved, and the wheels rolled. He took the car to the corner store. He drove it to a divorced-fathers meeting, his guitar shoved in the backseat, and showed it off to his daughter Jenny, although he wouldn't take her for a drive. Not yet — the car was still too dangerous. There were brake lights but only a partial electrical system, no paint on the sanded body. It may not have been pretty — not yet — but the Studebaker could breathe again.

A few weeks later, Glenn was under the dashboard, humming to himself and working on the wiring, when he felt something drop onto his chest. He looked up — nearly banging his head on the underside of the dash — straight into the eyes of an orange and white cat. The kitten was small, probably six or seven weeks old, and he was staring at Glenn with his head cocked to the side. Glenn had no idea where the kitten came from, but there was something about the color of his fur that reminded him of the Studebaker when they pulled it out of the weeds.

"Well, hey, Rusty, how are you?" he said, petting the kitten softly on the head.

The cat nuzzled Glenn's palm. Then it went back to staring. Finally, it lay down on Glenn's chest and began to purr. After a minute, Glenn shrugged and went back to work, the banging of tools and Rusty's rolling purr the only sounds in the empty garage.

The next night, the kitten was waiting when Glenn arrived. When he held out his hand, the cat walked over and rubbed against it. "Good to see you again, Rusty," Glenn said. Rusty looked at him with his head cocked, then meowed. "All right, all right," Glenn said. "I hear you." When Glenn slid under the dash, Rusty once again jumped on his chest and curled up for a nap. The next night, he was there again. After a week, Glenn realized the kitten was sleeping in the

Commander, waiting for him to arrive. He started offering him sandwich meat or bites of his snacks. Rusty sniffed everything avidly; he ate most things aggressively.

"Want to come to my house, Rusty?" Glenn asked one night. He had taken to talking to Rusty like an old friend while he was tinkering. Rusty had gone from staring with that curious head tilt to talking back. The cat always seemed to have something to say.

"Not interested?" Glenn asked when Rusty didn't follow him out the door at the end of the night. "That's fine. I'll see you tomorrow."

Glenn had a way with animals. As a child, he tried to bring home every stray that crossed his path. Jumper, an energetic Labrador, lasted only a few days before Glenn's father took her to a friend's farm. Glenn found a terrier bleeding on the side of the road and carried it to his basement. He gave it water and bandages, and when it survived the night, he named the dog Rocky. A year later, his old owners spotted Rocky playing with Glenn and reclaimed their dog. Soon after, Spook followed Glenn home. When Glenn's parents moved twice without telling him — once to an apartment in the same building, once to a house down the block — it was Spook's barking that told Glenn where to go. In Texas, he even befriended the lion owned by his friend (the lion later went to a zoo, but it was the 1970s; I guess lions lived in suburban Dallas houses back then), and the two of them would ride around together in Glenn's Pontiac Grand Prix, the lion's head hanging out the window on one side, his tail hanging out the other side.

So Glenn wasn't surprised when, a few nights after his first invitation, Rusty followed him home. Unfortunately, Glenn's mother already owned a cat. A mean, ornery, stand-offish cat. The year before, Glenn had found and rescued it after five weeks trapped in an abandoned cistern — it must have licked moisture from the walls and eaten bugs to survive, which is a great story for another time — but still, that cat wouldn't do him any favors. There was no way, just from pure territorial cussedness, it was letting Rusty into the house. Rusty was a good-size kitten, and he was the only one of the two cats with claws, but he wasn't a fighter. Not from fear or submission, he just . . . he didn't have an aggressive personality. He was a "live and let live" kind of cat.

Glenn apologized to Rusty, told him he could go back to the garage with the Commander, but Rusty decided to settle on the porch. He was always there when Glenn went to work, and he was always there when he came home in the evening. After dinner, they would walk together to the garage to work on the Studebaker; Glenn even considered, once or twice, bringing him to a divorced-dads meeting. That summer, the city started major repairs on Court Street, the large road beside Glenn's mother's house, so Rusty and Glenn got in the habit of walking nine blocks through the construction zone to Bill's beer bar. Rusty waited outside while Glenn grabbed a drink. Half the time, when Glenn came out, Rusty had made a friend.

"This your cat?" the woman would ask — and it was almost always a woman.

"Sure is."

"He is so cute. And friendly."

"Yep," Glenn said. "That's Rusty. He's a cool cat."

Eventually, autumn arrived, and the days got shorter. Court Street reopened to traffic, making it too dangerous for Rusty's walks. Glenn joined a band, just a few old friends jamming out the blues, and started spending a few nights away every week. Rusty took to jumping on the porch railing of the house, then onto the kitchen window frame to stare at the warm rooms inside. Every night, as he prepared for bed, Glenn saw Rusty watching him. When they made eye contact, the big orange cat always started meowing and scraping his paw on the glass.

"We've got to let him in, Mom," Glenn said. "It's cold out there."

Glenn's mom wouldn't hear of it, not with the way that cat of hers was behaving. So when a house came up for rent two blocks away, Glenn moved out. The new house was another version of his monk's cell, a small, unfurnished place, but at least Glenn had a roommate this time. He left a window open for Rusty, which the big cat used only when Glenn was gone. When Glenn was home, the cat always hung around. And he was especially partial to people food. Everything Glenn prepared, Rusty sniffed. If he liked the smell, he had to try it. If he liked the taste, he whined until Glenn gave him a plateful. After the dishes were washed, Glenn usually lay down on the sofa so that Rusty could climb up and knead his back with his claws. It was the world's best massage after a hard day of work.

At his mother's house, Glenn had played his guitar every night in bed. Half the time, he'd wake up in the morning and find the guitar cradled in his arms. "That guitar became my best friend," Glenn told me once.

Maybe, if you want to get psychological, that's why Rusty hated the guitar. At first, as soon as Glenn picked it up to practice a few songs, Rusty was out the window.

"It's only rock and roll," Glenn would call after him, laughing as he hit the first chord.

Eventually, Rusty stuck around. Whenever Glenn pulled the guitar out of its case, he sauntered over and stepped inside. Then he'd bat at the lid until it slammed shut. Glenn wasn't sure what the cat did in there, but as long as he played guitar, Rusty stayed in the case. As soon as Glenn opened the case to put his guitar away, Rusty jumped out. When Glenn went to bed, Rusty always climbed in beside him.

Even when Rusty got lazy and stopped accompanying him to the garage, Glenn kept working, painting the Studebaker matte black, not flashy but definitely cool. He still didn't trust all the systems, which had a tendency to misfire, but he no longer worked obsessively on the car either. Instead, Glenn spent more evenings in the backyard with Rusty. The rental was a shotgun close to the street, but the backyard was full of trees, flower beds, and Rusty's favorite: butterflies. At two years old, Rusty was pushing twenty pounds, and he was a gentle giant, too. He might hurt a fly, but not butterflies. On the rare occasions he snatched one out of the air, he always let it go. When a tree limb broke during a storm, Glenn secured it at an angle so burly Rusty could climb for a better view. He loved to sit in the branches and watch the birds, then stare over the fence into the neighbor's yard. Rusty knew every blade of grass in the lawn, but he never stepped off the property. Not one foot.

"I've watched him. That cat never leaves," the neighbor told Glenn in amazement.

Glenn shrugged. "That's Rusty," he said.

He was a loyal companion. Whenever Glenn talked — about his problems and triumphs, his gripes and rewards, the funny jokes he'd heard that day — Rusty listened. And responded. Rusty could talk through a whole meal and the dishes, too, if he was in the mood. Meow-meow-meow-meow-meow. When Glenn was down, Rusty knew it. He jumped on his lap and stared at him the way he had that first day in the Studebaker Commander: with his head cocked and those deep, intelligent eyes. Then he pushed his scent whiskers into Glenn's beard. That's a cat question. *You okay, buddy?* Glenn would respond by rubbing his beard against Rusty's face, telling him he was fine.

Rusty also helped Glenn with his daughter Jenny. Glenn had never been able to stay close to his other children; Jenny was his last chance to be the father he always wanted.

On court order, she spent every other weekend with him, and he gave her everything he could. Jenny adored her father, Glenn knew, but he worried about her drifting away like his other children had. Not with Rusty around, though. Jenny loved Rusty. Every time Glenn picked her up from her mother's house, she asked about him. When they saw each other, they started running. Jenny would hold out her arms, and Rusty would leap into them like a puppy.

Rusty was always, um, big-boned. At five, Glenn figured, the cat weighed twenty-five pounds easy, although Rusty refused to sit on a scale. Glenn thought it was all muscle, since Rusty was a forager and inveterate climber of trees, but even he had to admit that Rusty looked like a fat Buddha when he sat on his hind legs. Eight-year-old Jenny thought Rusty was flabby, and she took it upon herself to thin him down. She held his arms out in front of him, pushing them back and forth as if he were doing the cha-cha. Then she put him on his back, grabbed his legs, and pedaled them in circles as if he were riding a bicycle. She called them Rusty's Butterball Exercises.

"Time for your Butterball Exercises," she called to Rusty every Saturday morning after pancakes and syrup. He'd sort of sigh, hang his head, and trudge over, because no matter what Jenny wanted, Rusty obliged. And even after all those exercises, he curled up beside Jenny every night. He loved her; it was that simple. Loved her in a way Glenn understood, because he loved her that way, too. They were both disappointed every time her mother picked her up on Sunday night.

The years passed, with days at his mechanic jobs and evenings at his mother's house for dinner or chores. Nights he spent with Rusty or at divorced-dads meetings, where he felt more like a counselor than a survivor. He still worked on his Studebaker Commander, slowly but steadily. Fixed the steering, aligned the gear box, painted red flames on the side. He didn't have a final plan or destination. The Commander was a lifelong project, and he looked forward to always tinkering, always working, making it better. If a band he liked was playing, he drove down on Wednesday night to the Eagles dance hall. He had a lot of friends in the music scene, and often they'd call him up on stage to play a song or two. But he never danced. Women asked, but he shrugged them off. He didn't want to be rude; he just didn't have the energy. He was there for the music.

When an old friend, Norman Schwartz,

decided to start a dance hall in the small town of Waterbury, Nebraska — "We're going back to the fun days," Norm told him. "Nothing but old rock and roll and live bands" — Glenn figured he'd volunteer as muscle, helping Norm clear debris and install the wooden floor he'd bought out of the old gym at St. Michael's Church just before they tore it down.

"I thought you were allergic to manual labor," Norm said, clearly joking.

"I am," Glenn assured him, "but I'll suffer for a friend." They cracked a beer or three and drank to old times. He was pushing sixty, and the only women he'd ever have in his life now, Glenn figured, were his mother and daughter. His best friend, other than Norm, was a cat. A man could do worse. Much worse. So Glenn decided to retire. He figured he would head home to his Studebaker Commander, his support groups, and his nightly guitar. He'd fish when he wanted, help Norm at his dance hall, hang out with Rusty and his mom. But on his last day at work at the auto repair shop, a regular customer walked in and told him point-blank: "You're not retiring. You're coming to work for me."

The woman ran a job program for special-needs adults called New Perspectives. Glenn told her, "I appreciate the offer, but I'm sorry, I don't know anything about that line of work."

"You'll like it," she said. "Just come for a look."

New Perspectives was a series of low, concrete block buildings above a commercial strip in east Sioux City. It wasn't much, inside or out, but the people made it special. Bobby collected bottles for redemption with enthusiasm, calling out to everyone across the room. A young woman had lost most of her brain function when she was hit by a car, but she could remember everybody's birthday and tell them what day of the week it was going to fall on in any given year. They needed a strong man to hold Ross, a three-hundred-pound diabetic with Down syndrome, when he went into a seizure. As he walked the facility, as he met the special adults in the work program, Glenn felt a rising sense of joy and relief. He had been working all those years on his car, figuring out the systems. He'd spent all those years with Rusty, learning to live like a cat, without resentment or disappointment. He hadn't just been killing time. He'd been working on himself. He'd been working toward something. And this was it.

"You got me," Glenn said. "I'll start to-morrow."

Within a month, Glenn didn't need to hold Ross during his seizures; he knew the man so well, he could sense when they were coming and always had a candy in his pocket to raise his blood sugar. He introduced everybody to the young woman with brain damage, because he could tell she loved showing off her birthday skills. He came in one Monday morning and told Bobby the bottle collector, "I've got a present for you, buddy, but you gotta do me a favor."

"What's that, Glenn?"

"I gotta have your hat."

Bobby backed off. He wore the same filthy hat every day, and he wasn't going to give it up.

"I got a brand-new hat for you, Bobby, and it's got the tag still on it."

Glenn showed him a bright orange hunt-ing hat that said GRAHAM TIRE across the front. Bobby grabbed it and immediately put the brim to his nose; he had a habit of smelling everything. Then he turned away, slowly took off his filthy hat, and handed it to Glenn. When he turned back, he had the orange hat on his head and a huge smile on his face.

"We've been trying to get him to change

that hat for two years," the woman who had hired him said. "He wouldn't take it off for anybody."

After New Perspectives, Glenn cut back on his divorced-dads sessions. He started playing more seriously with the band, spending nights at the Eagles or other music clubs around town. When Storm'n Norman's Rock 'n' Roll Auditorium opened, Glenn not only played guitar with the band, he carried the keg and helped drain it, too. There was no official first dance; no advertising; no sign on the building; no arrows pointing the way through rolling hills of corn to a tiny Nebraska town. But somehow, more than one hundred fifty people showed up. There was no air-conditioning, not enough bathrooms, and the only chairs were borrowed from a funeral home — they even said "funeral home" on the back — but it was a heck of a good time.

I suppose you could say that, after years of work and decades of disappointment, Glenn's life was full. He had Rusty, his mother, his daughter Jenny, who was already in high school. He had friends and music. He worked an important job with people he loved. On the one night a month when Storm'n Norman's was open, he did chores: unclogging toilets, tending bar, "feeding the chickens" — a euphemism for sprinkling the dance floor with no-slip wax. After a while, he noticed that a lot of women managed to coax their husbands to Storm'n Norman's, but couldn't convince them to dance. So he added another job: one-song dance partner for the frustrated wives of Iowa and Nebraska, the tall good-looking gentleman who swept them away and let them cut loose, at least for a minute or two. Truth be told, though, he barely saw their faces. Dancing was another way to enjoy the music, to help a stranger, and pass the time. He loved dancing — he'd almost forgotten how nice it felt — but for Glenn Albertson the dance hall, despite the bright lights, was nothing more than a sea of gray.

Until one night, sixteen years after his last divorce and ten years after Rusty broke through the scars on his heart, Glenn Albertson saw a face. He was at the bar, mixing drinks, when he looked up and noticed her across the room. She was at a table on the edge of the dance floor, talking with a couple of friends, and it was if a spotlight was shining only on her. It was just a moment, a glancing chance, but it was something Glenn had never experienced before. In the gray sea of his life, this woman seemed to glow. And then their eyes met.

"Take over, Joe," he told his fellow bartender, "I'm gonna ask that woman to dance."

He did. She looked up at him, hesitated, then said, "Sure."

They walked quietly to the dance floor. She was smaller than he expected. The top of her head came only to the middle of his chest, and yet they seemed to fit together as they began to move silently across the floor. She was quiet, focused on something else perhaps, but when she looked into his face, her eyes seemed to take him in, to linger for a chorus, and then, reluctantly, to look away. When he swept her across the dance floor, she didn't feel like an obstacle. There was no resistance, no weight. There was only the feel of her warm hand, and the memory of her eyes staring into his own.

"I'm Glenn," he said.

"I'm Vicki," she replied.

He swept her around the dance floor a few more times, hardly noticing the sea of gray swirling around them. "Do you live around here?"

"In Spencer," she said.

When the song ended, he slipped his hand behind her waist. If she wanted to leave, he would let her, but she didn't. She leaned against his arm, allowing him to hold her.

Somewhere beyond them, in another world, the drummer beat time, and when the music started again, Glenn led her easily around the dance floor, holding her close as the band played something he never wanted to end.

"I had a good night," he told Rusty, when he finally got home. "A real good night."

The big cat looked at him, his eyes hooded and half awake, and meowed for some food.

PART II

I've always loved to dance. When I was a kid, Mom and Dad taught us to dance to the rhythms of the old radio in the family room of our farmhouse outside Moneta, Iowa. When I was nineteen and working in a box factory in Mankato, Minnesota, I danced my toes off every night. Dancing introduced me to my first husband, and it helped me through the dark days after my divorce. As a single mother attending college for the first time at the age of thirty, I didn't have time for so-called "leisure" pursuits, but dancing was never simple leisure to me. Dancing, to me, was essential. When I heard the music, when I got up to dance, I felt like myself — the good self, not the self that had been through six surgeries from a botched hysterectomy and spent almost a decade married to an alcoholic. Even on the darkest nights, after tucking my daughter into bed and scrubbing down the pots and writing that last class paper, I often went into the kitchen, put on a record, and danced all by myself.

I danced all through my years at the Spencer Public Library. After closing, Dewey and I danced in the library, just the two of us, hopping around between the books. At public events, I was known to cut loose with my male friends and my dates. I went to singles dances, too, although never in Spencer. It didn't seem right, somehow, for the town librarian to be seen cozying up to some man on a dance floor. People, as they say, would talk.

So I went out of town: the famous Roof Garden dance hall twenty miles away in the Iowa Lake Country; my friend Trudy's favorite spots in Worthington, Minnesota; the more respectable clubs in Sioux City. I dated, but the relationships never worked out. One suitor showed me his divorce certificate on the first night. That should have been a tip-off. The next day, his wife called and threatened my life. Apparently, her husband had the same name as his uncle. The man had shown me the papers from his uncle's divorce.

The Cowboy, a Sioux City blind date, drove me through the pens where the cows waited for slaughter because he thought they were beautiful in the moonlight. Then he took me to his house and showed me how to make bullets. A man from Minneapolis invited me for a weekend on his sailboat. A sudden storm blew in, and I got so seasick I vomited on my dress. The next morning, he told me his favorite place in the world was some spot in Italy. He asked my favorite place. I was in my thirties, and I'd never been anywhere but Iowa and Minnesota. I knew that relationship wasn't going to work out, either.

Not that I was focused on having a man. I had fun when they were around, especially the dancing, but I didn't spend my nights pining for them. I was too busy enjoying what I had: a meaningful job, a loyal family, great friends, and a wonderful library cat named Dewey Readmore Books. Sure, I was basically the person that answered his fan mail, but Dewey never treated me like the help. We were partners. I wasn't giving up anything by building my life around that partnership, and especially that job. I was gaining a life of contentment and laughter, a life where I didn't have to scatter my attention or waste my energy on something other well-meaning (and nosy) people told me I was supposed to want. Instead, I got to focus on what was important: supporting my daughter, caring for my parents, establishing deep friendships, and using my talents to build an institution that would provide for the citizens of Spencer. I was extremely happy as a mother and librarian by vocation, and a cat lover and a dancer by habit. I didn't want to be a girlfriend, too.

Then Dewey died.

My relationship with Dewey can't be summarized in a few sentences. I know that. And yet, I always come back to these few lines from my first book when I think of him: "Dewey was my cat. I was the person he came to for love. I was the person he came to for comfort. And I went to him for love and comfort, too. He wasn't a substitute husband or a substitute child. I wasn't lonely; I had plenty of friends. I wasn't unfulfilled; I loved my job. I wasn't looking for someone special. It wasn't even that I saw him every day. We lived apart. We could spend whole days together and hardly see each other. But even when I didn't see him, I knew he was there. We had chosen, I realized, to share our lives, not just tomorrow, but forever."

But nothing lasts forever, no matter how

strong your bond. Dewey was my best friend; he was my comfort and companion. He changed the library. He changed our town. And he was gone.

The job wasn't the same after that. I had been the library director for twenty years. I had dedicated more than two decades of my life to building the organization. Now, suddenly, it didn't feel like my library anymore. Part of that was my relationship with the library board, which had broken the moment they tried to remove Dewey because he was old. But there was also a coldness, a loneliness, an emptiness that had not existed within those walls for the nineteen years Dewey lived there.

As always, I threw myself into my work. I had projects to finish, goals I still wanted to achieve. I wanted to build on what Dewey and I had created, to continue to transform the library from a warehouse for books to a meetinghouse for souls.

I also wanted to write Dewey's story. I felt I owed it to him, because of what he had given to me and the town of Spencer. I owed it to his fans, who deserved the whole tale. His love, his companionship, his friendship — those were the reasons more than 270 newspapers printed his obituary and more than a thousand fans wrote letters and cards. That's why his life mattered. And that's what I wanted to share. I felt I owed the book to the world because I believed, and I still do, that there's an important message in Dewey's life: Never give up. Find your place. You can change your world.

But I was sick. After Dewey's death, I had developed an upper respiratory infection, and no matter what I tried, it would not go away. I had suffered for decades from serious illness, ever since that hysterectomy in my early twenties — a hysterectomy I didn't even know was going to be performed until I came out of the anesthesia — damaged my immune system. Every three or four years, what started as tonsillitis ended in the hospital. It was part of my life, part of what Dewey had helped me endure.

But this time was different. This time, I was sick in heart as well as body. In December, I drove myself hard to fulfill every Dewey-related request, but bitterly cold, post-holidays January found me tired and weak. In February, the weakness moved into my muscles and lungs. By March, I was barely making it out of bed. In April, I started working from home, at partial pay, to conserve my strength. My doctor tried all sorts of treatments, but my health deteriorated further. Nausea, headaches, fevers.

Most days, the only food I could keep down was saltines. My doctor performed tests. Colonoscopies, upper endoscopies, MRIs. There seemed to be no solution. I went back to work in May, but I wasn't myself. I was sent to specialists in Sioux City and Minnesota, but driving to the appointments wore me out. By summer, I was so weak I couldn't take a shower without having to lie down afterward for a rest.

Everyone thought I was depressed. And I *was* depressed. Dewey's death, combined with my problems with the library board, had collapsed my comfortable world. But I wasn't sick because I was depressed; I was depressed because I was sick. And nobody knew what was wrong with me. I thought, *This is it. This is how I'm going to be for the rest of my life. I can't get out of bed, I can't go anywhere, I can't see anybody. And then I'll die.*

Twenty years before, I had been a single mother making twenty-five thousand dollars a year. To keep my job, I had to earn a Master's degree in library science, which required a four-hour round trip to Sioux City every weekend for ten hours of class. At the same time, my daughter — the rock of my life — was growing apart from me. Maybe it was a natural part of growing up. Or maybe it was the fact that, because of everything I had to do to support her financially, I couldn't support her with my time. All I remembered for sure, years later, was the loneliness of my nights in the library, dead tired and struggling to complete my school papers and keep my priorities in order. I remembered the moments when it felt as if the weight was too much and the ceiling was caving in.

In those moments, Dewey came for me. He jumped on my lap; he knocked pens out of my hand; he flopped on the computer keyboard. He bumped me with his head until I relented, and then he streaked out of my office and down some dark aisle between two shelves of books. Sometimes I caught glimpses of him disappearing; sometimes, after five minutes, I still hadn't found him. Then, just when I was ready to quit, I'd turn around and he'd be standing right behind me. And I could swear he was laughing.

Now, once again, Dewey came to me. Before my health collapsed, I had committed to writing a book, and I was no quitter. Every evening, after working as much as I could for the library, I would sit at my kitchen table and talk with my cowriter, Bret Witter, about Dewey. And the more I talked about him, the more alive he became. I could see again the way he crouched when I dangled his red yarn and how, just when I turned away, he would leap at it with all four paws. I remembered the exact way his nose twitched as he sniffed his food — and then rejected it. I laughed at the memory of the poor cat soaking wet and angry after his twice yearly baths; the way his tongue would drag as he licked his toes; how he would jam those wet paws into his ears for a good cleaning. I smiled at the way he sniffed the air vent in my office three times every day, always protecting me.

Some nights the conversations were hard. My brother's suicide. My mother's death. I was most terrified, I think, to talk about my mastectomy. I had kept my surgery a secret, and even a decade later, I felt vulnerable and scarred. I was afraid to admit, even to myself, that when the doctor said breast cancer, I felt my world pull away. No one would touch me; no one wanted to say those words. Only Dewey was there for me, hour after hour, day after day. Only Dewey gave me the physical contact I craved.

Some days were even harder. The first time I talked about his death — how Dewey looked into my eyes and begged, *Help me, help me,* as I held him in the examination room — I bawled into the telephone. It had been months, but once again I felt flattened out, stretched to the point of breaking as Dr. Beale told me, "I feel a mass. It's an aggressive tumor. He's in pain. There's nothing we can do."

But opening that door brought back other memories, too. I remembered the cold of the examination table, the worn threads of Dewey's favorite blanket, the hum of his purring, the way he melted into my arms and laid his head against my skin. I remembered the trust in his golden eyes; the calm center beneath his terror; the closeness of our hearts as I whispered, "It's all right, Dewey. It's all right. Everything will be all right."

I remembered looking into his eyes and realizing I was alone.

It might seem that, in my weakened condition, all this talking, writing, and crying would have been too much. The truth was the opposite: The book was keeping me alive. When you are so sick that turning over in bed makes you throw up; when the only thing you can keep in your stomach is a few crackers; when no one can give you any assurance at all that your health will ever improve, it's easy to give up on the day. And once you start giving up on whole days, where does it end?

I never gave up on a day, because every

day I looked forward to my evenings with Dewey. Even on the days when I could do nothing more than crawl to the bathroom, I could lie on the couch, a phone to my ear, and talk about the Dew.

As I read the early drafts of the book, I could almost feel him on my shoulder reading along. *No,* Dewey would say, *that's not how it was.* When I heard that whisper of doubt in my mind, I would focus on that paragraph, or that sentence, or even that word. I had to get Dewey right. I knew that. He wasn't just the heart and soul of the book; he was everything. The more I focused on the details, the more he returned to my mind and heart. And the more I felt his presence, the more sure I was that everything in the book was right. It wasn't just the sight and sound; I was capturing the *feeling* of being around him — that old Dewey Magic — word by word.

In August, I made a decision. I was tired of listening to the experts. I was tired of driving two hours to explain my life history to a new doctor who couldn't figure out what was wrong with me. I was tired of falling to my knees in exhaustion at the end of the day, of pulling myself up from the sofa when the nausea overcame me. If I was going to get better, I realized, I needed to do it myself.

After six months of thinking about him, I was imbued with the spirit of Dewey. I really believe that. His can-do, always-keep-going, everything-will-be-fine spirit inspired me.

I retired from the library. I didn't slouch out a beaten woman; I went out on my terms, having accomplished all my major goals. The library board, God bless them, granted me that. With half the stress and a tenth the daily exposure to germs, I felt better immediately.

I changed my diet. I cut back on my medications. I stopped focusing on my limitations and started thinking about my strengths. I knew I needed to work my body, but I hated exercise. So I started dancing again. At first, I spent a few minutes shuffling around my living room with the music on. Then I'd collapse onto the sofa. Eventually, I started tapping my foot and swaying with the beat. After a few months — and yes, it was months — I started dancing. By myself, in the privacy of my house, but I was dancing.

By Christmas, I was well enough to start thinking about getting out on the dance floor. I wanted, though, for it to be the perfect night. My favorite local band, The Embers, at the best dance hall in the area: Storm'n Norman's Rock 'n' Roll Auditorium.

Storm'n Norman's was a very cool, almost secret dance club located in a former high school gym in a small town two hours from Spencer. You would never just wander into Storm'n Norman's by accident because when I say Waterbury, Nebraska, was small, I mean two blocks and one stop sign in the middle of nowhere small. I used to think it was a one-dog town, because I'd always see the same spotted mutt standing in the middle of the town's one intersection, but I walked the main street one afternoon and realized there were probably as many dogs in Waterbury as people. In a way, it reminded me of my hometown of Moneta, Iowa, which was a hearty five hundred people when I lived there in the 1950s but had since become so small (fewer than fifty people) that it was no longer even incorporated as a town. Moneta died when its heart, the redbrick Moneta School, was shut down by the state of Iowa in 1959. Waterbury hadn't died when its own school was closed by the state of Nebraska, but it was clearly limping along. There couldn't have been more than eighty people in town, and the only business (other than Storm'n Norman's) was the Buzzsaw Bar.

Storm'n Norman's didn't look like much from the outside. The former school gym was a squat, gray concrete block building on the edge of town, half hidden behind a clump of trees. The parking lot was the gravel road out front and a strip of grass. A wooden ramp led to the entrance, which was a plain metal door. Inside, a narrow hallway ended at the old gymnasium ticket window. Jeanette, Norman's wife, was usually collecting entrance fees.

Past the window, through a narrow door, you could look across the dance floor and catch your first glimpse of the stage. It was just a plain wooden auditorium stage, the kind built in just about every schoolhouse in America between about 1916 and 1983, except for the front end of a 1955 Chevy sticking out of the middle. The Chevy was black, with flames on the sides, and when the band hit a button, the engine would rev and the wheels would turn.

The Chevy set the mood, because when you're stepping through the doorway into Storm'n Norman's Rock N Roll Auditorium, it was like a gorgeous new world — the world of 1955 — exploded into life around you. The room was wide open and windowless, lit by hidden lamps and twenty strings of lights that connected above a disco ball in the middle of the high ceiling. The lights led your eyes down to the walls, where three 1950s American roadsters, two hot pink, sat on platforms twenty feet high. Underneath were signed guitars, statues, and black-and-white photographs of Marilyn, Elvis, and James Dean. Follow the walls around the room and you noticed first, over the entrance door, a vintage Chevy dashboard, then the rows of original, polished wooden gymnasium bleachers, perfect for lounging, along the back wall. There were two plain bars, in opposite corners, but the seating beside the wooden dance floor was neatly aligned and reminiscent of school tables and diner booths. Even the original basketball goals were still hanging from the walls. It was like walking into the idealized memory of your high school prom, but all grown up with nothing to prove. When two hundred people were crammed into Storm'n Norman's and a great band was belting classic rock and blues, there was no better place in the world.

I was determined to be there. I was determined to hear the Embers play. And I wasn't planning to be a wallflower, either. I was going to dance. Not to find a man, mind you, but to prove I could get off my sofa, heal my wounded body, and enjoy the rest of my life.

And that's how on March 15, 2008, sixteen months after Dewey's death sent my health into a spiral, I found myself riding toward Waterbury, Nebraska, with two of my best friends, Trudy and Faith. I still wasn't healthy — I was terribly weak, and I had to roll down the window a few times to keep from being queasy on the drive over — but I kept that to myself. I was tired of talking about my illness, tired of people asking how I felt, tired of trying to explain. I just wanted to enjoy myself, and the best way to do that was to pretend that everything was fine. Besides, I had talked Trudy and Faith into driving down from Minnesota, and there was no way I was turning back on them now.

We arrived early (a minor miracle with always-running-late Faith along), since I needed to sit, and tables next to the dance floor filled up fast. I didn't know what to expect, after a year in bed, but I could feel the energy in the room. As soon as the Embers launched into their playlist, my toes started tapping. By the second band break, I had danced with four men. I've always been small — just over five feet tall with a thin frame — but during my illness, I'd dropped to ninety-five pounds. I was too weak to climb stairs and standing made me dizzy. But there was something about dancing. As long as I was moving, and as long as I didn't complicate things by talking, my body felt strong. It was between songs, when the music stopped, that I started to collapse. When a guy asked for a second dance, I could barely force out the words, "Sorry, too tired," before wandering back to the table.

It was during one of my breaks, while trying to catch my breath, that he appeared. I don't remember him approaching. I'm sure I'd never seen him before, not even for a moment. I just looked up, and there he was, standing over me. He held out his hand and asked me to dance.

"Sure," I said.

He was tall and broad-shouldered but surprisingly light on the dance floor. We moved easily together, swept along by the music. I appreciated that he didn't try to stand too close, that he didn't try to push me around the floor, that he didn't feel the need to say something silly — or anything at all. We just drifted together, in a way that felt as natural as the sun. It must have been halfway through the song before I looked into his face. He was strikingly handsome, with an easy smile and a casual elegance beneath his bald head and well-groomed beard. But it was his eyes that startled me. They were the most gentle and caring eyes I had ever seen. And they were focused on me. Not the generic dance partner, but the real me inside. I knew, just by looking into them, that if he found out how sick I was, he'd take me straight back to my seat.

But for once, I didn't want to sit down. So when the music stopped, and I felt his arm slide around my waist, I leaned back and let him support my weight. He noticed something was wrong — I could see the concern in his eyes — but he didn't say anything. He just held me up. When the music started again, he pushed me into a two-step.

"I have to sit down," I said reluctantly, after four songs.

He escorted me to the table and sat across from me. Trudy and Faith, my protective friends, peppered him with questions. I was in a fog, unable to catch my breath, and his answers seemed to float away on the music, leaving only his good-natured smile. When the earth started to spin, I reached for my water glass, missed, and knocked it across the table. He reached over and scooped it up, found a rag and wiped down the table. We danced a few more songs, I'm not sure how many, because I only remember the music winding down and the crowd beginning to disperse.

"I'm gonna take off," he said. He grabbed my hand and kissed it. "It was a pleasure meeting you."

I was still thanking him for a lovely evening when I realized he had come around the table and was kissing me on the cheek. That normally would have put me off, a stranger being so forward, but my only thought as he disappeared into the crowd was, *Well, that was nice.*

"What was his name?" I asked my friends when we were outside and the cool March air had cleared my head. "Was it Paul?"

"For goodness' sakes, Vicki," Trudy said. "His name was Glenn."

I may not have remembered his name, but there was something about this Glenn fellow I just couldn't forget. Something that lifted my spirits, that made me think of him whenever my mind started to wander. Something that made the feel of his hands spring to mind at the strangest times.

That something was his eyes. It may sound strange, but when I looked into Glenn Albertson's eyes that night at Storm'n Norman's, I thought of Dewey. When I pulled Dewey out of the library book drop, wrapped him in a blanket, and held him against my chest, he was ice cold. His paws were literally frozen, and he barely had a pulse. He didn't know me, but he lifted his head and looked into my eyes with affection. I looked into his eyes and saw openness and trust.

I knew Glenn was a gentleman, because he never pushed me or tried to dance too close. I knew he was a thoughtful man, because of the way he supported me between songs. I knew he was a kind man, because of the way he spoke to my friends. But there was something else in his eyes. There was the calmness of the old soul, and an honest affection. Like Dewey, he wasn't just looking at me, he was *seeing* me. And he was letting me see him. Not just the kindness, but what lurked behind it: the fear and hurt, but also a deep sense of contentment and pride.

Dewey sent him, I thought, when I saw those eyes. It was just a moment, a sudden flash, before I realized it was merely a matter of similarity — they were alike, Dewey and Glenn. But the thought stuck with me. *Dewey sent him.* I knew it wasn't possible, but love is so wrapped up and complicated, so heartfelt and illogical, what can we really ever know for sure?

I knew one thing for sure: I wanted to see him again. So I called Norman's wife, Jeanette. "I met a fellow named Glenn at your place last week," I told her. "Tall with a beard, nice smile, good dancer."

"I know him," Jeanette said.

"Is he a good guy or a bad guy?"

"Oh, he's a good guy," Jeanette said, getting excited. "A really good guy." I didn't know Glenn had been helping out at the dance hall for years. I didn't know he had been friends with Jeanette and Norman since high school. At that point, I didn't know much about him at all, only that he was the most open and attentive man I'd ever met.

"I can set this up," Jeanette said, getting excited. "I used to do this all the time in high school. I'm really good at it. I can call him if you want."

A few hours later, Glenn called me. We talked for a half an hour, then longer a few nights later. Pretty soon, we were talking every night, then two or three times a day. We talked about everything — our work, our cats (although I never mentioned the book), even the biggies: politics and religion. When it was time for the next Storm'n Norman dance, we were both eager to see each other again. *Just for the dancing,* I told myself, *he's such a good dancer.* But my nervous energy as Trudy, Faith, and I took the long drive to Waterbury, Nebraska, told me that wasn't true. There were so many butterflies in my stomach, I could have lifted right out of the car.

We were late because of Faith (being on Faith time, we call it), and there was a line at the ticket window. When the couples cleared, I saw him standing on the other side of the door, waiting for me. He was wearing a nice pair of black jeans and a tucked-in black button-down shirt, and I could tell just by the way he held himself that he had spent a few extra minutes getting ready for the night. Then I saw the red rose in his hand, and the butterflies vanished. I walked up and, without hesitation, kissed him on the cheek. I can't remember what we said. I only remember dancing, because it was like we'd been doing it together all our lives. Somewhere in the middle of the night, when the band hit the opening chords of Ronnie Milsap's "Lost in the 50s Tonight," I remember looking into his eyes and seeing for the hundredth time the warmth — and an invitation. *I'm open,* they said. *I'm here. I'm for you. I'm never going to hurt you.*

"My favorite song," Glenn said, as the band sang *"shoo-bop, shoo-be-bop, so real, so right."*

"Mine, too," I said. Then I laid my head against his chest, just over his heart, and thought: *I'm home.*

If I had known then about his three marriages and five children? Well, I've got to admit, I still would have been interested in

Glenn Albertson. Maybe if I'd known before the first dance, things might have been different. But after the second night? At that point, there was no turning back. Even as we got to know each other over the coming weeks, and even as his life unspooled before me, I never doubted his character. One divorce is a mistake. Three divorces? That's when you stop pointing the finger at other people and start looking at yourself. But Glenn had done that work. That's why, the more I found out about his life, the more extraordinary he became. I had met plenty of guys who were closed off, who ran from their emotions and couldn't talk about much beyond sports. Glenn had gone through more than any of them, and yet he was willing to share that pain with me. He could lift me like a feather; he could take apart and repair my car; he could give me a wonderful massage and even cut my hair; he could give me a rose and a kiss and make me feel like the most beautiful woman in Iowa. But most important, he could be honest with me. He could show me his heart.

To ponder Glenn's life, though, is to ignore the biggest obstacle to our relationship: I was dead serious about my single life. I had lived it for so long, I had no intention of leaving. As my old saying goes (or went):

"I only want a man if I can hang him in my closet, like an old suit I can pull out when I want to dance." And I meant it. At almost sixty years old, with more than thirty years happily single, I didn't even want to contemplate bringing a man into my life. I had given the library and my daughter everything I had, and I felt pride and satisfaction in what I had accomplished. I was close to my family, especially my father, who needed me more than ever since my mother's death. I had great friends I'd known for decades, and who I could count on for love, support, and a belly-busting laugh. I had my daughter. And grandchildren. I made shadow boxes and had planned fourteen weddings (and counting), from the flowers to the invitations to the first song. I was retired, but I still served on several statewide library boards, so I traveled regularly. I will always remember tumbling into a taxi cab in New Orleans after a night of drinking and dancing with professional friends. The driver, after a few minutes, turned to us and said, "I can't believe you're librarians. You're having so much fun."

Of course we had fun! Librarians aren't ladies with bun hairdos who always say *shush*. We're highly educated men and women who manage businesses. We fight censorship. We are early adopters of e-books and computer networks. We market, we educate, we create. Our jobs are challenging and complex, even more so with a cat on staff, and that's why we love them so much.

I may not have been a working librarian anymore, and I may not have had Dewey anymore, but as long as I had my health, I was content. I had always packed as much living as I could into my days and appreciated my privacy at night. I could eat when I felt hungry, go to bed when I felt tired, and watch whatever I wanted on television. Why, oh why, would I want to risk all that for a man?

And yet, I was being swept away. And enjoying it! Sure, I tried to pull back a few times, to convince myself I didn't need this kind of relationship, but that feeling never seemed to last more than an hour or two. Glenn would call (we were up to seven calls a day at one point), and I'd always give in. Not to his pressure, or even to his charm, but to his tenderness. To his understanding. To his obvious love. When I talked about Dewey, I knew he didn't just listen. He asked questions. He understood. Some men would have been turned off by my love of a cat, but I always had the sense Glenn saw who I really was, and he liked what he saw.

And, of course, he had an important cat in his life, too. I knew that because of how much he talked about Rusty. He was a smart cat, he told me. He knew his name. He would come when called. I would like him. He always snuggled with strangers, guaranteed. And he wasn't just a shy house cat. Oh no. Rusty was quirky. He slept in a guitar case and ate nachos. He fought pit bulls but caught and released butterflies. Whenever Glenn yelled, "It's time for a bath, Rusty," he ran. Not away from the tub but *toward* it. Rusty loved water. Rusty would spread out in a bathtub full of water and *luxuriate*.

"You gotta see it," Glenn said. "It's something."

I think that's how he coaxed me to his house the first time, with the promise of meeting Rusty. I was still weak from my illness, and as soon as I sat down on Glenn's sofa for a rest, Rusty came right up and started rubbing against my legs. Soon, he was in my lap. He was a massive boy, at least three times the weight of Dewey. But he was a teddy bear, too, just like Glenn. Meeting Rusty confirmed all my instincts about the man I was, dare I say it, beginning to love.

After getting the nod from Rusty, Glenn took me to meet his mom. She was in her eighties, still living in her own house, still mowing her own grass. It could have been awkward, I suppose, meeting my boyfriend's beloved mother, except for one thing: She had followed Dewey's life in the newspaper for years. So I told her stories about Dewey: how he climbed into the jacket of a disabled girl and made her smile; how he entertained the children left in the library "day care" by their working parents; how he rode the left shoulder (always the left!) of the homeless man who came to the library every day for the sole purpose of talking to our cat. She listened. She smiled. She offered me coffee and homemade cake. I could tell Dewey's Magic was still at work, and it was working on both our hearts. How could I not love someone who loved Dewey? How could she not trust Dewey's mom?

When spring finally arrived, Glenn drove me to Pierce, where he had spent his childhood summers. He showed me his grandmother's old house, and the auto repair shop where he'd fallen in love with cars. We parked under the town's one big tree, near the intersection where Glenn had run to watch the train blow its huge cloud of steam as it crossed downtown, and kissed. We drove to Storm'n Norman's for a dance, and Glenn told Norman he was sorry, but he was too busy to bartend anymore. After dinner one night, he drove me to a big beautiful house in a suburban neighborhood.

"What's that?" I asked.

"My first ex-wife and I used to live there," he said. That was the one moment I was taken aback. The moment when I remembered, suddenly, that I didn't want a serious relationship with a man, and I remembered why: because they were unpredictable and complicated.

But it only lasted for a second. Because I knew the man beside me. Maybe not every fact, maybe not every decision in his life, but I knew his heart, and I felt more comfortable with him than with any man I'd ever met. I was reading the last drafts of *Dewey* that spring, and I could feel the confidence I always felt when that cat was near me. I read for the twentieth time the last page of the book, where I talked about the lessons Dewey taught me.

Find your place. Be happy with what you have. Treat everyone well. Live a good life. It isn't about material things; it's about love. And you can never anticipate love.

I invited Glenn to Spencer for Memorial Day. For every date, he went to the florist and chose the healthiest and brightest rose in the store, just as he had on our first "date" at Storm'n Norman's. I kept each one, drying them in my craft room for my curio boxes. This time, though, he arrived with two red roses. We were planning to visit my mother's grave near the town of Hartley, Iowa, so I assumed the second rose was for her. Glenn said he wanted to make another stop first. He drove to the library and walked to the large window where Dewey's grave was marked by a simple granite plaque. It was a cold December morning when, just as the sun rose, the assistant librarian and I had broken the frozen ground and laid Dewey's ashes to rest.

"You are always with us," I had said.

Glenn put the second red rose on Dewey's grave. "I know how much he means to you," he said, holding me tight.

I'm going to marry this man, I thought, and it didn't surprise me at all.

Glenn and I are now engaged, and I have never been happier. We are so sure of our love that we even bought a house together, a nice bungalow on the west side of Spencer. We figured we might as well go ahead and move in together, we'd be married soon, but it's been two years, and we still aren't married. I know that might strike a few people as immoral, even if we are a committed couple in our sixties, but I have my reasons.

My first wedding, back in 1969, was just our immediate families and a few friends. My dress was a hand-me-down my mom had bought cheap when a local girl's wedding fell through at the last minute. The reception was held at my husband's favorite restaurant, and more than half the guests were related to him. It was my wedding, but I can honestly say that nothing about it was mine. I always felt cheated.

I don't care if this is my second marriage; I'm not doing that again. This one is going to be special. I am going to personally plan every detail, from the flowers for the ceremony at the Catholic church in Milford to the color of the type on the invitations to the beautiful white dress I had always wanted to wear. Glenn will have to give up his black jeans for a tuxedo, and I'll convince the Embers to play the reception, which we'd hold at Storm'n Norman's Rock 'n' Roll Auditorium, of course, if it weren't so far for everyone to drive.

Unfortunately, I've been too busy to plan the perfect day I've waited a lifetime to enjoy. The month we moved into our new house, *Dewey*, the book I wrote as a tribute to my best friend and favorite library cat, a book that healed my body and heart, was published. It went straight to the top of national bestseller lists and stayed there for more than six months. Sometimes, it feels as if I've spent every day since on the road, but don't get me wrong; I'm not complaining. For the last two years, I've been doing the best thing in the world: talking about Dewey. My health is still precarious, and it always will be. I have to be careful not to overtax myself, and sometimes I have to cut appearances short, but I want to experience everything I possibly can. I want to see the world. I want to meet wonderful people who love Dewey as much as I do, even if they never met him. I want to talk about him and know that he is there — with me and for me. We are intertwined, Dewey and I, more than we've ever been.

Glenn doesn't mind sharing me. I told him straight away, on our first date: "I'm a package deal. My friends and family come with me." By the second date, he knew Dewey was part of the package, too — even though I didn't tell him about the book until we were engaged. He not only understands that Dewey will always be a part of my life, he embraces it. If I ever doubt my man, all I have to do is see him with animals. When I walk outside, the birds in our yard scatter. When Glenn walks outside, they stay where they are. In Florida, I once saw a squirrel eating cereal out of the palm of his hand.

That doesn't mean everything about our new life is easy, especially for Glenn. He didn't mind giving up his rental house, putting his 1953 Studebaker Commander into storage, and tooling around in his (much safer) Buick. But it was hard to leave the people he loved. He'd visited his mother almost every day since his father died almost twenty years before; now, with a two hour drive between them, he gets to see her only every few weeks. There was crying on both sides when he broke the news to Bobby, Ross, and the other disabled adults that he was leaving New Perspectives.

Moving away from his daughter Jenny, who was starting college in Sioux City, was especially difficult. Glenn has lost five children in his life; how can he not fear losing her, too? He knew Jenny and Rusty loved each other, and he knew he always wanted to maintain a presence in her life, so he made the ultimate sacrifice: He gave her Rusty. Now Glenn goes to her house every time he is in Sioux City, just to check on Rusty, he says. It is a transparent ploy, of course. Rusty is fine. Jenny already had two pets, but the big orange cat has them both trained. The dog is a wimp. Mama Kitty, an old blind cat, follows Rusty around the house as he meows.

Old Rusty loves having animals he can take care of and boss around — and since Jenny is older now, he doesn't even have to do his Butterball Exercises.

I knew Glenn missed Rusty. I could see it in his eyes whenever we left Jenny's house. And I could hear it in his voice when he said, every few days, "You know, as soon as this *Dewey* stuff dies down, we should volunteer at the animal shelter." I knew, in my heart, he wanted a cat of his own.

But that was where the problem started. You see, I didn't want another cat. I always told myself, *Someday. Someday I'll be ready.* But every time I thought about it, that day seemed a long way off. I had spent nineteen years with Dewey, and I still missed him terribly. I had owned cats all my life, and they had all died, of course, but Dewey was different. He was one of a kind. I had loved him so much, and thought of him so highly, that I had spent a year writing a book about him. Now I was spending much of my time at book events, talking about his life and legacy. I was attached to him, forever. It wouldn't be fair to adopt another cat. The new cat would always be compared to Dewey, and how could it ever compete?

Then one December morning, almost exactly two years after Dewey's death, a Japanese film crew arrived in Spencer. Dewey had been famous in Japan ever since, five years before, a crew had come from Tokyo to film him for a documentary. This second crew wanted follow-up footage of me at the library, but before I could take off my coat and settle in for the interview, the library staff grabbed me and pushed me back to my former office. I could tell they were excited, but I had no idea why. Then I saw a tiny kitten crouched in the back corner of the room.

Oh, she was cute. She had long copper fur, with a magnificent ruff at the neck. She weighed two pounds, maximum, and half of that was hair. But I didn't want another cat. And I definitely didn't want another cat that looked like Dewey. If I adopted another cat, I had always told myself, I needed a clean break from the memories. A black cat. A white and gray calico, maybe. But when I saw that little orange kitten huddled by the heater in the back corner of the office, my heart leapt. It was like seeing Dewey on his first morning: so tiny, so helpless, so wonderfully, beautifully ginger brown. She had green eyes instead of Dewey's gorgeous gold, and her tail was stubby instead of fluffy, but otherwise . . .

I picked the kitten up and cradled her in

my arms. She looked at me and began to purr. Just as with Dewey on his first morning, I melted.

Then I heard her story, a story so much like Dewey's story, in its way, that it made me hurt. After all, we were in the middle of another bitterly cold Spencer winter, and several feet of snow and ice had been on the ground for weeks. Sue Seltzer, a computer technician who worked occasionally at the library, had been edging her car down a side street in downtown Spencer, when she saw a truck swerve outside Nelson Hearing Aid Service. She thought there was a clump of ice in the road, so she slowed down. Then she saw the clump move. It was a bedraggled little kitten, shivering and staggering, with ice and twigs matted in its fur. She picked it up, looked in its face, and thought: Dewey. Sue had always been a big fan of the Dew.

Sue took the kitten to her office and bathed her. Like Dewey, the kitten purred in the warm water. Sue already had five cats, and her husband refused to entertain the thought of making it six, so she decided to take the kitten to the library. If any cat was destined to take Dewey's place, she figured, it was this tiny girl. But since the publication of *Dewey,* the Spencer Public Library had been deluged with cats. Two poor kittens, I regret to say, had even been shoved into the book drop. The only sensible thing was to implement and publicize a blanket No Cats policy. And that's why, when I finished my interview with the Japanese crew, the kitten was still waiting in the corner of the office. But now, she was sitting on Glenn's lap.

They both looked up at me. Glenn smiled and sort of shrugged. My heart melted for the second time. And the tiny kitten, so reminiscent of Dewey it was both scary and exciting, came home with me.

That night, I mentioned the kitten on Dewey's Web site. A boy named Cody wrote back to suggest the name Page. I was turning a new page in my life, he wrote; what could be more appropriate?

The next day, Page did something very Dewey-like: She appeared in the *Spencer Daily Reporter,* our little five-days-a-week newspaper. The story spread to the *Sioux City Journal.* Soon, an AP photographer was on his way to Spencer from Des Moines. Just like that, Page and I were appearing in hundreds of newspapers around the country. Librarian in Iowa adopts a cat! Sounds like hard-hitting national news, right?

"What's next?" Glenn joked. "Are they going to start reporting what you had for breakfast?"

That news report may have been the last Dewey-like thing my new cat ever did. Much to my relief, Page had a personality of her own. She wasn't like her older brother at all.

Well . . . in one regard maybe, because when we took her to the vet — the same vet who treated Dewey and discovered his tumor — we received a startling diagnosis. Page was a boy.

So Page Turner, as we renamed him, had boyness in common with Dewey, too. But beyond that? No. Beyond that, there was nothing Dewey about our new cat.

He was clumsy, for one thing. The first night he was at my house, he broke a ceramic angel when he jumped on my side table. The first night! Dewey was graceful. He had gone nineteen years without breaking anything. Page Turner wasn't even graceful when he lay down. Instead of easing himself down like a normal kitten, he flopped over on the ground like a hairy dust mop. And it's so not true that cats always land on their feet. Page Turner would be sitting on the back of the sofa and suddenly just fall off onto his back. He even fell off the bed when he was sleeping. Bam, right onto his back, and he never even woke up.

Dewey loved heat. He would get so hot

lounging in front of the library heater that you couldn't touch his fur. Page Turner hated heat. Even in winter, I found him curled up in the coldest place in the house: the basement stairs. He hated sunlight. He was skittish around strangers. And he never curled up in my lap, which was Dewey's favorite spot. Page Turner preferred to lie on top of my feet.

He didn't care about my rules. No matter how many times I put him down, he always jumped on the dinner table. He ran back and forth through the drapes, driving himself into a frenzy. Without fail, he chose my best furniture to sharpen his claws on. He chased his tail like a dog. He stared at the TV like a slack-jawed teenager. When I put ice in his water dish to keep it fresh, he fished it out and chased it around the house. Dewey hated water so much, he wouldn't even drink it. Page never cared about getting soaked. He never cared about being laughed at. Dewey was dignified. He couldn't stand being the butt of the joke. Page Turner never seemed to mind that I was doubled over laughing at his antics.

Thank goodness, I said to myself, *they didn't try to put this cat in the library.* It's a common misconception that just any old cat can live in a library. Page Turner, although appropriately named, was far too high-strung for the job. He was too distrustful and shy. He didn't have a quiet dignity about him. He wasn't Dewey, of course, but he wasn't Rusty, either. He wasn't cool. He didn't have empathy. He wouldn't rub against you when you were down. His advice, if he could have given any, would have been abysmal I'm sure. But we can't all be the prime rib on the plate of life, right? Some of us, like Page Turner, have to be the broccoli.

Find your place. That's one of the lessons Dewey taught me. We all have a place where we will thrive. By the summer of 2009 — when the book tours finally slowed and I started to think about writing this book — it was clear that Page Turner had mellowed out and found his place. He had been so unsure and frantic those first few months, I could now see, because life on the street had been hard. He ran from every creak because, I had no doubt, he had been hurt out there. He gulped food because he had been starving. On the day we took him home, I'm not sure he was ready to believe in anyone. But he had trusted Glenn. Just like Rusty, Page Turner could see the gentleness and love in the man's soul.

Sure, he's spoiled now. He interrupts our dinner until we give him a few bites to eat.

He licks the bottom of the cheese container that comes with my soft pretzel (my nightly vice!). He attacks my feet when I'm trying to sleep, lounges on my keyboard when I'm trying to write, and does nothing on Saturdays but watch NASCAR with Glenn. You may think this is somehow bad for him — unhealthy, unproductive, unnatural, and all the other insults that have been hurled at my treatment of Dewey since that book was published — but I know Page Turner is happy. At six weeks old, he was shivering in the middle of a Spencer street, filthy dirty, with ice clumps and sticks matted in his fur. Now he lives in a house with two people who adore him. He has cat food whenever he wants. He sleeps in a warm bed. He has toys to play with — even the kind with annoying bells! — and a microwave to watch. He hates strangers — I didn't see him for four days the first time my grandchildren came for a visit — but he has a little hidey-hole behind the suitcases in my closet where he can go whenever he feels afraid. He doesn't go outside, but in the summer we open a window so he can watch and listen and fantasize about the birds in the garden.

My friends think Page Turner looks like Dewey. I don't see it. They are both fluffy orange cats, but Page is a different shape (that would be 100 percent round). He's bigger than Dewey. And although his eyes are changing from green to Dewey's golden amber, they don't look anything like Dewey's eyes. Page is not an old soul. He is not wise. He is an energetic, sometimes naughty, often exasperating klutz. He makes me laugh and shake my head and wonder, *What the heck will that cat do next?* He's warm and loving and, let's face it, he gives Glenn and me something to focus on. Something that's ours. Together.

I'm not saying Page Turner is the child Glenn always wanted to have around. He's not even a new version of Rusty, if the truth be known. Rusty was Glenn's companion when he didn't want any company. For a while, he was the glue that held Glenn's life together. But they've both moved on. Whenever Glenn visits him now, Rusty looks him over, like he's checking his old friend's condition. They meow at each other — yes, Glenn meows — and Rusty hops into Glenn's arms and mashes his cheek into Glenn's beard. Then Rusty wanders off to his new life. He's an easygoing cat, the kind that can be happy almost anywhere, and he's found his place in Jenny's home.

And Glenn? Well, he's a sucker for Page Turner. Whenever we're away overnight, he's the one asking, "Have you called to check on Page? Is he all right?" He's the one always buying him little gifts and giving him extra bites of food. And please, do not ask to see pictures. Glenn has more than five hundred photographs of Page Turner stored on his camera, and he'll show you each one. He's got Page Turner's pictures on his cell phone, and I swear he changes the screen saver every day.

Rusty was Glenn's friend and confidante. Page Turner . . . he's more like Glenn's grandchild. And no, I'm not saying he's literally a grandchild or that he's a replacement for something Glenn was missing. Life, love, and desire are never that simple. Happiness is never something you can calculate. At its best, it's something that catches you unaware and that you never fully understand.

All I'm saying, I suppose, is that Dewey was the wise and caring cat, the one who helped me and the town of Spencer through some very tough times. Rusty was the cool dude that wandered in at the right time. Page Turner is a perpetual child. He's fun. He's foolish. He's dependent. And I wouldn't want him any other way.

So, no, Page Turner didn't help me get over the loss of Dewey. Time did that. Page Turner just eased me into the next part of my life. The part with Glenn. And grand-kids. And travel. And good health that I do have to constantly monitor and for that reason will always cherish. We've built a new life together, Glenn and I. We've bought a house. Page Turner made that house a home and our little trio a family.

What more should we ever ask of our cats?

ACKNOWLEDGMENTS

My utmost thanks to the people who opened their lives so that their stories could be told in this book, and to all the people who helped fill out those stories with additional information, such as Adrienna (Sweetie) Case, Dr. Niki Kimling, and Harris Riggs. And, of course, a special thank you to all the wonderful cats who are the heart and soul of these stories; without them, none of this would have been written. This book is, truly, for all the cats around the world that brighten and enhance our lives.

To Peter McGuigan, my agent and friend, how can I thank you enough? Thank you to all the wonderful people at Foundry Literary + Media, especially Hannah Brown-Gordon, Stephanie Abou, and Dan McGillivray.

To Carrie Thornton, my editor, for always believing in this idea, and to Brian Tart, who seems to run the whole show from behind a mysterious curtain, for his support of her enthusiastic support. Lily Kosner — you are cool. Thank you Christine Ball (Publicity), Carrie Swetonic (Marketing), Monica Benalcazar (Art), and Susan Schwartz and Rachael Hicks (Managing Editorial): there would be no Magic without you.

Thank you, as always, to my friend and cowriter, Bret Witter, to his family — Beth, Lydia, and Isaac — and to his cats — Blackie and Ally. I know Bret wants to say thank you as well to Kayla Voskuhl, whom he met during an appearance at the Kentucky School for the Blind and whose laughter, optimism, and love of her cat, Ralph, inspired him. I am so sorry we didn't have room to include that story in this book.

To my own new little family, Glenn Albertson and Page Turner — I couldn't do all this without your love and constant support.

To all the Dewey fans who have written or e-mailed but didn't make this book. Your stories have touched my heart and proved to me that Dewey's Magic continues to touch lives around the world. Thank you for your kind words.

And last but certainly not least, to Dewey Readmore Books. His legacy of love and acceptance still teaches me important life lessons. I miss you, my friend.

ANIMALS IN NEED

Many of the relationships in this book, like thousands of others around the world, were made possible by the hard work of organizations dedicated to helping abused and homeless animals. The following is a list of groups that changed the lives of the animals in this book — and their owners — forever. If you are inspired by these stories, I hope you will consider giving of your time and resources to these or other similar organizations around the world.

Siouxland Humane Society
1015 Tri-View Ave., Sioux City, Iowa
   51103
www.siouxlandhumanesociety.org

North Shore Animal League
25 Davis Avenue, Port Washington, NY
   11050
www.nsalamerica.org

Humane Society of Kodiak
2409 Mill Bay Road, Kodiak, AK
   99615
www.kodiakanimalshelter.com

Northwest Wildlife Rehabilitation Center
P.O. Box 4273, Bellingham, WA 98227
www.northwestwildlife.org

Adopt-A-Pet
13575 N. Fenton Road, Fenton, MI
   48430
www.adoptapetfenton.com

Humane Society of Huron Valley
3100 Cherry Hill Road, Ann Arbor, MI
   48105
www.hshv.org

People for Pets
2312 Highway Boulevard, Spencer, IA
   51301
www.peopleforpets.com

ABOUT THE AUTHOR

Vicki Myron was thirty-four when she went to college, eventually receiving a master's degree. She was director of the Spencer Public Library for twenty years. Myron lives in Spencer, Iowa.